Selected Writings
and Speeches of
MARCUS GARVEY

DOVER·THRIFT·EDITIONS

Selected Writings and Speeches of MARCUS GARVEY

Edited by
BOB BLAISDELL

DOVER PUBLICATIONS, INC.
Mineola, New York

DOVER THRIFT EDITIONS

General Editor: Paul Negri
Editor of This Volume: Thomas Crawford

Bibliographical Note

Selected Writings and Speeches of Marcus Garvey is a new compilation, first published by Dover Publications, Inc., in 2004.

Library of Congress Cataloging-in-Publication Data

Garvey, Marcus, 1887–1940.
    [Selections. 2004]
    Selected writings and speeches of Marcus Garvey / Marcus Garvey ; edited by Bob Blaisdell.
        p. cm. (Dover thrift editions)
    ISBN-13: 978-0-486-43787-3 (pbk.)
    ISBN-10: 0-486-43787-6 (pbk.)
    1. African Americans—Politics and government—20th century. 2. African Americans—Civil rights—History—20th century. 3. Black nationalism—United States—History—20th century. 4. African-Americans—Social conditions—To 1964. 5. United States—Race relations. 6. Racism—United States—History—20th century. 7. Garvey, Marcus, 1887–1940. 8. Universal Negro Improvement Association. I. Blaisdell, Robert. II. Title. III. Series.

E185.97.G3A25 2004
320.54'6—dc22   2004056231

Manufactured in the United States by Courier Corporation
43787609   2014
www.doverpublications.com

Introduction

IN 1965 to honor the memory of Jamaica's hero of African redemption, Martin Luther King, Jr., told an assembly in Kingston, "Marcus Garvey was the first man of color in the history of the United States to lead and develop a mass movement. He was the first man, on a mass scale, and level, to give millions of Negroes a sense of dignity and destiny, and make the Negro feel that he was somebody."[1] Those who have revered Garvey have similarly expressed themselves. A Harlem member of Garvey's Universal Negro Improvement Association remembers the effect Garvey made after arriving in New York City in the late 1910s: ". . . a deep consciousness was awakened in me. . . . He raised in me a certain knowledge of me belonging to people all over the world, the African people, and he gave me pride, and he gave me a great knowledge of the history of the wealth of Africa."[2] After thousands of black soldiers had gone off to fight for American democracy in World War I, only to return home after 1918 to encounter an even more ruthless racism than they had left, and with economic and social prospects worse than ever, Black America was receptive to a stronger stance and message than, for instance, the National Association for the Advancement of Colored People's cautious and careful advocacy of social progress. A Southern woman who joined the U.N.I.A. said, "Garvey is giving my people backbones where they had wishbones."[3] Harlem was the heart of black America, and would bring forth the great Harlem Renaissance in the arts (a contemporary renaissance with which Garvey had little sympathy) as well as political and social consciousness. And while the mass movements and revolutions in Russia, Ireland, and India were making news, Garvey saw and extended the call

---

[1] Amy Jacques Garvey. *Garvey and Garveyism.* New York: Collier Books. 1970. 308.
[2] Ula Yvette Taylor. *The Veiled Garvey: The Life and Times of Amy Jacques Garvey.* University of North Carolina Press. 2002. 41.
[3] *Garvey and Garveyism.* 29.

for revolution to all black people who lived in or descended from Africa. He told the audience in 1921 at the Second International Convention of the Negro Peoples of the World in New York City, "At this moment methinks I see Ethiopia stretching forth her hands unto God, and methinks I see the Angel of God taking up the standard of the Red, the Black and the Green, and saying, 'Men of the Negro Race, Men of Ethiopia, follow me.' Tonight we are following. We are following 400,000,000 strong. We are following with a determination that we must be free before the wreck of matter, before the crash of worlds."[4]

The first and greatest black orator of the twentieth century was not, as a young printer in Jamaica, a natural speaker; this private, intense activist taught himself through trial and humiliation until he learned to speak with fiery immediacy to audiences of any size. "The excellence and power of Garvey's oratory was probably the single most uncontroversial of his attributes," a historian has observed.[5] Garvey's enemies were as dazzled by his speeches as his admirers. We have learned from his widow that this amazing orator "could not speak from notes; they handicapped his ready flow of thoughts. . . . He memorized only the outlines of very important speeches."[6] For several years his newspaper, *The Negro World,* used a team of shorthand writers to take down his every word for publication. "The fluency of his speeches lay in the fact that he had something to say, something which touched him so deeply that it constituted an outpouring from the heart and found response in his hearers."[7] As for his editorial articles, once when his wife tried to suggest that he moderate some of his expressions, he explained to her, "I am writing for the masses—people who have not been accustomed to serious reading matter—I must hammer in what I want to impress on their minds."[8] Garvey was delighted and fascinated by all history, and loved retelling and citing events and episodes from the lives of various peoples and heroes in his speeches and writings. To the end of his life he was an advocate of self-education, in 1937 telling an audience in St. Kitts, British West Indies, "Read! read! read! and never stop until you discover the knowledge of the Universe."[9]

---

[4] "Negroes Will Stop at Nothing Short of Redemption of Motherland and Establishment of African Empire," August 14, 1921. (This speech appears on page 44 of this volume.)

[5] Tony Martin. *Race First: The Ideological and Organizational Struggles of Marcus Garvey and the Universal Negro Improvement Association.* Dover, Massachusetts: The Majority Press. 1986. 100.

[6] *Garvey and Garveyism.* 132.

[7] *Ibid.*

[8] *Ibid.* 131.

[9] *Ibid.* 242.

★

Born on August 17, 1887, Garvey grew up in St. Ann's Bay, Jamaica, British West Indies. He was an ambitious, bookish boy, who scarcely knew there was such a thing as racial prejudice until he was fourteen. He became a printer's apprentice in 1901, and left school around 1903. After moving to Kingston in 1906 to work as a printer, he became active in the printers union. He started his first (very short-lived) newspaper when he was twenty-one, and left Jamaica soon after in 1911 for Costa Rica and Panama, where he edited newspapers before returning to Jamaica. He sailed to England in 1912 to further his education, and took classes at the Birkbeck College in London. After travels through Western Europe, he returned to Jamaica in 1914 with a new purpose, inspired, he said, by the American Booker T. Washington's *Up from Slavery.* Through this book, "my doom—if I may so call it—of being a race leader dawned upon me . . ."[10] Upon arrival in Kingston, Garvey immediately founded the "Universal Negro Improvement Association and African Communities (Imperial) League . . . with the program of uniting the Negro peoples of the world into one great body to establish a country and government absolutely their own."[11]

To raise money for the organization, he traveled to the United States in 1916 (he also had hoped to meet Booker T. Washington, with whom he had corresponded, but the elderly head of the Tuskegee Institute died at the end of 1915). To Garvey's surprise, he found the perfect atmosphere in America for his boundless energy and ambitious plans. Starting as an unknown, unsung West Indian, addressing church groups and street-corner gatherings, Garvey eventually directly addressed and mesmerized tens of thousands in hundreds of speeches and millions more through newspapers, and by 1919 he had soared to prominence and was renowned throughout the world for his message of black pride. His now New York City-based Universal Negro Improvement Association already had, he estimated (his estimates were, by his own admission, imprecise—and, as more meticulous observers have said, likely exaggerated) two million members. When he survived an assassination attempt in his offices in Harlem on October 14, 1919 (due in part to the heroics of a secretary, Amy Ashwood, who tackled the would-be murderer), his fame was further intensified. There seemed no stopping this charismatic, contentious, controversial figure, who enjoyed baiting his enemies and

---

[10] "The Negro's Greatest Enemy," *Current History Magazine,* September 1923. (This essay appears on page 1 of this volume.) It is Garvey's most extended piece of autobiography, and the title is ironic.

[11] "The Negro's Greatest Enemy."

shocking his allies. He trusted his own star, and he rode it higher than anyone except himself expected. From 1919 the United States Bureau of Investigation (later known as the F.B.I.) began gathering information about Garvey as a "radical" for the purpose of deporting him. Garvey toured the United States, speaking to audiences north, south, east and west, spurring enrollment in and donations to the U.N.I.A. The center of his movement, however, because he lived and was based there, was Harlem, where he published his pamphlets, magazines, and his resounding weekly newspaper propaganda organ, *The Negro World*. He also presided there over Liberty Hall, an auditorium at 114 West 138th Street that became the political center of the U.N.I.A., which he operated as President-General. (In the midst of his whirlwind activism, he married Amy Ashwood on Christmas Day, 1919, and less than four months later, separated from her.)

In 1920, he organized and the U.N.I.A. sponsored the First Annual Convention of the Negro Peoples of the World, in New York City: "Garvey's address at his inauguration as Provisional President of Africa in 1920 demonstrated his strong belief in a personal destiny as the liberator of Africa. 'The signal honor of being Provisional President of Africa is mine,' he exulted. 'It is a political calling for me to redeem Africa. It is like asking Napoleon to take the world. . . . He failed and died at St. Helena. But may I not say that the lessons of Napoleon are but stepping stones by which we shall guide ourselves to African liberation?'"[12] (Because of Colonial Africa's fear and mistrust of Garvey, however, he was never allowed into a single African country.) At this convention, and in the "Declaration of Rights of the Negro Peoples of the World," he introduced the flag of the Red, Black and Green, "the most enduring of the U.N.I.A.'s external trappings of nationhood . . . as the official colors of the African race."[13] The principles of the U.N.I.A. were agreed upon by officers, but they were Garvey's own, as they developed and changed and veered in him. In early 1921, he sent a U.N.I.A. delegation to Liberia, West Africa, to negotiate the establishment of a U.N.I.A. community there. Meanwhile, Garvey traveled back to Jamaica and Central America to lecture, while one of the Black Star Line's ships sailed for the Caribbean, where it suffered several mishaps, much to Garvey's distress and frustration. Garvey, with the Black Star Line in dire financial straits, returned to New York that summer for the second annual Convention of the Negro Peoples of the World.

---

[12] E. David Cronon. *Black Moses: The Story of Marcus Garvey and the Universal Negro Improvement Association*. Madison: University of Wisconsin Press. 1969. 185.
[13] *Race First*. 43.

Garvey's goals and ambitions for the U.N.I.A. changed as opportunities and challenges arose, and the Universal Negro Improvement Association's philosophy became known as "Garveyism" for good reason, as he was its primary creator and developer, and was worshipped by some then (and later) as more than a man: "Not surprisingly," writes Tony Martin, "such fierce unswerving loyalty was often branded 'fanaticism' by Garvey's critics, and enemies did not hesitate to describe the style of leadership existing within Garvey's provisional African nation as fascist. These accusations were helped along by a strain of violence that seemed to run among Garveyites. . . . Garveyites, particularly in the United States, were often implicated in violent confrontations with rival persons and groups."[14] His most famous and bitter enemy was W. E. B. Du Bois, head of the N.A.A.C.P., who would characterize Garvey as "without doubt, the most dangerous enemy of the Negro race in America."[15] Though Garvey was himself Christian, he became more and more critical of the constraints Christianity placed upon the black race. His two minds about Christianity did not prevent him from occasionally representing himself as a prophet of a cause beyond or beside Christianity: "I am speaking to you as the man who founded and organized the Universal Negro Improvement Association, as the man who sacrificed and suffered to bring into existence the Universal Negro Improvement Association. I had a motive and a purpose; it was not the money, because I could have gotten that for myself and been satisfied; it was not position, because I could have got that for myself. What is it? It was the crying voice from the grave that said, 'Garvey, we have suffered for 250 years for your day and for your time; we expect something from you at this hour.'"[16]

Never one to take counsel or advice, Garvey continually battled with subordinates and dissenters. He was rarely cautious and always bold, but without his focus and dedication the U.N.I.A. could not have exerted its extraordinary influence over the black diaspora of his time and of the time to come. This, however, led to critical problems. "Garveyism," says a biographer, "was greatly handicapped by the fact that it always remained the personal crusade of a single leader whose autocratic methods and slipshod financial practices alienated much of the support the movement might otherwise have received."[17] His business venture into the Black Star Line shipping company was successful as far as promoting

---

[14] *Race First.* 58.
[15] In an article in *Crisis,* May 1924.
[16] "Biggest Case in History of Negro Race." May 20, 1923. (This speech appears on page 126 of this volume.)
[17] *Black Moses.* 200.

the possibilities of black economic power, but a disaster as far as it concerned the financial capabilities of the U.N.I.A. and Garvey's own legal status in America. J. Edgar Hoover, later famous as the head of the F.B.I., was
the Bureau of Investigation agent assigned to investigate and help eliminate
Garvey from the American scene, and because of the careless and inept
business practices of the Black Star Line, Hoover was able to bring about
Garvey's arrest in 1922 and in 1923 his conviction (on very flimsy charges
of mail fraud, related to sales of shares in the Black Star Line) and sentence
of five years' imprisonment. At his 1923 trial, Garvey acted as his own
lawyer, and while this enabled him to make impressive statements about his
beliefs and actions, it probably did his case more harm than good. Garvey,
who lived modestly and abstemiously, was notoriously inattentive to financial matters, but almost always refused to acknowledge his own complicity
in hiring loyal but incompetent or remarkably inexperienced followers for
positions of power and responsibility. "The most important consequence
of Garvey's trial and conviction," writes Tony Martin, "was that it finally
cleared the way for his deportation."[18]

It was on his cross-country speaking tour in 1922 that he began his dis-
turbingly close associations with white racist groups. Without apologizing for such dealings, he insisted that white racist organizations were the
only honest representatives of American sentiment, and compared the
beliefs of the U.N.I.A. with those of such groups: "The Ku Klux Klan is
the invisible government of the United States of America. The Ku Klux
Klan expresses to a great extent the feeling of every real white American.
. . . The attitude of the Universal Negro Improvement Association is in a
way similar to the Ku Klux Klan. Whilst the Ku Klux Klan desires to
make America absolutely a white man's country, the Universal Negro
Improvement Association wants to make Africa absolutely a black man's
country."[19] This avowed kinship with white supremacists dismayed many
of his followers and sympathizers and left his opponents in the N.A.A.C.P.
and the Communist Party volubly outraged. Garvey tried to make his
pow-wows with racists sound simply pragmatic: "So you realize that the
Universal Negro Improvement Association is carrying out just what the
Ku Klux Klan is carrying out—the purity of the white race down
South—and we are going to carry out the purity of the black race not
only down South, but all through the world."[20] Garvey's stance on miscegenation and "racial purity" was a position that Garvey's greatest scholar,

---

[18] *Race First*. 196.
[19] "Hon. Marcus Garvey Tells of Interview with the Ku Klux Klan," July 9, 1922. (This
speech appears on page 74 of this volume.)
[20] *Ibid.*

Robert A. Hill, believes tripped up the momentum of the Universal Negro Improvement Association and kept it from extending beyond what Hill calls the "propaganda stage": that is, ". . . the disintegration of the U.N.I.A. as a radical political force began the moment Garvey resorted to the ideology of racial purity."[21]

In the summer of 1922, the Black Star Line's onboard and boardroom mismanagement put it out of business, but Garvey, never daunted, would continue over the next two years to try to take on various business ventures, including another in shipping. Garvey unrelentingly promoted the right of sovereignty of the African peoples, and sent a delegation from the U.N.I.A. to the League of Nations meeting in Geneva. When the Liberian government, pressured by European governments and also, perhaps, fearing a coup d'état as the ultimate political intention of the U.N.I.A., denied the U.N.I.A. a settlement, Garvey was furious but not defeated.[22] While imprisoned in the Manhattan House of Detention ("The Tombs") during the summer of 1923, he continued to write editorials for *The Negro World,* attacking enemies, rallying his forces, and, through the work of his second wife, Amy Jacques Garvey, to promote his ideas and at the same time present a less radical image of himself to the American public in the first volume of *The Philosophy and Opinions of Marcus Garvey.* From The Tombs, he declared, "I am here because I dared to tell the Negro that the time has come for him to lift his head and be a man."[23] Out on bail in September, for the next fifteen months he resumed his usual tireless efforts as a one-man political machine.

After his imprisonment for the mail fraud conviction in the Atlanta Federal Penitentiary in February 1925, Amy Jacques Garvey unsuccessfully petitioned the U.S. Government for a pardon, and meanwhile strove to follow her husband's many orders. In December 1925 she published the second volume of *The Philosophy and Opinions of Marcus Garvey,* subtitled "Or, Africa for the Africans." The U.N.I.A., on the other hand, splintered and staggered without Garvey's immediate directing influence and his ability to raise money. Soon his hold over it and its allegiance to him disappeared. An unlikely and unpleasant show of support for Garvey's release came from white supremacist groups, which continued to see Garvey as a fellow soldier in their war against miscegenation. In November 1927, President Calvin Coolidge pardoned Garvey for the purpose of deporting him immediately to Jamaica. Well-wishers saw him

---

[21] *The Marcus Garvey and Universal Negro Improvement Association Papers.* Volume 1. Edited by Robert A. Hill. Berkeley: University of California Press. LXXXIV.

[22] See *Race First,* 133.

[23] *Race First,* 196.

off at a ship at New Orleans on December 3, and he would never again set foot in the United States. Garvey's remaining dozen years show signs of life but also a depressing and distressing fall. After spending several months traveling and lecturing in Europe and Canada in 1928 with his wife, he tried from Jamaica to reform the U.N.I.A. into the force it had been while he was active in Harlem, but he could not. In 1930 he and Amy Jacques Garvey had their first son, Marcus, Jr. (In 1933, their second son, Julius, was born.) In Kingston, Garvey entered local politics, but was stymied there, and after further business enterprises failed, he left his wife and sons for London in 1935. He had once explained to Amy, "Sometimes I like what I do. Other times I hate like hell to do the things I have to; but in my work I must get the best use of every human being with whom I come in contact. I thought you realized that long ago."[24] Her husband, said his widow, "had submerged 'the roles of husband and father' and sacrificed 'his family on the altar of African redemption.'"[25] Garvey acknowledged this sacrifice himself, many years before, from Atlanta Federal Penitentiary when he wrote asking his followers to "give protection to my wife, whom I neglected and cheated for the cause that I so much love."[26]

His hard, long-standing, and narrow adherence to, and belief in, nationalism now led him to identify and sympathize with such European tyrants as Benito Mussolini, the Fascist dictator of Italy, and Nazi leader Adolph Hitler, of Germany. In March 1934, in Garvey's magazine, *The Black Man,* he recommended that his readers peruse *Mein Kampf,* expressing his hope that one day the black race would produce its own Hitler: "Hitler has a lesson to teach and he is teaching it well."[27] To a long-time U.N.I.A. supporter in 1937, Garvey boasted, "We were the first Fascists. We had disciplined men, women and children in training for the liberation of Africa. The black masses saw that in this extreme nationalism lay their only hope and readily supported it. Mussolini copied fascism from me, but the Negro reactionaries sabotaged it."[28]

He continued to travel to Canada and the Caribbean to lecture, and to write and edit newspapers and journals, and in 1937 began his School of African Philosophy, training several young men through classes and correspondence courses to disseminate his teachings. His sons and wife came to London to live with him in 1937, but left within a year to return

---

[24] *Garvey and Garveyism.* 197.

[25] *The Veiled Garvey.* 138.

[26] August 1, 1925. (This article appears on page 186 of this volume.)

[27] *The Marcus Garvey and Universal Negro Improvement Association Papers.* Volume 7. 580–581.

[28] J. A. Rogers, *World's Great Men of Color* (1947) [quoted by Tony Martin in *Race First,* 60]. Garvey's most fervent admirers have not been able to explain away these deplorable alliances and sentiments.

to Jamaica. He never corresponded with his wife again, but wrote fond notes to his sons. He suffered a cerebral hemorrhage in January of 1940, which resulted in partial paralysis, and he died on June 10, only fifty-three years old. He was buried in a London cemetery. Because of funding difficulties and legal problems between his wives, his body was not returned to Jamaica until 1964, when it was reburied with hero's honors.

Even though his influence seemed to have disappeared with his deportation and then his death, it was apparently only underground, awaiting a new spring, and revived, partly with the aid of his radicalized old foe, W. E. B. Du Bois, and his wife, ever a proponent of "Garveyism." From the 1920s, Garvey influenced the Kenyan Jomo Kenyatta's aspirations for his country's independence as well as Kwame Nkrumah, of Ghana, who said that *The Philosophy and Opinions of Marcus Garvey* "fired" his "enthusiasm."[29] "Every time you see another nation on the African continent become independent," said Malcolm X, whose father had been in the U.N.I.A., "you know that Marcus Garvey is alive."[30] In the 1960s, particularly in the United States and Jamaica, Garvey's message flourished again. Tony Martin concludes his history of Garvey and the U.N.I.A., saying, "It took the Black Power revolution of the 1960s with its revival of Garvey's red, black and green, his race pride, his self-reliance, his separatism, his anti-imperialism and his revolutionary nationalism to belatedly return to Garvey the recognition he deserves as a major, if not *the* major black figure of the century."[31]

*

Amy Jacques Garvey's two volumes of *The Philosophy and Opinions of Marcus Garvey, Or, Africa for the Africans* (1923 and 1925) were hastily arranged and edited from, for the most part, her husband's undated speeches and writing, and yet the collection has been the primary source for Garvey's ideas ever since. My goal in this shorter, chronologically arranged collection of Garvey's work has been to select the most famous and representative of the datable writings and speeches from *The Philosophy and Opinions of Marcus Garvey, or Africa for the Africans* and to supplement it with other vital articles and speeches from Garvey's Harlem years. (Regrettably, the years between 1917 and 1920 are poorly represented in this volume, not at all for their lack of importance in understanding Garvey but because of a lack of access to documents from those years in originals or microform.) I have added representative quo-

---

[29] *The Veiled Garvey*. 216.
[30] *The Veiled Garvey*. 229.
[31] *Race First*. 360.

tations from the speeches and articles to help readers identify the primary topics and have left off the newspaper subheadings.

Any serious student of Garvey and the Universal Negro Improvement Association, however, must turn to and rely on Professor Robert A. Hill's comprehensive scholarly edition, *The Marcus Garvey and Universal Negro Improvement Association Papers* (particularly Volumes 1–7, University of California Press, 1983–1990). Almost every extant document concerning Garvey and the organization is represented and scrupulously edited and noted. I am indebted to it not only for its help in dating the selections in Amy Jacques Garvey's book but for its clarifications of faint and difficult readings in the microforms of *The Negro World*. I also thank the librarians of Lehman College, City University of New York, and the Schomburg Research Center of the New York City Public Library for making the microforms of *The Negro World* and *The Champion Magazine* available, and for their help in copying rare documents.

For analyses of Garvey's time and politics, Tony Martin's *Race First* (1976) is very good. Amy Jacques Garvey's *Garvey and Garveyism* (1970) is less satisfactory in its analyses, but revealing, at odd moments, of her strong and mixed feelings about her husband. The only collection of writings from Garvey's post-American years (1928–1940) is Robert A. Hill's *Marcus Garvey: Life and Lessons.* Biographically, E. David Cronon's *Black Moses: The Story of Marcus Garvey* (1969) is readable, slim and interesting, focusing on Garvey as a political and ideological phenomenon. Cronon's compilation, *Marcus Garvey, Great Lives Observed,* and John Henrik Clarke's *Marcus Garvey and the Vision of Africa* are useful. Ula Yvette Taylor's *The Veiled Garvey: The Life and Times of Amy Jacques Garvey* (2002) is a fine illumination not only of Amy Jacques Garvey but of Garvey as a husband and father—features of the man scarcely touched upon in previous biographies. One hopes a comprehensive biography of Marcus Garvey will soon spring from the vast soil and materials of Professor Hill's work.

Contents

The Negro's Greatest Enemy

". . . my doom—if I may so call it—of being
a race leader dawned upon me . . ."

Current History Magazine,
September 1923

I WAS born in the Island of Jamaica, British West Indies, on August 17, 1887. My parents were black Negroes. My father was a man of brilliant intellect and dashing courage. He was unafraid of consequences. He took human chances in the course of life, as most bold men do, and he failed at the close of his career. He once had a fortune; he died poor. My mother was a sober and conscientious Christian, too soft and good for the time in which she lived. She was the direct opposite of my father. He was severe, firm, determined, bold and strong, refusing to yield even to superior forces if he believed he was right. My mother, on the other hand, was always willing to return a smile for a blow, and ever ready to bestow charity upon her enemy. Of this strange combination I was born thirty-six years ago, and ushered into a world of sin, the flesh and the devil.

I grew up with other black and white boys. I was never whipped by any, but made them all respect the strength of my arms. I got my education from many sources—through private tutors, two public schools, two grammar or high schools and two colleges. My teachers were men and women of varied experiences and abilities; four of them were eminent preachers. They studied me and I studied them. With some I became friendly in after years, others and I drifted apart, because as a boy they wanted to whip me, and I simply refused to be whipped. I was not made to be whipped. It annoys me to be defeated; hence to me, to be once defeated is to find cause for an everlasting struggle to reach the top.

I became a printer's apprentice at an early age, while still attending school. My apprentice master was a highly educated and alert man. In the affairs of business and the world he had no peer. He taught me many things before I reached twelve, and at fourteen I had enough intelligence and experience to manage men. I was strong and manly, and I made them respect me. I developed a strong and forceful character, and have maintained it still.

To me, at home in my early days, there was no difference between white and black. One of my father's properties, the place where I lived most of the time, was adjoining that of a white man. He had three girls and two boys; the Wesleyan minister, another white man whose church my parents attended, also had property adjoining ours. He had three girls and one boy. All of us were playmates. We romped and were happy children playmates together. The little white girl whom I liked the most knew no better than I did myself. We were two innocent fools who never dreamed of a race feeling and problem. As a child, I went to school with white boys and girls, like all other Negroes. We were not called Negroes then. I never heard the term Negro used once until I was about fourteen.

At fourteen my little white playmate and I parted. Her parents thought the time had come to separate us and draw the color line. They sent her and another sister to Edinburgh, Scotland, and told her that she was never to write or try to get in touch with me, for I was a "nigger." It was then that I found for the first time that there was some difference in humanity, and that there were different races, each having its own separate and distinct social life. I did not care about the separation after I was told about it, because I never thought all during our childhood association that the girl and the rest of the children of her race were better than I was; in fact, they used to look up to me. So I simply had no regrets.

After my first lesson in race distinction, I never thought of playing with white girls any more, even if they might be next-door neighbors. At home my sister's company was good enough for me, and at school I made friends with the colored girls next to me. White boys and I used to frolic together. We played cricket and baseball, ran races and rode bicycles together, took each other to the river and to the sea beach to learn to swim, and made boyish efforts while out in deep water to drown each other, making a sprint for shore crying out "shark, shark, shark." In all our experiences, however, only one black boy was drowned. He went under on a Friday afternoon after school hours, and his parents found him afloat half eaten by sharks on the following Sunday afternoon. Since then we boys never went back to sea.

At maturity the black and white boys separated, and took different courses in life. I grew up then to see the difference between the races more and more. My schoolmates as young men did not know or remember me any more. Then I realized that I had to make a fight for a place in the world, that it was not so easy to pass on to office and position. Personally, however, I had not much difficulty in finding and holding a place for myself, for I was aggressive. At eighteen I had an excellent position as manager of a large printing establishment, having under my control several men old enough to be my grandfathers. But I got mixed up with public life. I started to take an interest in the politics of my country, and then I saw the injustice done to my race because it was black, and I became dissatisfied on that account. I went traveling to South and Central America and parts of the West Indies to find out if it was so elsewhere, and I found the same situation. I set sail for Europe to find out if it was different there, and again I found the stumbling-block—"You are black." I read of the conditions in America. I read *Up From Slavery,* by Booker T. Washington, and then my doom—if I may so call it—of being a race leader dawned upon me in London after I had traveled through almost half of Europe.

I asked, "Where is the black man's Government?" "Where is his King and his kingdom?" "Where is his President, his country, and his ambassador, his army, his navy, his men of big affairs?" I could not find them, and then I declared, "I will help to make them."

Becoming naturally restless for the opportunity of doing something for the advancement of my race, I was determined that the black man would not continue to be kicked about by all the other races and nations of the world, as I saw it in the West Indies, South and Central America and Europe, and as I read of it in America. My young and ambitious mind led me into flights of great imagination. I saw before me then, even as I do now, a new world of black men, not peons, serfs, dogs and slaves, but a nation of sturdy men making their impress upon civilization and causing a new light to dawn upon the human race. I could not remain in London any more. My brain was afire. There was a world of thought to conquer. I had to start ere it became too late and the work be not done. Immediately I boarded a ship at Southampton for Jamaica, where I arrived on July 15, 1914. The Universal Negro Improvement Association and African Communities (Imperial) League was founded and organized five days after my arrival, with the program of uniting all the Negro peoples of the world into one great body to establish a country and government absolutely their own.

Where did the name of the organization come from? It was while speaking to a West Indian Negro who was a passenger on the ship with me from Southampton, who was returning home to the West Indies from Basutoland with his Basuto wife, that I further learned of the horrors of native life in Africa. He related to me in conversation such horrible and pitiable tales that my heart bled within me. Retiring from the conversation to my cabin, all day and the following night I pondered over the subject matter of that conversation, and at midnight, lying flat on my back, the vision and thought came to me that I should name the organization the Universal Negro Improvement Association and African Communities (Imperial) League. Such a name I thought would embrace the purpose of all black humanity. Thus to the world a name was born, a movement created, and a man became known.

I really never knew there was so much color prejudice in Jamaica, my own native home, until I started the work of the Universal Negro Improvement Association. We started immediately before the war. I had just returned from a successful trip to Europe, which was an exceptional achievement for a black man. The daily papers wrote me up with big headlines and told of my movement. But nobody wanted to be a Negro. "Garvey is crazy; he has lost his head," "Is that the use he is going to make of his experience and intelligence?"—such were the criticisms passed upon me. Men and women as black as I, and even more so, had believed themselves white under the West Indian order of society. I was simply an impossible man to use openly the term "Negro;" yet every one beneath his breath was calling the black man a Negro.

I had to decide whether to please my friends and be one of the "black-whites" of Jamaica, and be reasonably prosperous, or come out openly and defend and help improve and protect the integrity of the black millions and suffer. I decided to do the latter, hence my offence against "colored-black-white" society in the colonies and America. I was openly hated and persecuted by some of these colored men of the island who did not want to be classified as Negroes, but as white. They hated me worse than poison. They opposed me at every step, but I had a large number of white friends, who encouraged and helped me. Notable among them were the then Governor of the Colony, the Colonial Secretary and several other prominent men. But they were afraid of offending the "colored gentry" that were passed for white. Hence my fight had to be made alone. I spent hundreds of pounds (sterling) helping the organization to gain a footing. I also gave up all my time to the promulgation of its ideals. I became a marked man, but I was determined that the work should be done.

The war helped a great deal in arousing the consciousness of the colored people to the reasonableness of our program, especially after the British at home had rejected a large number of West Indian colored men who wanted to be officers in the British army. When they were told that Negroes could not be officers in the British army they started their own propaganda, which supplemented the program of the Universal Negro Improvement Association. With this and other contributing agencies a few of the stiff-necked colored people began to see the reasonableness of my program, but they were firm in refusing to be known as Negroes. Furthermore, I was a black man and therefore had absolutely no right to lead; in the opinion of the "colored" element, leadership should have been in the hands of a yellow or a very light man. On such flimsy prejudices our race has been retarded. There is more bitterness among us Negroes because of the caste of color than there is between any other peoples, not excluding the people of India.

I succeeded to a great extent in establishing the association in Jamaica with the assistance of a Catholic Bishop, the Governor, Sir John Pringle, the Rev. William Graham, a Scottish clergyman, and several other white friends. I got in touch with Booker Washington and told him what I wanted to do. He invited me to America and promised to speak with me in the Southern and other states to help my work. Although he died in the fall of 1915, I made my arrangements and arrived in the United States on March 23, 1916.

Here I found a new and different problem. I immediately visited some of the then so-called Negro leaders, only to discover, after a close study of them, that they had no program, but were mere opportunists who were living off their so-called leadership while the poor people were groping in the dark. I traveled through thirty-eight states and everywhere found the same condition. I visited Tuskegee and paid my respects to the dead hero, Booker Washington, and then returned to New York, where I organized the New York division of the Universal Negro Improvement Association. After instructing the people in the aims and objects of the association, I intended returning to Jamaica to perfect the Jamaica organization, but when we had enrolled about 800 or 1,000 members in the Harlem district and had elected the officers a few Negro politicians began trying to turn the movement into a political club.

Seeing that these politicians were about to destroy my ideals, I had to fight to get them out of the organization. There it was that I made my first political enemies in Harlem. They fought me until they smashed the first organization and reduced its membership to about fifty. I started again, and in two months built up a new organization of about 1,500 members. Again the politicians came and divided us into two factions. They took away all the books of the organization, its treasury and all its belongings. At that time I was only an organizer, for it was not then my intention to remain in America, but to return to Jamaica. The organization had its proper officers elected, and I was not an officer of the New York division, but President of the Jamaica branch.

On the second split in Harlem thirteen of the members conferred with me and requested me to become President for a time of the New York organization so as to save them from the politicians. I consented and was elected President. There then sprung up two factions, one led by the politicians with the books and the money, and the other led by me. My faction had no money. I placed at their disposal what money I had, opened an office for them, rented a meeting place, employed two women secretaries, went on the streets of Harlem at night to speak for the movement. In three weeks more than 2,000 new members joined. By this time I had the association incorporated so as to prevent the other faction using the name, but in two weeks the politicians had stolen all the people's money and had smashed up their faction.

The organization under my Presidency grew by leaps and bounds. I started *The Negro World.* Being a journalist, I edited this paper free of cost for the association, and worked for them without pay until November, 1920. I traveled all over the country for the association at my own expense, and established branches until in 1919 we had about thirty branches in different cities. By my writings and speeches we were able to build up a large organization of over 2,000,000 by June, 1919, at which time we launched the program of the Black Star Line.

To have built up a new organization, which was not purely political, among Negroes in America was a wonderful feat, for the Negro politician does not allow any other kind of organization within his race to thrive. We succeeded, however, in making the Universal Negro Improvement Association so formidable in 1919 that we encountered more trouble from our political brethren. They sought the influence of the District Attorney's office of the County of New York to put us out of business. Edwin P. Kilroe, at that time an Assistant District Attorney, on the complaint of the Negro politicians, started to investigate us and the association. Mr. Kilroe would constantly and continuously call me to his office for investigation on extraneous matters without coming to the point. The result was that after the eighth or ninth time I wrote an article in our newspaper, *The Negro World,* against him. This was interpreted as a criminal libel, for which I was indicted and arrested but subsequently dismissed on retracting what I had written.

During my many tilts with Mr. Kilroe, the question of the Black Star Line was discussed. He did not want us to have a line of ships. I told him that even as there was a White Star Line, we would have, irrespective of his wishes, a Black Star Line. On June 27, 1919, we incorporated the Black Star Line of Delaware, and in September we obtained a ship.

The following month (October) a man by the name of Tyler came to my office at 56 West 135th Street, New York City, and told me that Mr. Kilroe had sent him to "get me," and at once fired four shots at me from a .38-calibre revolver. He wounded me in the right leg and the right side of my scalp. I was taken to the Harlem Hospital, and he was arrested. The next day it was reported that he committed suicide in jail just before he was to be taken before a City Magistrate.

The first year of our activities for the Black Star Line added prestige to the Universal Negro Improvement Association. Several hundred thousand dollars worth of shares were sold. Our first ship, the steamship *Yarmouth,* had made two voyages to the West Indies and Central America. The white press had flashed the news all over the world. I, a young Negro, as President of the corporation, had become famous. My name was discussed on five continents. The Universal Negro Improvement Association gained millions of followers all over the world. By August,

1920, over 4,000,000 persons had joined the movement. A convention of all the Negro peoples of the world was called to meet in New York that month. Delegates came from all parts of the known world. Over 25,000 persons packed the Madison Square Garden on Aug. 1 to hear me speak to the first International Convention of Negroes. It was a record-breaking meeting, the first and the biggest of its kind. The name of Garvey had become known as a leader of his race.

Such fame among Negroes was too much for other race leaders and politicians to tolerate. My downfall was planned by my enemies. They laid all kinds of traps for me. They scattered their spies among the employees of the Black Star Line and the Universal Negro Improvement Association. Our office records were stolen. Employees started to be openly dishonest; we could get no convictions against them; even if on complaint they were held by a magistrate, they were dismissed by the Grand Jury. The ships' officers started to pile up thousands of dollars of debts against the company without the knowledge of the officers of the corporation. Our ships were damaged at sea, and there was a general riot of wreck and ruin. Officers of the Universal Negro Improvement Association also began to steal and be openly dishonest. I had to dismiss them. They joined my enemies, and thus I had an endless fight on my hands to save the ideals of the association and carry out our program for the race. My Negro enemies, finding that they alone could not destroy me, resorted to misrepresenting me to the leaders of the white race, several of whom, without proper investigation, also opposed me.

With robberies from within and from without, the Black Star Line was forced to suspend active business in December 1921. While I was on a business trip to the West Indies in the spring of 1921, the Black Star Line received the blow from which it was unable to recover. A sum of $25,000 was paid by one of the officers of the corporation to a man to purchase a ship, but the ship was never obtained and the money was never returned. The company was defrauded of a further sum of $11,000. Through such actions on the part of dishonest men in the shipping business, the Black Star Line received its first setback. This resulted in my being indicted for using the United States mails to defraud investors in the company. I was subsequently convicted and sentenced to five years in a Federal penitentiary. My trial is a matter of history. I know I was not given a square deal, because my indictment was the result of a "frame-up" among my political and business enemies. I had to conduct my own case in court because of the peculiar position in which I found myself. I had millions of friends and a large number of enemies. I wanted a colored attorney to handle my case, but there was none I could trust. I feel that I have been denied justice because of prejudice. Yet I have an abundance of faith in the courts of America, and I hope yet to obtain justice on my appeal.

The temporary ruin of the Black Star Line has in no way affected the larger work of the Universal Negro Improvement Association, which now has 900 branches with an approximate membership of 6,000,000. This organization has succeeded in organizing the Negroes all over the world and we now look forward to a renaissance that will create a new people and bring about the restoration of Ethiopia's ancient glory.

Being black, I have committed an unpardonable offense against the very light-colored Negroes in America and the West Indies by making myself famous as a Negro leader of millions. In their view, no black man must rise above them, but I still forge ahead determined to give to the world the truth about the new Negro who is determined to make and hold for himself a place in the affairs of men. The Universal Negro Improvement Association has been misrepresented by my enemies. They have tried to make it appear that we are hostile to other races. This is absolutely false. We love all humanity. We are working for the peace of the world which we believe can only come about when all races are given their due.

We feel that there is absolutely no reason why there should be any differences between the black and white races, if each stop to adjust and steady itself. We believe in the purity of both races. We do not believe the black man should be encouraged in the idea that his highest purpose in life is to marry a white woman, but we do believe that the white man should be taught to respect the black woman in the same way as he wants the black man to respect the white woman. It is a vicious and dangerous doctrine of social equality to urge, as certain colored leaders do, that black and white should get together, for that would destroy the racial purity of both.

We believe that the black people should have a country of their own where they should be given the fullest opportunity to develop politically, socially and industrially. The black people should not be encouraged to remain in white people's countries and expect to be presidents, governors, mayors, senators, congressmen, judges and social and industrial leaders. We believe that with the rising ambition of the Negro, if a country is not provided for him in another 50 or 100 years, there will be a terrible clash that will end disastrously to him and disgrace our civilization. We desire to prevent such a clash by pointing the Negro to a home of his own. We feel that all well-disposed and broad-minded white men will aid in this direction. It is because of this belief no doubt that my Negro enemies, so as to prejudice me further in the opinion of the public, wickedly state that I am a member of the Ku Klux Klan, even though I am a black man.

I have been deprived of the opportunity of properly explaining my work to the white people of America through the prejudice worked up against me by jealous and wicked members of my own race. My success as an organizer was much more than rival Negro leaders could tolerate. They, regardless of consequences, either to me or to the race, had to destroy me by fair means or foul. The thousands of anonymous and other hostile letters written to the editors and publishers of the white press by Negro rivals to prejudice we in the eyes of public opinion are sufficient evidence of the wicked and vicious opposition I have had to meet from among my own people, especially among the very light-colored. But they went further than the press in their attempts to discredit me. They organized clubs all over the United States and the West Indies, and wrote both open and anonymous letters to city, state and federal officials of this and other governments to induce them to use their influence to hamper and destroy me. No wonder, therefore, that several judges, district attorneys and other high officials have been against me without knowing me. No wonder, therefore, that the great white population of this country and of the world has a wrong impression of the aims and objects of the Universal Negro Improvement Association and of the work of Marcus Garvey.

Having had the wrong education as a start in his racial career, the Negro has become his own greatest enemy. Most of the trouble I have had in advancing the cause of the race has come from Negroes. Booker Washington aptly described the race in one of his lectures by stating that we were like crabs in a barrel, that none would allow the other to climb over, but on any such attempt all would continue to pull back into the barrel the one crab that would make the effort to climb out. Yet, those of us with vision cannot desert the race, leaving it to suffer and die.

Looking forward a century or two, we can see an economic and political death struggle for the survival of the different race groups. Many of our present-day national centres will have become overcrowded with vast surplus populations. The fight for bread and position will be keen and severe. The weaker and unprepared group is bound to go under. That is why, visionaries as we are in the Universal Negro Improvement Association, we are fighting for the founding of a Negro nation in Africa, so that there will be no clash between black and white and that each race will have a separate existence and civilization all its own without courting suspicion and hatred or eyeing each other with jealousy and rivalry within the borders of the same country.

White men who have struggled for and built up their countries and their own civilizations are not disposed to hand them over to the Negro or any other race without let or hindrance. It would be unreasonable to expect this. Hence any vain assumption on the part of the Negro to imagine that he will one day become president of the nation, governor of the state, or mayor of the city in the countries of white men, is like waiting on the devil and his angels to take up their residence in the Realm on High and direct there the affairs of Paradise.

Great Ideals Know No Nationality

"All intelligent people know that one's nationality has nothing to do with great ideals and great principles."

The Philosophy and Opinions of Marcus Garvey, or Africa for the Africans, Volume 1, 1923

MY enemies in America have done much to hold me up to public contempt and ridicule, but have failed. They believe that the only resort is to stir up national prejudice against me, in that I was not born within the borders of the United States of America.

I am not in the least concerned about such a propaganda, because I have travelled the length and breadth of America and I have discovered that among the fifteen million of my race, only those who have exploited and lived off the ignorance of the masses are concerned with where I was born. The masses of the people are looking for leadership, they desire sincere, honest guidance in racial affairs. As proof of this I may mention, that the largest number of members in the Universal Negro Improvement Association (of which I am President-General) are to be found in America, and are native-born Americans. I know these people so well and I love them so well, that I would not for one minute think that they would fall for such an insidious propaganda.

All intelligent people know that one's nationality has nothing to do with great ideals and great principles. If because I am a Jamaican the Negro should not accept the principle of race rights and liberty, or the ideal of a free and independent race; then you may well say that because Jesus was a Nazarene the outside world should not accept His doctrine of Christianity, because He was an "alien."

Because Martin Luther was born in Germany, the world should not accept the doctrine of Protestantism.

Because Alexander Hamilton and Lafayette were not born in America, Americans should not accept and appreciate the benefits they bestowed upon the nation.

Because Marconi was an Italian, we of the New World should not make use of wireless telegraphy. Again I say, great principles, great ideals know no nationality.

I know no national boundary where the Negro is concerned. The whole world is my province until Africa is free.

I Am a Negro

"We did not come here of our own free will. We were brought here, and so the question of birth does not enter into the question."

From His Closing Address to the Jury at His Trial: New York City
June 15, 1923

The Philosophy and Opinions of Marcus Garvey, or Africa for the Africans,
Volume 2

I AM a Negro. I make absolutely no apology for being a Negro because my God created me to be what I am, and as I am so will I return to my God, for He knows just why He created me as He did. So, gentlemen, you will understand that behind the whole business proposition lies the spirit of the movement. I have no time to go into the work of the Universal Negro Improvement Association, but I say this: I know there are certain people who do not like me because I am black; they don't like me because I am not born here, through no fault of mine.

I didn't bring myself into this Western world. You know the history of my race. I was brought here; I was sold to some slave master in the island of Jamaica. Some Irish slave master who subsequently gave my great-grandfather his name. Garvey is not an African name; it is an Irish name, as Johnston is not an African name, Garcia is not an African name, Thompson and Tobias are not African names. Where did we get those names from? We inherited them from our own slave masters, English, French, Irish or Scotch. So, if I was born in Jamaica, it was no fault of mine. It was because that slave ship which took me to Jamaica did not come to American ports. That is how some Negroes of America were not born in the West Indies.

We did not come here of our own free will. We were brought here, and so the question of birth does not enter into the question of the Negro. It was a matter of accident. Will you blame me for the accident of being a Jamaican Negro and not an American Negro? Surely you will not. But there is a bigger question involved. It is a question of race. What are you going to do with this question of race? You may sit quietly by, but it is going to be serious later on, and that is why the Universal Negro Improvement Association is endeavoring to assist you in solving the Negro problem by helping the Negro to become enterprising, independent politically, and by having a country of his own. If you follow me down the ages you will see within a hundred years you are going to have a terrible race problem in America, when you will have increased and the country will become over-populated. It will be a fight for existence between two opposite races. The weak will have to go down in defeat before the strong. In the riots of Washington, East St. Louis, Chicago, Tulsa, study the race question and you will find that some serious thinking must be done now to solve this problem; otherwise our children will be confronted with it. Do you know when you want bread and the other fellow wants it, when there is only one loaf—what is going to happen? Enmity and pressure is going to spring up and a fight will ensue. That is why the Universal Negro Improvement Association has started this proposition to redeem Africa and build up a country of our own, so as not to molest you in the country your fathers founded hundreds of years ago.

Some Negroes believe in social equality. They want to intermarry with the white women of this country, and it is going to cause trouble later on. Some Negroes want the same jobs you have. They want to be presidents of the nation. What is going to be the outcome? Study the race question and you will find that the program of the Universal Negro Improvement Association and the Black Star Line is the solution of the problem which confronts us, not only in this country, but throughout the world.

Folks try to misrepresent me and say I don't like white people. That is not true. Some of the best friends I have are white men. The bishop who testified here has been my friend from youth. He said other things that some of us did not understand. I asked him, Do you know Marcus Garvey?—he said yes. What is the opinion of him? He said doubtful. Now probably you didn't understand what he meant. Garvey was a public man. Opinions differ. He was a priest and he had to tell the truth. Surely some men are doubtful of Marcus Garvey, and there are some who are not doubtful. He didn't say that Garvey was doubtful. He gives it as it was, when I asked him about his personal opinion I was not allowed because it was not the proper question, the court ruled. He said, however, Garvey was a worthy man, so I trust you will not have the wrong impression.

Now, gentlemen, I will not touch on the other witnesses, I leave it all to you. But, gentlemen, remember this, I assure you that you are all at this time to judge a man, to judge me by the testimony, by what has been brought here, by your judgment of what is right and what is wrong. You condemn the body but not the soul. It is not in your power to condemn a soul, it is only the power of God. You can only condemn the body, but God condemns the soul. Yes, judge me and God will judge you for judging Marcus Garvey. You can believe me, it is satisfactory to Marcus Garvey because some writer says, "What greater breastplate than a heart untainted. Thrice is he armed who hath his quarrel just and he but naked—though locked up in steel whose conscience with injustice is corrupted." I stand before you and the honorable court for your judgment and I do not regret what I have done for the Universal Negro Improvement Association; for the Negro race, because I did it from the fullness of my soul. I did it with the fear of my God, believing that I was doing the right thing. I am still firm in my belief that I served my race, people, conscience and God. I further make no apology for what I have done. I ask for no mercy. If you say I am guilty, I go to my God as I feel, a clear conscience and a clean soul, knowing I have not wronged even a child of my race or any member of my family. I love all mankind. I love Jew, Gentile, I love white and black.

I have respect for every race. I believe the Irish should be free; they should have a country. I believe the Jew should be free and the Egyptian should be free, and the Indian and the Poles. I believe also that the black man should be free. I would fight for the freedom of the Jew, the Irish, the Poles; I would fight and die for the liberation of 400,000,000 Negroes. I expect from the world for Negroes what the world expects from them.

I thank you for your patience, gentlemen, and his Honor for the patience he has exhibited also. There has been some differences, but I have great respect for this court. I respect the constitution of this great country, the most liberal constitution in the world. This great government, the most liberal in the world. Could I go to Washington without paying my homage and respect to that hero, George Washington, and Abraham Lincoln, the emancipator of our million slaves? Then, how dare anyone accuse me of being disrespectful to the United States or the courts—I feel that my rights are infringed upon. If I differed from the judge, it is but human. I know you are business men just as I am. My business has been going to pieces and I know how much yours is going to pieces, but if you were to be tried and I were a juror I would give you the same consideration as you have given me, therefore, I leave myself to you, feeling that you should judge me as your God shall judge you, not for friendship, not for satisfying the whims of someone, but because of truth and justice.

The District Attorney will tell you it is Garvey, Garvey, Garvey, Garvey is the mastermind, Garvey is the genius; Garvey is but a man. Garvey is but human. But Garvey must be destroyed, but in destroying the physical in Garvey, you cannot destroy the soul and I feel you, gentlemen, will not do anything except that which is prompted by justice, truth and the law, as you know the law is but an expression of truth, of justice, and of thought. The law demands truth and justice so that justice can be done.

I leave myself to you. I have not denied anything that I know of and have done.

West Indies in the Mirror of Truth

"The Negroes of the West Indies have been sleeping for seventy-eight years and are still under the spell of Rip Van Winkle."

The Champion Magazine,
Chicago, January 1917

I HAVE been in America eight months. My mission to this country is to lecture and raise funds to help my organization—the Universal Negro Improvement Association of Jamaica—to establish an industrial and educational institute to assist in educating the Negro youth of that island. I am also engaged in the study of Negro life in this country.

I must say, at the outset, that the American Negro ought to compliment himself, as well as the early prejudice of the South, for the racial progress made in fifty years, and for the discriminating attitude that had led the race up to the high mark of consciousness preserving it from extinction.

I feel that the Negro who has come in touch with western civilization is characteristically the same, and but for the environment there would have been no marked difference between those of the scattered race in the Western hemisphere. The honest prejudice of the South was sufficiently evident to give the Negro of America the real start—the start with a race consciousness, which I am convinced is responsible for the state of development already reached by the race.

A Fred Douglass or a Booker Washington never would have been heard of in American national life if it were not for the consciousness of the race in having its own leaders. In contrast, the West Indies has produced no Fred Douglass or Booker Washington after seventy-eight years of emancipation, simply because the Negro people of that section started out without a race consciousness.

I have traveled a good deal through many countries, and from my observations and study, I unhesitatingly and unreservedly say that the American Negro is the peer of all Negroes, the most progressive and the foremost unit in the expansive chain of scattered Ethiopia. Industrially, financially, educationally and socially, the Negroes of both hemispheres have to defer to the American brother, the fellow who has revolutionized history in race development inasmuch as to be able within fifty years to produce men and women out of the immediate bond of slavery, the latchets of whose shoes many a "favored son and daughter" has been unable to loose.

As I travel through the various cities I have been observing with pleasure the active part played by Negro men and women in the commercial and industrial life of the nation. In the cities I have already visited, which include New York, Boston, Philadelphia, Pittsburgh, Baltimore, Washington and Chicago, I have seen commercial enterprises owned and managed by Negro people. I have seen Negro banks in Washington and Chicago, stores, cafés, restaurants, theaters and real estate agencies that fill my heart with joy to realize, in positive truth, and not by sentiment, that at one center of Negrodom, at least, the people of the race have sufficient pride to do things for themselves.

The acme of American Negro enterprise is not yet reached. You have still a far way to go. You want more stores, more banks, and bigger enterprises. I hope that your powerful Negro press and the conscientious element among your leaders will continue to inspire you to achieve; I have detected, during my short stay, that even among you there are leaders who are false, who are mere self-seekers, but on the other hand, I am pleased to find good men and, too, those whose fight for the uplift of the race is one of life and death. I have met some personalities who are not prominently in the limelight for whom I have a strong regard as towards their sincerity in the cause of race uplift, and I think more of their people as real disciples working for the good of our race than many of the men whose names have become nationally and internationally known. In New York, I met John E. Bruce, a man for whom I have the strongest regard inasmuch as I have seen in him a true Negro, a man who does not talk simply because he is in a position for which he must say or do something, but who feels honored to be a member. I can also place in this category Dr. R. R. Wright, Jr., Dr. Parks, vice-president of the Baptist Union, and Dr. Triley of the M. E. Church of Philadelphia, the Rev. J. C. Anderson of Quinn Chapel and Mrs. Ida Wells Barnett of Chicago. With men and women of this type, who are conscientious workers and not mere life service dignitaries, I can quite understand that the time is at hand when the stranger, such as I am, will discover the American Negro firmly and strongly set on the pinnacle of fame.

The West Indian Negro who has had seventy-eight years of emancipation has nothing to compare with your progress. Educationally, he has, in the exception, made a step forward, but generally he is stagnant. I have discovered a lot of "vain bluff" as propagated by the irresponsible type of West Indian Negro who has become resident of this country—bluff to the effect that conditions are better in the West Indies than they are in America. Now let me assure you, honestly and truthfully, that they are nothing of the kind. The West Indies in reality could have been the ideal home of the Negro, but the sleeping West Indian has ignored his chance ever since his emancipation, and today he is at the tail end of all that is worthwhile in the West Indies. The educated men are immigrating to the United States, Canada and Europe; the laboring element are to be found by the thousands in Central and South America. These people are leaving their homes simply because they haven't pride and courage enough to stay at home and combat the forces that make them exiles. If we had the spirit of self-consciousness and reliance, such as you have in America, we would have been ahead of you, and today the standard of Negro development in the West would have been higher. We haven't the pluck in the West Indies to agitate for or demand a square deal and the blame can be attributed to no other source than indolence and lack of pride among themselves.

Let not the American Negro be misled; he occupies the best position among all Negroes up to the present time, and my advice to him is to keep up his constitutional fight for equity and justice.

The Negroes of the West Indies have been sleeping for seventy-eight years and are still under the spell of Rip Van Winkle. These people want a terrific sensation to awaken them to their racial consciousness. We are throwing away good business opportunities in the beautiful islands of the West Indies. We have no banks of our own, no big stores and commercial undertakings, we depend on others as dealers, while we remain consumers. The file is there open and ready for anyone who has the training and ability to become a pioneer. If enterprising Negro Americans would get hold of some of the wealthy Negroes of the West Indies and teach them how to trade and to do things in the interest of their people, a great good would be accomplished for the advancement of the race.

The Negro masses in the West Indies want enterprises that will help them to dress as well as the Negroes in the North of the United States; to help them to live in good homes and to provide them with furniture on the installment plan; to insure them in sickness and death and to prevent a pauper's grave.

Declaration of the Rights of the Negro Peoples of the World

". . . we, the duly elected representatives of the Negro peoples of
the world, invoking the aid of the just and Almighty God, do
declare all men, women, and children of our blood throughout
the world free citizens, and do claim them as free citizens of
Africa, the Motherland of all Negroes."

International Convention of the Negroes of the World, New York City,
August 31, 1920

The Philosophy and Opinions of Marcus Garvey, or Africa for the Africans,
Volume 2

DRAFTED and adopted at Convention held in New York, 1920, over which Marcus Garvey presided as Chairman, and at which he was elected Provisional President of Africa.

Be it Resolved, That the Negro people of the world, through their chosen representatives in convention assembled in Liberty Hall, in the City of New York and United States of America, from August 1 to August 31, in the year of our Lord, one thousand nine hundred and twenty, protest against the wrongs and injustices they are suffering at the hands of their white brethren, and state what they deem their fair and just rights, as well as the treatment they propose to demand of all men in the future.

We complain:

I. That nowhere in the world, with few exceptions, are black men accorded equal treatment with white men, although in the same situation and circumstances, but, on the contrary, are discriminated against and denied the common rights due to human beings for no other reason than their race and color.

We are not willingly accepted as guests in the public hotels and inns of the world for no other reason than our race and color.

II. In certain parts of the United States of America our race is denied the right of public trial accorded to other races when accused of crime, but are lynched and burned by mobs, and such brutal and inhuman treatment is even practiced upon our women.

III. That European nations have parcelled out among themselves and taken possession of nearly all of the continent of Africa, and the natives are compelled to surrender their lands to aliens and are treated in most instances like slaves.

IV. In the southern portion of the United States of America, although citizens under the Federal Constitution, and in some states almost equal to the whites in population and are qualified land owners and taxpayers, we are, nevertheless, denied all voice in the making and administration of the laws and are taxed without representation by the state governments, and at the same time compelled to do military service in defense of the country.

V. On the public conveyances and common carriers in the Southern portion of the United States we are Jim-Crowed and compelled to accept separate and inferior accommodations and made to pay the same fare charged for first-class accommodations, and our families are often humiliated and insulted by drunken white men who habitually pass through the Jim-Crow cars going to the smoking car.

VI. The physicians of our race are denied the right to attend their patients while in the public hospitals of the cities and states where they reside in certain parts of the United States.

Our children are forced to attend inferior separate schools for shorter terms than white children, and the public school funds are unequally divided between the white and colored schools.

VII. We are discriminated against and denied an equal chance to earn wages for the support of our families, and in many instances are refused admission into labor unions, and nearly everywhere are paid smaller wages than white men.

VIII. In Civil Service and departmental offices we are everywhere discriminated against and made to feel that to be a black man in Europe, America and the West Indies is equivalent to being an outcast and a leper among the races of men, no matter what the character and attainments of the black man may be.

IX. In the British and other West Indian Islands and colonies, Negroes are secretly and cunningly discriminated against, and denied those fuller rights in government to which white citizens are appointed, nominated and elected.

X. That our people in those parts are forced to work for lower wages than the average standard of white men and are kept in conditions repugnant to good civilized tastes and customs.

XI. That the many acts of injustice against members of our race before the courts of law in the respective islands and colonies are of such nature as to create disgust and disrespect for the white man's sense of justice.

XII. Against all such inhuman, un-Christian and uncivilized treatment we here and now emphatically protest, and invoke the condemnation of all mankind.

In order to encourage our race all over the world and to stimulate it to a higher and grander destiny, we demand and insist on the following Declaration of Rights:

1. Be it known to all men that whereas, all men are created equal and entitled to the rights of life, liberty and the pursuit of happiness, and because of this we, the duly elected representatives of the Negro peoples of the world, invoking the aid of the just and Almighty God, do declare all men, women and children of our blood throughout the world free citizens, and do claim them as free citizens of Africa, the Motherland of all Negroes.

2. That we believe in the supreme authority of our race in all things racial; that all things are created and given to man as a common possession; that there should be an equitable distribution and apportionment of all such things, and in consideration of the fact that as a race we are now deprived of those things that are morally and legally ours, we believe it right that all such things should be acquired and held by whatsoever means possible.

3. That we believe the Negro, like any other race, should be governed by the ethics of civilization, and, therefore, should not be deprived of any of those rights or privileges common to other human beings.

4. We declare that Negroes, wheresoever they form a community among themselves, should be given the right to elect their own representatives to represent them in legislatures, courts of law, or such institutions as may exercise control over that particular community.

5. We assert that the Negro is entitled to even-handed justice before all courts of law and equity in whatever country he may be found, and when this is denied him on account of his race or color such denial is an insult to the race as a whole and should be resented by the entire body of Negroes.

6. We declare it unfair and prejudicial to the rights of Negroes in communities where they exist in considerable numbers to be tried by a judge and jury composed entirely of an alien race, but in all such cases members of our race are entitled to representation on the jury.

7. We believe that any law or practice that tends to deprive any African of his land or the privileges of free citizenship within his country is unjust and immoral, and no native should respect any such law or practice.

8. We declare taxation without representation unjust and tyrannous, and there should be no obligation on the part of the Negro to obey the levy of a tax by any law-making body from which he is excluded and denied representation on account of his race and color.

9. We believe that any law especially directed against the Negro to his detriment and singling him out because of his race or color is unfair and immoral, and should not be respected.

10. We believe all men entitled to common human respect, and that our race should in no way tolerate any insults that may be interpreted to mean disrespect to our color.

11. We deprecate the use of the term "nigger" as applied to Negroes, and demand that the word "Negro" be written with a capital "N."

12. We believe that the Negro should adopt every means to protect himself against barbarous practices inflicted upon him because of color.

13. We believe in the freedom of Africa for the Negro people of the world, and by the principle of Europe for the Europeans and Asia for the Asiatics; we also demand Africa for the Africans at home and abroad.

14. We believe in the inherent right of the Negro to possess himself of Africa, and that his possession of same shall not be regarded as an infringement on any claim or purchase made by any race or nation.

15. We strongly condemn the cupidity of those nations of the world who, by open aggression or secret schemes, have seized the territories and inexhaustible natural wealth of Africa, and we place on record our most solemn determination to reclaim the treasures and possession of the vast continent of our forefathers.

16. We believe all men should live in peace one with the other, but when races and nations provoke their ire of other races and nations by attempting to infringe upon their rights, war becomes inevitable, and the attempt in any way to free one's self or protect one's rights or heritage becomes justifiable.

17. Whereas, the lynching, by burning, hanging or any other means, of human beings is a barbarous practice, and a shame and disgrace to civilization, we therefore declare any country guilty of such atrocities outside the pale of civilization.

18. We protest against the atrocious crime of whipping, flogging and overworking of the native tribes of Africa and Negroes everywhere. These are methods that should be abolished, and all means should be taken to prevent a continuance of such brutal practices.

19. We protest against the atrocious practice of shaving the heads of Africans, especially of African women or individuals of Negro blood, when placed in prison as a punishment for crime by an alien race.

20. We protest against segregated districts, separate public conveyances, industrial discrimination, lynchings and limitations of political privileges of any Negro citizen in any part of the world on account of race, color or creed, and will exert our full influence and power against all such.

21. We protest against any punishment inflicted upon a Negro with severity, as against lighter punishment inflicted upon another of an alien race for like offense, as an act of prejudice and injustice, and should be resented by the entire race.

22. We protest against the system of education in any country where Negroes are denied the same privileges and advantages as other races.

23. We declare it inhuman and unfair to boycott Negroes from industries and labor in any part of the world.

24. We believe in the doctrine of the freedom of the press, and we therefore emphatically protest against the suppression of Negro newspapers and periodicals in various parts of the world, and call upon Negroes everywhere to employ all available means to prevent such suppression.

25. We further demand free speech universally for all men.

26. We hereby protest against the publication of scandalous and inflammatory articles by an alien press tending to create racial strife and the exhibition of picture films showing the Negro as a cannibal.

27. We believe in the self-determination of all peoples.

28. We declare for the freedom of religious worship.

29. With the help of Almighty God, we declare ourselves the sworn protectors of the honor and virtue of our women and children, and pledge our lives for their protection and defense everywhere, and under all circumstances from wrongs and outrages.

30. We demand the right of unlimited and unprejudiced education for ourselves and our posterity forever.

31. We declare that the teaching in any school by alien teachers to our

boys and girls, that the alien race is superior to the Negro race, is an insult to the Negro people of the world.

32. Where Negroes form a part of the citizenry of any country, and pass the civil service examination of such country, we declare them entitled to the same consideration as other citizens as to appointments in such civil service.

33. We vigorously protest against the increasingly unfair and unjust treatment accorded Negro travelers on land and sea by the agents and employees of railroad and steamship companies and insist that for equal fare we receive equal privileges with travelers of other races.

34. We declare it unjust for any country, state or nation to enact laws tending to hinder and obstruct the free immigration of Negroes on account of their race and color.

35. That the right of the Negro to travel unmolested throughout the world be not abridged by any person or persons, and all Negroes are called upon to give aid to a fellow Negro when thus molested.

36. We declare that all Negroes are entitled to the same right to travel over the world as other men.

37. We hereby demand that the governments of the world recognize our leader, and his representatives chosen by the race to look after the welfare of our people under such governments.

38. We demand complete control of our social institutions without interference by any alien race or races.

39. That the colors, Red, Black and Green, be the colors of the Negro race.

40. Resolved, That the anthem, "Ethiopia, Thou Land of Our Fathers," etc., shall be the anthem of the Negro race.

The Universal Ethiopian Anthem
(Poem by Benjamin Burrell and
U.N.I.A. music director Arnold J. Ford.)

I

Ethiopia, thou land of our fathers,
Thou land where the gods loved to be,
As storm cloud at night suddenly gathers
Our armies come rushing to thee.
We must in the fight be victorious
When swords are thrust outward to gleam;
For us will the vict'ry be glorious
When led by the Red, Black and Green.

Chorus

Advance, advance to victory,
Let Africa be free;
Advance to meet the foe
With the might
Of the Red, the Black and the Green.

II

Ethiopia, the tyrant's falling,
Who smote thee upon thy knees,
And thy children are lustily calling
From over the distant seas.
Jehovah, the Great One has heard us,
Has noted our sighs and our tears,
With His spirit of Love he has stirred us
To be One through the coming years.
CHORUS—Advance, advance, etc.

III

O Jehovah, thou God of the ages
Grant unto our sons that lead
The wisdom Thou gave to Thy sages
When Israel was sore in need.
Thy voice thro' the dim past has spoken,
Ethiopia shall stretch forth her hand,
By Thee shall all fetters be broken,
And Heav'n bless our dear fatherland.
CHORUS—Advance, advance, etc.

41. We believe that any limited liberty which deprives one of the complete rights and prerogatives of full citizenship is but a modified form of slavery.

42. We declare it an injustice to our people and a serious impediment to the health of the race to deny to competent licensed Negro physicians the right to practice in the public hospitals of the communities in which they reside, for no other reason than their race and color.

43. We call upon the various governments of the world to accept and acknowledge Negro representatives who shall be sent to the said governments to represent the general welfare of the Negro peoples of the world.

44. We deplore and protest against the practice of confining juvenile prisoners in prisons with adults, and we recommend that such youthful prisoners be taught gainful trades under humane supervision.

45. Be it further resolved, that we as a race of people declare the League of Nations null and void as far as the Negro is concerned, in that it seeks to deprive Negroes of their liberty.

46. We demand of all men to do unto us as we would do unto them, in the name of justice; and we cheerfully accord to all men all the rights we claim herein for ourselves.

47. We declare that no Negro shall engage himself in battle for an alien race without first obtaining the consent of the leader of the Negro people of the world, except in a matter of national self-defense.

48. We protest against the practice of drafting Negroes and sending them to war with alien forces without proper training, and demand in all cases that Negro soldiers be given the same training as the aliens.

49. We demand that instructions given Negro children in schools include the subject of "Negro History," to their benefit.

50. We demand a free and unfettered commercial intercourse with all the Negro people of the world.

51. We declare for the absolute freedom of the seas for all peoples.

52. We demand that our duly accredited representatives be given proper recognition in all leagues, conferences, conventions or courts of international arbitration wherever human rights are discussed.

53. We proclaim the 31st day of August of each year to be an international holiday to be observed by all Negroes.

54. We want all men to know we shall maintain and contend for the freedom and equality of every man, woman and child of our race, with our lives, our fortunes and our sacred honor.

These rights we believe to be justly ours and proper for the protection of the Negro race at large, and because of this belief we, on behalf of the four hundred million Negroes of the world, do pledge herein the sacred blood of the race in defense, and we hereby subscribe our names as a guarantee of the truthfulness and faithfulness hereof in the presence of Almighty God, on the 13th day of August, in the year of our Lord one thousand nine hundred and twenty.

Marcus Garvey, James D. Brooks, James W. H. Eason, Henrietta Vinton Davis, Lionel Winston Greenidge, Adrion Fitzroy Johnson, Rudolph Ethelbert Brissaac Smith, Charles Augustus Petioni, Thomas H. N. Simon, Richard Hilton Tobitt, George Alexander McGuire, Peter Edward Baston, Reynold R. Felix, Harry Walters Kirby, Sarah Branch, Marie Barrier Houston, Geoge L. O'Brien, F. O. Ogilvie, Arden A. Bryan, Benjamin Dyett, Marie Duchaterlier, John Phillip Hodge, Theophilus H. Saunders, Wilford H. Smith, Gabriel E. Stewart, Arnold Josiah Ford, Lee Crawford, William McCartney, Adina Clem. James, William Musgrave La Motte, John Sydney de Bourg, Arnold S. Cunning, Vernal J. Williams, Frances Wilcome Ellegor, J. Frederick Selkridge, Innis Abel Horsford, Cyril A. Chrichlow, Samuel McIntyre, John Thomas Wilkins, Mary Thurston, John G. Befue, William Ware, J. A. Lewis, O. C. Kelly, Venture R. Hamilton, R. H. Hodge, Edward Alfred Taylor,

Ellen Wilson, G. W. Wilson, Richard Edward Riley, Nellie Grant Whiting, G. W. Washington, Maldena Miller, Gertrude Davis, James D. Williams, Emily Christmas Kinch, D. D. Lewis, Nettie Clayton, Partheria Hills, Janie Jenkins, John C. Simons, Alphonso A. Jones, Allen Hobbs, Reynold Fitzgerald Austin, James Benjamin Yearwood, Frank O. Raines, Shedrick Williams, John Edward Ivey, Frederick Augustus Toote, Philip Hemmings, F. F. Smith, E. J. Jones, Joseph Josiah Cranston, Frederick Samuel Ricketts, Dugald Augustus Wade, E. E. Nelom, Florida Jenkins, Napoleon J. Francis, Joseph D. Gibson, J. P. Jasper, J. W. Montgomery, David Benjamin, J. Gordon, Harry E. Ford, Carrie M. Ashford, Andrew N. Willis, Lucy Sands, Louise Woodson, George D. Creese, W. A. Wallace, Thomas E. Bagley, James Young, Prince Alfred McConney, John E. Hudson, William Ines, Harry R. Watkins, C. L. Halton, J. T. Bailey, Ira Joseph Touissant Wright, T. H. Golden, Abraham Benjamin Thomas, Richard C. Noble, Walter Green, C. S. Bourne, G. F. Bennett, B. D. Levy, Mary E. Johnson, Lionel Antonio Francis, Carl Roper, E. R. Donawa, Philip Van Putten, I. Brathwaite, Jesse W. Luck, Olivier Kaye, J. W. Hudspeth, C. B. Lovell, William C. Matthews, A. Williams, Ratford E. M. Jack, H. Vinton Plummer, Randolph Phillips, A. I. Bailey, duly elected representatives of the Negro people of the world.

Sworn before me this 15th day of August, 1920.

[Legal Seal]
JOHN G. BAYNE.
Notary Public, New York County.

New York County Clerk's No. 378; New York County Register's No. 12102. Commission expires March 30, 1922.

Unemployment

"Let a man lose his confidence in his people and in a God, and chaos is ushered in and anarchy sweeps the world and human society is destroyed."

Liberty Hall, New York City
February 11, 1921

The Negro World,
February 26, 1921

I DESIRE to speak to you this evening in a heart-to-heart manner, because just at the time we are facing critical conditions, and it is but right that we should talk to each other, counsel each other, and get to understand each other, so that all of us may be able to work from one common understanding for the good of all.

I desire to appeal to the memory of the members of this association. You will remember that in the years immediately preceding the great war in Europe there was a great industrial stagnation among Negroes in the United States of America, and that we then faced a hard and difficult task industrially, economically, and we saw no hope, and we had none. Then immediately, whilst undergoing our hard and difficult experience, the war broke out in Europe. Germany declared war, and nearly all the European powers were dragged into the bloody conflict. Immediately the war started in Europe, the participants rushed a large number of orders for war supplies and munitions to the United States of America, that was then neutral in the war. By the abnormal demands for the industrials of these United States of America, a great industrial wave swept the country, and untold opportunities were opened up to Negroes everywhere in these United States of America; not only to Negroes, but those untold opportunities were opened up to all races, to peoples within the confines of this country. Factories and mills and industrial plants sprang up everywhere in the great industrial centers, and men who never had employment, men who never had any occupations prior to that time, found opportunities then. Men for years who never had the chance of earning a decent wage, found jobs ranging in weekly salaries or wages from $25 to $100, and some $200 a week. Men everywhere were employed, and even the peons and the serfs of the South broke loose from the South and ran North, where these great industrial opportunities had opened up themselves for each and every one. Men came from the West Indies; men came from all parts of the world to America to enjoy the benefits of the new industrial opportunities offered in America. These opportunities opened up larger and larger, and out of the wealth that was poured out of the great war some of the people who enjoyed the distribution of that wealth conserved the portion they got or received, such as the Jews, the Italians, the Irish and the Poles. Their leaders in the pulpits, through periodicals, through magazines, and from platforms and classrooms, taught their respective groups the value of conserving the wealth that was then poured out into their pockets in the form of salaries and wages, to prepare for the rainy day that would come. Negroes, however, in the most loose, the most slack, the most indifferent manner, received their portion of the wealth that was poured out, and they made absolutely no effort to conserve it. They distributed it as quickly as they received it; they paid it out back to the employer, or to his friend, or to his brother, or some of his relatives, as quickly as they received it from him. And just at the time a large number of the leaders of the country said nothing. They had no advice to give. The preachers said nothing, and they gave no advice to the people.

Just about that time the Universal Negro Improvement Association came upon the scene, with an active propaganda. It taught preparedness—industrial preparedness among the Negroes then. It warned them, and told them that they should prepare to start industries of their own, to save their money, and to make every effort to protect themselves; because after the war there would be a great industrial dearth; there would be a great industrial stagnation. We taught that doctrine; we preached it; we wrote it in the newspapers; we scattered it near and far; we sent the doctrine everywhere and everywhere we got the retort that we were crazy; that we were a bunch of lunatics. The man who inspired the movement was a crazy man and a fit subject for the lunatic asylum. They said all manner of things against him, because we dared then, when no others would do so, to teach the doctrine of industrial, economic preparedness. The people, however, could not see, and they believed we were crazy. But we stuck to our doctrine, we adhered to our belief, and we were able to convert four million people scattered all over the world to our doctrine and to our belief. But we did not convert the four million people at one time; it took us four years to convert them. Some became converted immediately, and assumed the burden and responsibility of carrying and conveying the doctrine to others. Hence tonight I am able to look into the faces of some of the people who started with me when we organized the Universal Negro Improvement Association; people who have made the sacrifices I made—sacrifices in money and in time. They bore the brunt of the situation, because on them laid the responsibility to finance and support the propaganda so as to carry the propaganda to others. And they have borne the price of the propaganda for four years reaching the four millions. But it reached the four millions only too late, because the war and the opportunities were over, and when it reached them they could ill afford to support the doctrine to convey it unto others. Hence the present situation that confronts us now.

There are hundreds and thousands, and later on millions of men in this country of Negro blood who will be thrown out—thrown out into the cold. We anticipated it; we saw it, and we warned the people against it. We did it with the feeling of our sympathies for our own; we did it with the feelings of conviction that the men with whom we mingled during the war paid us large wages, paid us large salaries with a vengeance, but they were forced, they were compelled to do so, and they did it with a spite and with a vengeance. Some did not see it, and did not appreciate the fact of those who saw it and warned the people against it. The attitude of the employers in this country was to pay the Negro as small a wage as possible on which he could hardly subsist or hardly live, because he desired to keep the Negro as an industrial peon, as an industrial serf, and make it impossible for him to rise in the great industrial, economic ladder of life. He kept him down, not because the Negro before the war was not worth more than he was paid for his labor, for at all times the Negro is worth more than twenty, thirty or forty dollars a month. Yet that was all that was paid to us prior to the war, and all of you know it. It was paid to the elevator men, to the porter men, and everybody nearly got the maximum of forty dollars or fifty dollars, or sixty dollars a month from his employer prior to the war, not because we were not worth more than that for our labor, but because the other man was prejudiced against paying us more than that. He desired not to give us a chance to rise in the industrial and economic world. But the war came, and we compelled him by conditions, we forced him by conditions to pay us $100 a week, to pay us $50 a week, to pay us $60 a week, and some of us mechanics forced him to pay us $200 a week, and he paid it, but with a bitter anguish; he paid it with great reluctance; he paid it with a vengeance and he said: "I am going to get even with the Negro." He knew the Negro better than the Negro knew himself. He knew the Negro would spend every dollar, every nickel, every penny he earned which he was compelled to pay him. He laid the plan by which the Negro would spend every nickel, but the Negro hadn't sense sufficient to see it and know it. Now, what was the object and purpose of it? To take back every nickel that he paid him. When he raised the cost of living, when he raised the cost of bread, when he raised the cost of butter and of eggs, and of meat, and of other necessities of life, what did he mean? He meant that we should return to him every penny of that which we got from him, and that the Negro had not sense enough to see it. He raised the price of everything; he raised the price of luxuries, for he knew well that, above all other peoples, Negroes love luxuries, and he taxed us in the districts where Negroes live, for you paid more for the luxuries you received in your district than the white folks paid for the same luxuries in their district. The white people planned to get every nickel that they paid to you; and we fell for it. We bought silk shirts at $10 apiece, and $15 apiece. We bought shoes at $30 and $25 a pair. We bought ladies' dresses at $100 a suit; we bought the most expensive hats, silk socks at $3 a pair, at $2 a pair, and $1.50 a pair {*laughter*}, and we took automobile rides and paid $24 for a Sunday afternoon ride, and we did all kinds of things of that sort. Some of us had six girls and gave presents to each of them. {*Laughter.*} Thus we spent every nickel of what we received.

Did anyone else live at the same rate at which the Negro then lived? Did the Italian live at that rate? Did the Jew live at that rate? They did not. The Jews saved at least fifty percent of what they earned. The Italian saved at least sixty percent of what he earned. The Irish saved at least fifty percent of what he earned. And at the end of the war every one of them had a bank account to show. Every one of them had some investment in Irish interests to show. How much did we save? What interest have we to show? Absolutely none. Whose fault is it? It is the fault of the people; it is the fault, more, of the leaders. You cannot so much blame the people, because the bulk of the people do not think, the bulk of the people follow the advice of their leaders, and the people of that race that has no leaders is a race that is doomed. Negroes never had any leaders at any time. That is why we have always been doomed. When we preached the doctrine of preparedness, men like Du Bois criticized the U.N.I.A. and its leader. All of you can remember that when we started the propaganda of the U.N.I.A. and the Black Star, every newspaper and magazine in New York tried to down us. The *Amsterdam News* wrote against us; the *New York News* wrote against us; the *Crusade* wrote against us; the *Challenge* wrote against us; the *Emancipator* wrote against us; every one of them wrote against us, and discouraged the people. Whose fault is it now?

That is the question, and you yourselves must give the answer. They all said, and pointed to us, saying that we were a crazy bunch of people. What did we tell you during the war period? And immediately following the war, when you were still employed? Didn't we tell you that there was a Black Star Line? Did we not tell you that its capital was $10,000,000? Did we not throw away, during the war, $50 and $100 and more at different times for mere pleasure and expensive, fashionable clothing? And had we invested that money which we then spent so lavishly and foolishly, to subscribing to the capital stock of the Black Star Line, what would have happened? With $10,000,000 of its stock subscribed and paid for, we would tonight have twenty ships that would belong to us as ours, each worth half a million dollars. And what kind of ships would they be? They would be ships of a tonnage of five thousand to eight or ten thousand tons. They would be ships each able to accommodate at least 500 to 1,000 passengers. If we had twenty ships, each able to accommodate a thousand passengers across the Atlantic Ocean, what would happen today? Every day in the week, or every other day of the week, a ship of the Black Star Line would sail out of New York port with at least a thousand unemployed men from New York to Liberia, West Africa. {*Applause.*} That is what we saw. That is what we tried to tell the people and teach the people. How many of us would be unemployed tonight if the capital stock of the Black Star Line had been subscribed for two years ago? I hardly believe that there would be an unemployed Negro here. Because if we have ten thousand unemployed Negroes in Harlem tonight, we could call up ten ships of the Black Star Line, and say to the captain of those ships that we have ten thousand Negro men unemployed to send to Liberia. Take them! But you did not subscribe the capital; you paid it out in silk shirts; you paid it out in expensive socks. And who made those factory silk shirts and those fancy silk socks that you purchased and paid for? White men. Who sold them to you? White men. Where is the money you paid for them? Gone back to white men, and you are still the paupers that you were prior to the war in 1914. Whose fault is it? That is the answer you must give yourselves.

It pains me, it grieves me, it brings tears to my eyes when I see a race, not of children, but of matured minds, of full grown men and women, playing with and threatening their lives and the destiny of themselves and of posterity. What more can we do as leaders of the Universal Negro Improvement Association than to open the eyes of the people by talking to them, preaching to them, pleading with them, and writing to them concerning that which we know, that which we see? That is all we can do. Some of you are crazy now, as crazy as you were, some of you, four years ago. {*Laughter.*} And those of you who are old members of the U.N.I.A. can remember Marcus Garvey in the streets of Harlem. When you had your fat jobs downtown, earning $100 a week, and in other parts of the country, I could have done the same. But I saw the threatening disaster. And what did I do? I had as much ability as the average man; I had as much skill as the average man. The average man was going his way, making his pile, and enjoyed himself when he was at leisure. People would walk up and down Lenox Avenue and see Marcus Garvey on a stepladder, and would say: "Look at that crazy black fool!" {*Laughter.*} (They called me all kinds and all manner of names standing up there talking about Africa!) Look at his coat! Look at his shoes, and everything he has on! They said all those things about me. But I saw the future collapse. I saw the results that would follow the then period of prosperity that was only transitory. I saw the day when the very big Negro who then got his pay envelope on a Saturday night of $100 and believed he was the biggest thing in Harlem—I foresaw when he would be the smallest thing in Harlem; that he would be the man without a nickel, because I knew the war would soon be over, and I knew the white man would then throw him aside as soon as hostilities were over and there was a slackening in the demand for the commodities or munitions he was then making and give the preference to white men; and that has been the white man's policy ever since his contact with the Negro. That has been his program, and that will be his program always, so long as Negroes are foolish enough to allow him to use them for what he wants.

I am sounding the second warning, and I want you to take it from a man who feels the consciousness of what he says. I am not pretending to be a prophet; I am not pretending to be a sage or a philosopher. I am but an ordinary man with ordinary common sense who can see where the wind blows, and the man who is so foolish as not to be able to see and understand where the wind blows, I am sorry for him; his senses are gone. I can feel; and the man who cannot feel now I am sorry for his dead sense. I can see where the wind is blowing, and it is because of what I see that I am talking to you like this. There are some Negroes in Harlem who are working and some who save money. They believe they are always going to have jobs; they believe they are always going to have money. You will always have money if you know how to use it. There are some men who have money and then lose all they have because they never know how to use it. There are some men who never had and they get and always have it. Now, I want you to realize this one truth that I am endeavoring to point out to you. There are a large number of unemployed Negroes in New York and there are hundreds of thousands of unemployed Negroes in different parts of the country. I have been traveling for the last couple of months and in all of the Western states I have been I have seen Negroes out of work by the hundreds in centers like around the Western and mid-Western states. So that whether we live in New York or somewhere else, conditions are just as bad. So you might as well stay where you are and face the situation. What we want Negroes who are still working and who have money to do is to decide upon some wise plan to save the situation. Negroes do not like to help Negroes anyhow; but perforce we will have to help each other or otherwise something will happen to surprise us. I told you but recently that when a man is hungry he is the respecter of no person. A hungry man forgets the look of his father. Understand that. There are some Negroes who believe they should not take interest in other Negroes. Now, let me tell you that we are going to face a situation, the most critical ever experienced by this race of ours in these United States of America. I told you some time ago that it is a question of dog eating dog. You know how bad a situation that must be. What I mean by it is just that: that there are some Negroes who are too big, who are too aristocratic and too dicty* to take interest in other Negroes. I am going to tell you what I believe will happen to such Negroes later on, if they do not get busy now and do something for all Negroes irrespective of what class these Negroes belong to. No community is safe if in its midst there are thousands of hungry men. I do not care where that community is, it is an unsafe community and especially at midnight. Let the big dicty Negroes say, "What do I care for that good-for-nothing Negro; he is nothing." That poor Negro who has never had a square meal for four days goes to that big dicty Negro—I am trying to picture the conditions later on—he goes to that big dicty Negro and asks for a quarter or 50 cents and he drives him away. That Negro after not having a square meal for two, three or four days, turns away and loses heart and nothing in the world is too desperate for him not to do. To find bread a man is driven to the farthest extreme and at midnight or even in the daylight he resorts to violence and cares not what the result be so long as he finds bread to satisfy his hungry heart and soul. I have just come from Chicago and there I heard of a hungry Negro who never had a square meal for two or three days. He had begged everybody around town and everybody drove

---

*According to *Webster's Third New International Dictionary,* "dicty" means "high-toned."

him away. He said, "Why should I die for hunger when somebody can give me bread? Since they have refused me, I will take it," and he goes to the house of a preacher somewhere in the outskirts of Chicago and he gets into the house where sleeps the lonely preacher and at midnight what did that hungry Negro do? He took a razor or some sharp instrument and severed the head of that sleeping preacher from the body to get two dollars. He got $2, and killed a man for $2 as to find bread. When he had spent that two dollars and could not get any more bread he called the police and said, "I will confess to you what I did if you give me a square meal." He was given a meal of chicken and something else and confessed that he killed the man. Those are the conditions that hungry men are not responsible for. I do not care how religious a man is or how many Sunday schools he goes to; I do not care how long he can pray, when that man is hungry he is a dangerous character. And that is the practical common-sense issue that you have to face in a practical common-sense way. White folks have stopped looking out for Negroes; they stopped before there was a war.

The war robbed them of all that there was in the world. Now they have nothing because they have used up all that is in the world. It is a question now of every man looking out for himself. That is all. The white man is deaf to your sympathy and to your cries. You may cry and beg for jobs he will not give you except you are the only fellow who can fill that job that he wants done. But the first man of his own race he finds able to fill that same job with the same ability as you have, you are gone. And he does not wait to ask where the white man comes from. He only wants to know he is a white man, and out you go. He does not wait to know where you are from. He says you are a Negro, and out you go.

"Now what do we do?" we are saying to the men of the Universal Negro Improvement Association and to the Negro race. I am speaking only to those who have confidence. If you do not have any confidence in yourselves, if you do not have any confidence in your own race movements, I am sorry for you, and I would ask you to go your way. Men must have confidence in something and in someone. Without confidence the world is lost. Mankind has retrograded and the world has gone back. The world is built upon confidence—confidence in someone, confidence in some institution, confidence in something. We live as rational human beings, social human beings, because we have confidence in people and in God the creator. Let a man lose his confidence in his people and in a God, and chaos is ushered in and anarchy sweeps the world and human society is destroyed. It is only the belief and the confidence that we have in a God why man is able to understand his own social institutions and move and live like rational human beings. Take away the highest ideal—the highest faith and confidence in God, and mankind at large is destroyed. As with your confidence in God, as with your confidence in religion, whether it be Christianity or any other religion, so must you have confidence in your institutions that mean anything to you as individuals and as a community.

Now I am saying to you who have confidence in the Universal Negro Improvement Association—and if you have no confidence you should not be here. I am here because I have confidence that the men and the women who make up the movement will continue and continue until victory be written on the banner of the Red, the Black and the Green. {*Cheers.*} I am here because I have confidence in humanity; I am here because I have confidence in God, and I expect that all those who wear the Red, the Black and the Green are here because they have confidence in the ultimate triumph of this great cause of ours. {*Cheers.*} If you have confidence; if you have faith in it as you have confidence and faith in your religion, therefore it is time for you to support the movement and make it the success that you want it to be, make your support not a half-hearted one, but make it a whole-hearted one. You have seen the first practical demonstration of the utility of the Universal Negro Improvement Association. You have seen the first mistake made by this race of ours, as I have tried to preach to you in these few years—the mistake during the war period. I am asking you now not to repeat or not to make the same mistake. I know as I look into the face of many of you that there are hundreds of you members of the Universal Negro Improvement Association who have not done anything yet for the practical carrying out of the program of this organization. I have asked many of you if you have your Liberty bonds, and you say no. I ask why? You say, well, because you are not able just now to buy. You rate your ability to buy on the surplus money you have. When you bought a share or two in the Black Star Line for $5 or $10 two years ago you did it when you were getting a salary of probably $100 or $50 a week, and you said, "I will invest $10 in the Black Star Line," because you had your work and so much surplus cash. Now it is not a question of surplus cash; it is a question of duty. It is a question of your own interest. I am saying to the men and women of the Negro race there is but one salvation for the Negro as I see it now, and that is the building of Liberia, West Africa. The only salvation for Negroes now is opening up industrial and economic opportunities somewhere, and I don't see it around here. You will have to create another war for it, or you will have to get another kaiser before I will see it around here. I have no objection to seeing another kaiser, and I feel sure you would have no objection either, whether he comes from Japan or anywhere, but on the second coming I believe you will be better prepared than the first coming. "Once bitten, twice shy." But you have to bite Negroes a hundred times before they get shy. We have been bitten for 300 years and up to now we are not shy yet. What do I mean? I want you members to act as living missionaries to convince others. There are still Negroes here who can help and buy shares in the Black Star Line. Those of you who have done your duty, I am not speaking to you; but there are thousands who can subscribe to the Liberian Construction Loan. There is a hungry man, he has not a nickel in his pocket and he is begging bread. There is another man with a thousand dollars. The one man without money to buy bread can neither help himself nor his fellow men. The man with a thousand dollars cannot only help himself, but he can help dozens of others; but he is too selfish. He, like the other man, has no money, has no job, and he says: "I have a thousand dollars, but I have no job. I am just going to hold on to this thousand dollars." And every day he spends $3, $4, $5 out of it and still has no job. Every day $5 has gone and he is too selfish to think about the other man.

He is too selfish to think about anybody else he meets, and every day $5 goes out of his thousand dollars, and at the end of the year he still has no job. His thousand dollars is gone, and he is like the other fellow, without a nickel. Both of them face each other—two hungry men; one cannot help the other; but that man who had the thousand dollars, if he were a wise man, a man of common, ordinary sense, what would he have done when he finds himself without a job and with a thousand dollars only left out of his years of earnings? He would say: Is there an organization around that is endeavoring to do some good? Are there any other men around who want to do some good? If so, I will go and link up with them and do some good. Yes, he would say, there is an organization over there. What are they trying to do? They are trying among other things to raise two million dollars or ten million dollars to put a line of steamships on the ocean to carry hundreds of men from these ports of the world to Africa, where they are going to build factories, mills, railroads, etc., and find employment for hundreds of men. They are crying for money to put over the scheme. I will find out how far they have gone, and if it is possible that they can carry it through I will put in $500, and if the other fellow who has his thousand will also put in $500 and others will do likewise $10,000,000 will be subscribed to buy ships and $2,000,000 will be subscribed to buy railroad and building materials, and we will be ready to ship men to Africa to work from January to December and open up opportunities immediately. That is what I am trying to get you to understand. A thousand dollars in your pocket without a job may find you worse off at the end of six months. A thousand dollars or $200 or $100 invested in an organization in which you have confidence may save yourself, your children and posterity. If you have no confidence I cannot advise you because I will do nothing myself except I have confidence in it. A man's confidence is his guide; a man's faith is his guide. I am only speaking to those who have faith in the Universal Negro Improvement Association. If you have faith, if you respect the success that we have made in three years when we started without anything and have reached where we are now; if you have faith that we can continue where we are to the greater success to be, I am asking you to support the program of the Universal Negro Improvement Association. I want to find out how many of you have confidence and faith in the Universal Negro Improvement Association. Hold your hands up. {*Simultaneously hands go up from all parts of the hall.*} I thank you for your faith. I thank you for your confidence; but men and women, remember it is not a question of Marcus Garvey or any other man. It is a question of yourselves. What will you do to save yourselves? Marcus Garvey cannot save anybody because Marcus Garvey is but human like every other man. Jesus Christ is the only man who has the power to save. I am but a man. I cannot save you; you must save yourselves. I am only trying to advise you the way how all of us can save ourselves. If you do not heed it will not be my fault. I have stood by; I have listened and I have heard all kinds of people blaming me . . . What can I do? I have advised you all the time how to get jobs. That is all I did. If you do not have jobs now it is not my fault. I advised you to put the money you saved into a great corporation—into a great corporation of which you are members; not in some strange thing that you did not know anything about—but in your own organization. Every member of the organization has a right to know everything about the organization, so that when you put your money into it you are putting your money in your own hands. I am but one individual who helped to carry on the work of the organization, and if you do not trust yourselves, who is to blame? You did not have confidence in yourselves.

I am giving you a message that you may impart it to others and tell them there is still a chance; because we have not reached the worst yet; but that chance you must grasp in the next sixty days. I have met men coming to the office who have been out of work for three months and two months and one month. It brings tears to my eyes to see them. I saw a fellow whom I believe four years ago was raising "Cain" up in Harlem. He used to look at me on the street and laugh and walk on; but now he has been reduced to dire straits, and he came to the office and would not leave until I gave him 50 cents. That is the way with the majority of Negroes. That fellow earned as much money as any other man around here, and every evening you saw him on the avenue with . . . a new girl. {*Laughter.*} The girls are belonging to somebody else and he is down and out. {*Laughter.*} And that is the situation, not with one man but with hundreds of our men.

I am going to give this one advice. I have been waiting for the last 60 days to see what the politicians would do in making an effort to present the case of the Negro to the proper authorities. I have searched all the papers, and I have not seen anything done—no attempt made; and because they have done nothing I have to start to do something. You will all understand that I am an African citizen, and I am not supposed to interfere in domestic politics; but if the other fellow will not start out, before I see the people perish, I will take my chance. I know that this nation owes a solemn obligation to the Negro, and I could not stand and see the Negro perish without a hearing; and since the politicians have not spoken we shall send a delegation of the Universal Negro Improvement Association to the Governor of New York to find out what he means by allowing Negroes to be closed out of jobs, when Negroes and especially the boys of the New York 15th fought so nobly in France and Flanders for the preservation of American freedom. What does the state mean by allowing the politicians and citizens of the state to close out Negroes and give alien enemies jobs now? {*Cheers.*} We will send a deputation to Albany to ask Albany, "Will you want us again?" And we will expect a direct answer from Albany. We will ask Albany, "Will you want us in the American-Japanese war? Will you want us in the Anglo-American war?" Because David Lloyd George is scheming now to write off the war debt, and no American citizen is going to stand for it. Therefore, it may end somewhere else. "Will you want us then?" And we will listen for the answer from Albany; and from Albany we will send the same deputation to Washington a couple of days after to ask the same question. {*Cheers.*}

This is no time for bowing and scraping and pussyfooting. It is time to let the other fellow know that you are alive. {*Great applause.*} Negroes do not want to beg jobs; Negroes must demand jobs; that is all there is about it. {*Applause.*} But you must demand jobs in the proper way. Let the leaders of the race, if they are leaders, as Du Bois, and men like Moton, go out and let President Harding know that ten or fifteen million Negroes stood behind the country in time of war, and they must now stand behind those ten or fifteen million Negroes. {*Applause.*} If you have any men posing as leaders who are going about among white people bowing and scraping they will brush you aside. You must have as your leaders and representatives men who will let our high officials and other influential white people know that you are alive, and that you are going to stay alive. I cannot see the philosophy of taking any other stand but this. I cannot see the reason for it—that Negroes should be drafted and sent three thousand miles away to fight and die at the command of their country, to help make conditions and life safe for other people; that Negroes, those whom their Government did not send to war, remained at home and engaged in making munitions and other necessities for carrying on the war, so as to win the victory—I repeat, I cannot see wherein Negroes who have made sacrifices such as these for their country, now that the war is over and a condition of business depression exists through the country, should be discriminated against, and in favor of other men who were their country's foes, and who have no other claim to preferential consideration than the color of their skin happens to be white. I cannot see the consistency, the right of it. Your men must not yield up your jobs so easily. You have a right to them, and it is a question what you must make up your minds to do; and that is, to demand what is yours; that is all. If you are too cowardly you will never get anything. It is better to die demanding what is yours than starve getting nothing. That's how I feel, and since they have done nothing, in another ten or fifteen days we will have a delegation up in Albany, and from Albany the delegation will go to Washington and ask what do they mean. We preserved the nation and the nation must preserve us.

Men, you have the balance of power in America, and we are the balance of power over the world. Do not let the world bluff you. The American writers themselves acknowledge that the only people they could depend on in America for loyalty to the flag are the fifteen million Negroes in America {*applause*}; because they cannot tell the enemy in that he is white; the German is white; and they have had a hard time finding Germans. But they could tell who were Negroes, and the kaiser was not from the Negro, either. So they knew the Negro was their friend. When the white man came, they had to ask: "Who comes there?"—and he had to answer: "Friend." But they did not have to ask that when they saw the black man coming, they knew before he came that he was a friend. However, we are going to ask them a question, as I told you a while ago, for since the politicians have not done anything we have got to play a little politics now. But, above all, men, I want you to remember that now is the time for you to support the Universal Liberian Construction Loan—you men who have fifty dollars; you men who have a hundred dollars; you men who have three hundred dollars or two hundred dollars. Now is the time for you to invest part of your money so as to enable us in another couple of weeks to secure the ship which we want to go to Africa. The ship is right down at the foot of Eighty-Second Street now. We can have it under contract this very hour; but the ship has to go for another twenty-six days, because we haven't the money to sign up the contract. The ship costs $500,000. Oh, some of you think a ship can be bought for $500. {*Laughter.*} Ships in these days cost a million, two million dollars, five hundred thousand dollars, two hundred and fifty thousand dollars, and so on; and when you get a ship for $250,000 you have got a cheap ship. We have been negotiating for the ship, the kind of beautiful ship that we want—a ship with everything on it that we want; but we just had to look and wait awhile, because Negroes wouldn't subscribe enough to buy it.

If we had the money with which to buy the ship we could send three hundred men tomorrow morning to Africa. The ship can carry three hundred passengers at one time; and the money for it is right here in Harlem! Some of you say we are crazy. I cannot do better than tell you what we are planning, what we are hoping, what we are doing, what lies before us all in the future, and what we should do to attain the destiny that God has mapped out for us. We are hoping that we will realize the money between now and the 19th of March to complete the contract. But God Almighty knows it depends upon the people. If they will not support the Universal Liberian Construction Loan I cannot work miracles; I cannot take blood out of a stone. Therefore, for this reason I have spoken to you tonight, and I am asking you to advise your friends, those of you who have already subscribed, or who have already invested in the Universal Liberian Construction Loan, to appeal to them and urge them to join in the support of this very necessary and much needed and most worthy object, by subscribing to the Loan and investing whatever money they can at this time in the enterprise so that we can put this great program over.

I thank you very much for your attention. Goodnight, all! {*Great applause.*}

Leadership

"The leadership of the past has been a leadership more destructive than constructive—a leadership that misrepresented the true desires, the true hopes of this struggling race of ours."

Liberty Hall, New York City,
July 23, 1921

The Negro World,
July 30, 1921

RIGHT Honorable Members of the Executive Council, Members and Friends of the Universal Negro Improvement Association: I am pleased to be with you tonight. I desire to speak for a short while from the subject of "Leadership": that is, as far as that leadership relates to the great movement known as the Universal Negro Improvement Association, and as that leadership affects the Negro race at large. You will realize as a serious group of people that you are living in a serious age, in a serious world—a world without sympathy—a world without charity, a world without love; a selfish, heartless world. This world in which we live is divided up into separate and distinct national groups. It is also divided up into great human groups. Each and every one of these national groups, and each and every one of these many race groups is fighting for its own interests; fighting for those things that are dear to it. This conflict of groups and conflict of nations has called for the best in each group and the best in each nation. If you were to take a survey of humanity—if you were to take a survey of the world politically, you will find every little group of humanity striking out in its own domain, whether it be in England, France, Italy, the United States of America, or in Japan. Each and every one is striking out for its own protection. Let it be Jew, let it be Anglo-Saxon, let it be Teuton, let it be Chinese or Japanese, each and every group is striking out in its own interest. Under the principle of self-interest, under the principle of national interest, the Universal Negro Improvement Association strikes out in behalf of the Negro the world over with an interest that is clear to each and every one. It has a national hope that is clear to each and every one of us.

At this hour Frenchmen are determined that there shall be a France—a nation second to none in the world; Englishmen are determined that there shall be a greater Britain, an empire second to none in the world; the Japanese are determined that there shall be a Japan, an empire second to none in the world. The republic known as the United States of America, under whose flag of protection we live, is determined that America shall be the greatest republic in the world, second to none. And a new hope seems to be springing up throughout the universe among the despised group of humanity that has been kept back for the last 300 years. The hope of that group is that there shall be an African republic second to none in the world. {*Cheers.*} In the performance of these desires the Anglo-Saxons of Great Britain present within their ranks the best of their statesmanship. They give us a David Lloyd George, they give us an Arthur J. Balfour, they give us an Earl Reading. We turn to the statesmanship of the great republic known as the United States of America, and they give us a Warren G. Harding, Charles Evans Hughes, Leonard Wood, a William Howard Taft, a William Randolph Hearst. We turn to the great empire and kingdom of Italy, and they give us . . . an Orlando and a Marconi. We turn to the French Republic that desires to live forever, and they give us a Joffre, they give us a Clemenceau, and we turn to this rising race of ours and up to now we cannot discover a man. We have searched the world—400,000,000 of us—and we have not yet found the leaders worthy of leadership of a great race like the Negro race. When we come to match the statesmanship of the world, Englishmen are able to match their intellect to protect the interests of their government—to match the intellect of any other statesmanship representing any other government in the world, and simultaneously you will find other governments and other races able to present men capable of foresight, men capable of leading a race and a nation to greater destiny. But apparently it will appear that whenever fools are to be made everybody turns to the Negro.

The leadership of the past has been a leadership more destructive than constructive—a leadership that misrepresented the true desires, the true hopes of this struggling race of ours. At no time in the history of creation has the Negro ever made up his mind to be a slave; at no time in the history of creation has the Negro ever made up his mind to be a serf or peon; at no time in the history of creation has the Negro ever made up his mind to take a back place in the onward march of humanity. And these things have happened in the past because we have not the kind of leadership to represent the true sentiments of the Negro. {*Cheers.*} . . . The Negroes of Central America, the Negroes in the West Indies have absolutely no compromise to make on the question of liberty, freedom and democracy for the 400,000,000 Negroes of the world; and I take it also to be the desire and the sentiment of 15,000,000 Negroes in these United States of America.

The world has reached the turning point of humanity. The world has reached the crossroads of humanity, when each race will travel in its own direction, when each national group will travel in its own avenue. Let the Anglo-Saxon go the way he desires to go. Let the Frenchman go the way he desires; let the Teuton go the way he desires to go; we are now organizing the 400,000,000 Negroes so that they can go the way they desire to go. {*Cheers.*} Now, we cannot travel that way without leadership. Where is the leadership? I call upon Du Bois, who for years represented himself as a leader, and I ask him, "In what direction are you traveling?" and his answer is, "Wheresoever my master leads I will follow." I call upon Kelly Miller and ask him, "Whither leadest thou?" and he says, "By the bidding of my master shall I follow." And I come back to the 400,000,000 Negroes of the world and I ask, "Are you prepared to be led that way?" and a universal answer comes to me, "No! We shall not be led in that direction." And by that answer I realize that you demand a new leadership—a leadership that will not give up when the hour seems dark; a leader that will start and continue the journey until victory perches upon the banner of the Red, the Black and the Green. {*Cheers.*} A leadership that counts not for a dark hour is a leadership misplaced, because in all leadership that leads to liberty, freedom and human emancipation there has always been a dark hour. All victories have been won just at the turning point of the dark hour. There is always a silver lining, and the leader who thinks that the dark hour will not come in the struggle of the Negro is a leader who is indeed misplaced. We have seen experiences and trials in the Universal Negro Improvement Association, but our dark hour has not yet come. The dark hour is the hour when you apparently seem to be losing out, yet you have courage enough to fight on until victory comes your way. That is the dark hour which each and every one of you must prepare for. That dark hour may be tomorrow; that dark hour may be five or ten years or twenty years from now; but I want you to realize that you must prepare for the dark hour. It may meet you in America; it may meet you in the West Indies; it may meet you on the battle plains of Africa; but wheresoever it meets, you must be ready. {*Cheers.*} And you would not be true and loyal members of the U.N.I.A. if you did not count for a dark hour. The dark hour may never come, but it is best to prepare for that hour as you march on from one success to the other, because the history of the Universal Negro Improvement Association reveals one continuous line of success—one triumph after another. How many fights and battles have we won? Innumerable battles and fights we have won and there are other battles still to be encountered—other fights still to be won. Let us prepare for them.

If I can interpret correctly the spirit of Negroes, it is for me to say that Negroes everywhere are determined to be free, determined to be liberated; liberated from lynch law, liberated from mob rule, liberated from segregation, liberated from Jim Crowism, liberated from injustice. That is the spirit of Negroes everywhere. It is not found in any one country because Negroes have been taken advantage of everywhere. It is a universal desire and it is a universal program that seeks to liberate Negroes everywhere.

It is well the world knows and understands that as men we are determined to live as men and determined to die as men. {*Cheers.*} We recognize no superman in creation; we recognize the equality of men and because man is equal we feel that man has no right to take advantage of man. . . . Let the world understand that 400,000,000 Negroes are determined to die for liberty. If we must die we shall die nobly. We shall die gallantly fighting on the battle heights of Africa to plant the standard that represents liberty. {*Cheers.*}

Some people seem to misunderstand us in this African question. They desire us to locate the part of Africa we intend to fight. {*Laughter.*} Now, you know that no general is going to give away his plans, and we never told anybody we are going to fight, anyhow. We only say that if you remain there until we get there, what happens to you is not our fault. That is all we say. If you want to interpret that as fighting, that is your business. Now listen, some people try to misrepresent us by saying that we are going to locate ourselves at a certain place in Africa and start fighting from there. I want to disavow any knowledge of any particular place where we are going to start from, because anywhere I land I am going to start to fight right there. {*Cheers and laughter.*}

We feel that the time has come for universal action. I really would like to have the world understand the Negro so that there can be no blame given to the Negro for hiding his attitude, for suppressing his intention, for stultifying his desires. The old leadership represented us as a race of beggars. The old leadership represented us as wanting only an industrial school and a few churches; the old leadership said we were satisfied to shout, "Give me Jesus and take the world." {*Laughter.*} The old leadership represented us as wanting to have no hand in politics, but that we were satisfied to cast our vote for Tom, Dick and Harry of any other race without trying to exercise it in our own behalf. That is a misrepresentation of the new Negro, and if any of the old leaders make any such representations they are misinterpreting the spirit of the new Negro. That is a warning to civilization; that is a notice to the world. We no longer are satisfied with industrial schools and churches only; we are no longer satisfied to have the vote and not to exercise it in our own behalf. The vote represents political liberty and the new Negro desires to give his ballot for an alderman of his race, for a congressman of his race, for a senator of his race, and for a president of his race. {*Loud cheers.*} He says if you will not give me an opportunity because you outnumber me by mob violence—if you will not give me an opportunity to cast my vote for my own alderman, congressman, senator or president in one part of the world, I will make it possible to cast it in another part of the world. {*Cheers.*} The new Negro says, not only churches, not only industrial schools, but we want parliament houses, houses of Congress, national museums, national art galleries, great institutions of learning of our own. The old Negro representing the Negro as being satisfied to be a subject without rights is a misrepresentation. The new Negro demands a leadership which will establish his right to rule. If it is right for the yellow man to rule, it is also right for the black man to rule. {*Cheers.*} We say rule on, great white man; rule on, great yellow man, and we are now saying rule on, great 400,000,000 black men. Creation opened with many distinct races; I cannot enumerate them, but creation will also close with those many distinct races, and when the end comes and other races answer here, I am quite sure the Negro will be among those who will answer, "Here." They may exterminate the North American Indian; they may exterminate the aborigines of Australia; they may exterminate the aborigines of the various countries they have conquered, but there is one race that they shall never—will never exterminate, and that is the Negro race. {*Cheers.*} I would like to see the race that would be so audacious as to make the attempt to exterminate the black race of today—a race of warriors who have never fought—warriors whose deeds in war have never been reckoned because they have never been performed. They talk about the New York 15th; that was only an experiment in warfare. {*Cheers.*} They talk about the Illinois 8th; that was only a pastime for the boys. They talk about the prowess of the West Indian regiments; those fellows were only having a picnic; it was a gala day. No man has ever yet seen the Negro fighting at his best, because the Negro has never yet fought for himself. {*Loud and prolonged cheers.*}

Civilization and statesmanship have flattered themselves that there shall be peace, but intelligent students of political economy and political science know that there will be war and rumors of war. And all political students know that the world is more preparing for war today than ever before. And all students of political history and political science know that at any moment humanity will face its common battleground. The world of political scientists know that the conflict may originate in Asia as well as it may originate in Europe; but to be originated we know it will; and all races and all peoples are preparing for it. The old leadership of the Negro prepared for nothing. We foresee the conflict of races, and we know that no conflict in the future or at the present can be successfully decided except the Negro casts his vote. I do not only mean politically this time by going to the ballot box, but cast his vote on the battlefield. No conflict can be successfully decided until the Negro has put his hand in it. And I am warning the races and nations of the world not to forget and not to ignore the Negro.

The old leadership of Negroes recorded nothing. They have no record of lynch law; they have no record of mob violence; they have no record of injustice; they have no record of segregation; they have no record of brutalizing the Negro; but the New Negro has a record of everything that is done to him {*cheers*}, and when anything goes on later on, the first thing the Negro is going to do is to present his record, and he is going to ask you what you are going to do about it, and you have to decide clearly and positively before he will lend his hand. We appreciate and we love the civilization that we gave to the world. Thousands of years ago when the white man was a savage the Negro was the custodian of civilization. The Negro held civilization and in turn handed it to the white man to keep. You will always love your property anywhere you see it. If I have a suit of old clothes and I give it to somebody, anytime I see that suit I smile, because I loved it before I bought it. And this civilization that the white man has was not originally his. The Negro gave it to him; therefore, the Negro loves the civilization as held today by the white man, and the Negro when fighting will always fight to preserve the civilization that he gave to the white man, that is, to maintain it and keep it; but since the white man has it and claims it, we want him to understand that we are going to fight for it on condition. It is an easy thing to take away something you gave to somebody else. We do not want to take away civilization; we want to shore it up. We say to the white man, take a part of civilization and whenever your civilization is in trouble you can call on us and we will help you out of it; but the condition is, give us what is belonging to us. That is all we ask. I feel sure that there is no statesman in the world foolish enough to ignore the fighting force or power of the Negro. I cannot see where narrow-minded men get their argument from; brutalizing the Negro and legalizing it; Jim-Crowing the Negro and legalizing it, when they know that the Negro is a man and nothing can be decided in the world except the Negro is in it. {*Cheers.*} In the time of peace you kick down a man, you slap him in the face, and when you are in trouble you want that man to help you; are you not a fool? I trust the world will understand the new attitude of the Negro. We are not giving to you more than you give to us. Give us a kick and we return the kick; give us a smile and we return the smile—and you know nobody can smile like the Negro. {*Laughter.*} He smiles broadest and he fights longest.

I feel that we are nearing the point where all the races will get together and compromise the issue of life; but not until the Negro is lifted to the highest standard of humanity; not until the Negro is given the privileges and opportunities of other races; not until then will we sit around the table of peace—the table at which humanity will end its troubles. This is my message to you tonight, and I trust you will keep it with you and transmit it to your friends or colleagues or co-workers in the cause of African freedom. Realize, men, that the call of this hour is for new leadership, not the leadership Du Bois gives, not the leadership Moton gives—the leadership that is satisfied with industrial schools and the leadership that is satisfied with an annual donation from the white philanthropists, and so long as that donation comes regularly we are satisfied and come to a compromise and want us to "close ranks" at a time when we ought to open ranks. Remember that the Negro cannot be bought by charity alone; in fact, we want no charity; we are not beggars, we are not paupers, we are not lepers; we only want a chance.

At this time some of the white people say, "You Negroes are getting too impertinent and because of that, we are going to turn you out of your jobs and give them to white folks." They don't know that they are doing a dangerous thing. Do you know what government means? Government means the protection of human rights. Government means the protection of the property of the people who make up the nation. Do you know why they keep soldiers and battleships? Not for ornaments, but to protect the nation's property. Just a few years ago the property of the world was in danger, and they would have lost every penny they ever had were it not for the fact that 2,000,000 black men went to France and Flanders and drove the Teutons out of France and Belgium when white men failed to do it. {*Cheers.*} Do you know that were it not for the 2,000,000 Negroes who fought in the war the white men who fought on the side of the Allies would have lost everything they had; they would have had to pay over to Germany a huge war indemnity? Do you know that 2,000,000 black men left their business in Africa, in the West Indies and America and went over to France and Flanders and Mesopotamia and fought and saved the Allied nations? Let me tell you this: If you are employed by white men and they choose to dismiss you because of color tell him, "Brother, you remember the last war; all right, another one may come." That is your trump card. You are not begging for jobs; you demand jobs because you made it possible for them to live in peace. {*Cheers.*} Otherwise the Germans would have been at their door. You have a fair exchange for the money that is given to you. Let them know this: that your future service depends upon their present good treatment.

Now I must close for tonight. On Monday, the 1st of August, the biggest convention of races will assemble in New York with 50,000 delegates representing the Negro peoples of the world, who will assemble here to sit for 31 days and 31 nights to discuss the problems that confront this race of ours. We are coming to create new legislation for the government of 400,000,000 Negroes, and already some of the delegates are here, and they are coming from all quarters. By next Saturday we will have between 30,000 and 50,000 delegates here in New York. Monday week at 9:30 we will assemble in this hall for a religious service to open the convention. At one o'clock we will—50,000 of us—join in a great parade and march through the district of Harlem. At 8 o'clock the same night we will assemble at the 12th Regiment Armory at 62nd Street and Columbus Avenue, where we will officially celebrate the opening of the second International Convention of Negroes. It will be declared opened by His Highness, the Potentate, Hon. Gabriel Johnson, Mayor of Monrovia, Liberia. I trust all of you will do your best to scatter the information to advertise the convention so as to make a success of it.

Negroes Will Stop at Nothing Short of Redemption of Motherland and Establishment of African Empire

". . . methinks I see the Angel of God taking up the standard
of the Red, the Black and the Green, and saying,
'Men of the Negro Race, Men of Ethiopia, follow me.'"

The Second International Convention of Negroes of the World,
Liberty Hall, New York City,
August 14, 1921

The Philosophy and Opinions of Marcus Garvey, or Africa for the Africans,
Volume 1

FOUR years ago, realizing the oppression and the hardships from which we suffered, we organized ourselves into an organization for the purpose of bettering our condition, and founding a government of our own. The four years of organization have brought good results, in that from an obscure, despised race we have grown into a mighty power, a mighty force whose influence is being felt throughout the length and breadth of the world. The Universal Negro Improvement Association existed but in name four years ago, today it is known as the greatest moving force among Negroes. We have accomplished this through unity of effort and unity of purpose, it is a fair demonstration of what we will be able to accomplish in the very near future, when the millions who are outside the pale of the Universal Negro Improvement Association will have linked themselves up with us.

By our success of the last four years we will be able to estimate the grander success of a free and redeemed Africa.¹ In climbing the heights to where we are today, we have had to surmount difficulties, we have had to climb over obstacles, but the obstacles were stepping stones to the future greatness of this cause we represent? Day by day we are writing a new history, recording new deeds of valor performed by this race of ours. It is true that the world has not yet valued us at our true worth, but we are climbing up so fast and with such force that every day the world is changing its attitude towards us. Wheresoever you turn your eyes today you will find the moving influence of the Universal Negro Improvement Association among Negroes from all corners of the globe. We hear among Negroes the cry of "Africa for the Africans." This cry has become a positive, determined one. It is a cry that is raised simultaneously the world over because of the universal oppression that affects the Negro. You who are congregated here tonight as delegates representing the hundreds of branches of the Universal Negro Improvement Association in different parts of the world will realize that we in New York are positive in this great desire of a free and redeemed Africa. We have established this Liberty Hall as the center from which we send out the sparks of liberty to the four corners of the globe, and if you have caught the spark in your section, we want you to keep it a-burning for the great cause we represent.

There is a mad rush among races everywhere towards national independence. Everywhere we hear the cry of liberty, of freedom, and a demand for democracy. In our corner of the world we are raising the cry for liberty, freedom and democracy. Men who have raised the cry for freedom and liberty in ages past have always made up their minds to die for the realization of the dream. We who are assembled in this convention as delegates representing the Negroes of the world give out the same spirit that the fathers of liberty in this country gave out over one hundred years ago. We give out a spirit that knows no compromise, a spirit that refuses to turn back, a spirit that says "Liberty or

Death," and in prosecution of this great ideal—the ideal of a free and redeemed Africa, men may scorn, men may spurn us, and may say that we are on the wrong side of life, but let me tell you that way in which you are travelling is just the way all peoples who are free have travelled in the past. If you want liberty you yourselves must strike the blow. If you must be free you must become so through your own effort, through your own initiative. Those who have discouraged you in the past are those who have enslaved you for centuries and it is not expected that they will admit that you have a right to strike out at this late hour for freedom, liberty and democracy.

At no time in the history of the world, for the last five hundred years was there ever a serious attempt made to free Negroes. We have been camouflaged into believing that we were made free by Abraham Lincoln. That we were made free by Victoria of England, but up to now we are still slaves, we are industrial slaves, we are social slaves, we are political slaves, and the new Negro desires a freedom that has no boundary, no limit. We desire a freedom that will lift us to the common standard of all men, whether they be white men of Europe or yellow men of Asia; therefore, in our desire to lift ourselves to that standard we shall stop at nothing until there is a free and redeemed Africa.

I understand that just at this time while we are endeavoring to create public opinion and public sentiment in favor of a free Africa, that others of our race are being subsidized to turn the attention of the world toward a different desire on the part of Negroes, but let me tell you that we who make up this organization know no turning back, we have pledged ourselves even unto the last drop of our sacred blood that Africa must be free. The enemy may argue with you to show you the impossibility of a free and redeemed Africa, but I want you to take as your argument the thirteen colonies of America that once owed their sovereignty to Great Britain, that sovereignty has been destroyed to make a United States of America. George Washington was not God Almighty. He was a man like any Negro in this building, and if he and his associates were able to make a free America, we too can make a free Africa. Hampden, Gladstone, Pitt and Disraeli were not the representatives of God in the person of Jesus Christ. They were but men, but in their time they worked for the expansion of the British Empire, and today they boast of a British Empire upon which "the sun never sets." As Pitt and Gladstone were able to work for the expansion of the British Empire, so you and I can work for the expansion of a great African Empire. Voltaire and Mirabeau were not Jesus Christs, they were but men like ourselves. They worked and overturned the French monarchy. They worked for the democracy which France now enjoys, and if they were able to do that, we are able to work for a democracy in Africa. Lenin and Trotsky were not Jesus Christs, but they were able to overthrow the despotism of Russia, and today they have given to the world a socialist republic, the first of its kind. If Lenin and Trotsky were able to do that for Russia, you and I can do that for Africa. Therefore, let no man, let no power on earth, turn you from this sacred cause of liberty. I prefer to die at this moment rather than not to work for the freedom of Africa. If liberty is good for certain sets of humanity it is good for all. Black men, Colored men, Negroes have as much right to be free as any other race that God Almighty ever created, and we desire freedom that is unfettered, freedom that is unlimited, freedom that will give us a chance and opportunity to rise to the fullest of our ambition and that we cannot get in countries where other men rule and dominate.

We have reached the time when every minute, every second must count for something done, something achieved in the cause of Africa. We need the freedom of Africa now; therefore, we desire the kind of leadership that will give it to us as quickly as possible. You will realize that not only individuals, but governments are using their influence against us. But what do we care about the unrighteous influence of any government? Our cause is based upon righteousness. And anything that is not righteous we have no respect for, because God Almighty is our leader and Jesus Christ our standard bearer. We rely on them for that kind of leadership that will make us free, for it is the same God who inspired the Psalmist to write, "Princes shall come out of Egypt and Ethiopia shall stretch out her hands unto God." At this moment methinks I see Ethiopia stretching forth her hands unto God, and methinks I see the Angel of God taking up the standard of the Red, the Black and the Green, and saying "Men of the Negro Race, Men of Ethiopia, follow me." Tonight we are following. We are following 400,000,000 strong. We are following with a determination that we must be free before the wreck of matter, before the crash of worlds.

It falls to our lot to tear off the shackles that bind Mother Africa. Can you do it? You did it in the Revolutionary War. You did it in the Civil War. You did it at the Battles of the Marne and Verdun. You did it in Mesopotamia. You can do it marching up the battle heights of Africa. Let the world know that 400,000,000 Negroes are prepared to die or live as free men. Despise us as much as you care. Ignore us as much as you care. We are coming 400,000,000 strong. We are coming with our woes behind us, with the memory of suffering behind us—woes and suffering of three hundred years—they shall be our inspiration. My bulwark of strength in the conflict for freedom in Africa will be the three hundred years of persecution and hardship left behind in this Western Hemisphere. The more I remember the suffering of my fore-fathers, the more I remember the lynchings and burnings in the Southern States of America, the more I will fight on even though the battle seems doubtful. Tell me that I must turn back, and I laugh you to scorn. Go on! Go on! Climb ye the heights of liberty and cease not in well doing until you have planted the banner of the Red, the Black and the Green on the hilltops of Africa.

The Handwriting Is on the Wall

"No portion of humanity, no group of humanity, has an abiding
right, an everlasting right, an eternal right to oppress
other sections or portions of humanity."

The Second International Convention of Negroes of the World
Liberty Hall, New York City
August 31, 1921

The Negro World,
September 10, 1921

The Negro World *account describes how Garvey got up to deliver this speech, before the cheering crowd, "smiling and bowing to the right and then to the left like a black Napoleon, whereupon the audience again broke into great cheering and hurrahing, followed by the association yell of the Junior Motor Corps girls."*

WE are assembled here tonight to bring to a close our great convention of thirty-one days and thirty-one nights. Before we separate ourselves and take our departure to the different parts of the world from which we came, I desire to give you a message; one that you will, I hope, take home and propagate among the scattered millions of Africa's sons and daughters.

We have been here, sent here by the good will of the 400,000,000 Negroes of the world to legislate in their interests, and in the time allotted to us we did our best to enact laws and to frame laws that in our judgment, we hope, will solve the great problem that confronts us universally. The Universal Negro Improvement Association seeks to emancipate the Negro everywhere, industrially, educationally, politically and religiously. It also seeks a free and redeemed Africa. It has a great struggle ahead; it has a gigantic task to face. Nevertheless, as representatives of the Negro people of the world we have undertaken the task of freeing the 400,000,000 of our race, and of freeing our bleeding Motherland, Africa. We counseled with each other during the thirty-one days; we debated with each other during the thirty-one days, and out of all we did, and out of all we said, we have come to the one conclusion—that speedily

Africa must be redeemed! {*Applause.*} We have come to the conclusion that speedily there must be an emancipated Negro race everywhere {*applause*}; and on going back to our respective homes we go with our determination to lay down, if needs be, the last drop of our blood for the defense of Africa and for the emancipation of our race.

The handwriting is on the wall. You see it as plain as daylight; you see it coming out of India, the tribes of India rising in rebellion against their overlords. You see it coming out of Africa, our dear motherland, Africa; the Moors rising in rebellion against their overlords, and defeating them at every turn. {*Applause.*} According to the last report flashed to this country from Morocco by the Associated Press, the Moors have again conquered and subdued the Spanish hordes. The same Associated Press flashes to us the news that there is a serious uprising in India, and the English people are marshaling their troops to subdue the spirit of liberty, of freedom, which is now permeating India. The news has come to us, and I have a cable in my pocket that comes from Ireland that the Irish are determined to have liberty and nothing less than liberty. {*Applause.*}

The handwriting is on the wall, and as we go back to our respective homes we shall serve notice upon the world that we also are coming; coming with a united effort; coming with a united determination, a determination that Africa shall be free from coast to coast. {*Applause.*} I have before me the decision of the League of Nations. Immediately after the war a Council of the League of Nations was called, and at that council they decided that the territories wrested from Germany in West Africa, taken from her during the conflict, should be divided between France and England—608,000 square miles—without even asking the civilized Negroes of the world what disposition shall be made of their own homeland, of their own country. An insult was hurled at the civilized Negroes of the world when they thus took upon themselves the right to parcel out and apportion as they pleased 608,000 square miles of our own land; for we never gave it up; we never sold it. It is still ours. {*Cries of "Yes!"*} They parceled it out between these two nations—England and France—gave away our property without consulting us, and we are aggrieved, and we desire to serve notice on civilization and on the world that 400,000,000 Negroes are aggrieved. {*Cries of "Yes!" and applause.*}

And we are the more aggrieved because of the lynch rope, because of segregation, because of the Jim Crowism that is used, practiced and exercised here in this country, and in other parts of the world by the white nations of the earth, wherever Negroes happen accidentally or otherwise to find themselves. If there is no safety for Negroes in the white world, I cannot see what right they have to parcel out the homeland, the country of

Negroes, without consulting Negroes and asking their permission to do so. Therefore, we are aggrieved. This question of prejudice will be the downfall of civilization {*Applause*}, and I warn the white race of this, and of their doom. I hope they will take heed, because the handwriting is on the wall. {*Applause.*} No portion of humanity, no group of humanity, has an abiding right, an everlasting right, an eternal right to oppress other sections or portions of humanity. God never gave them the right, and if there is such a right, man arrogated it to himself, and God in all ages has been displeased with the arrogance of man. I warn those nations which believe themselves above the law of God, above the commandments of God. I warn those nations that believe themselves above human justice. You cannot ignore the laws of God; you cannot long ignore the commandments of God; you cannot long ignore human justice, and exist. Your arrogance will destroy you, and I warn the races and the nations that have arrogated to themselves the right to oppress, the right to circumscribe, the right to keep down other races. I warn them that the hour is coming when the oppressed will rise in their might, in their majesty, and throw off the yoke of ages.

The world ought to understand that the Negro has come to life, possessed with a new conscience and a new soul. The old Negro is buried, and it is well the world knew it. It is not my purpose to deceive the world. I believe in righteousness; I believe in truth; I believe in honesty. That is why I warn a selfish world of the outcome of their actions towards the oppressed. There will come a day, Josephus Daniels wrote about it, a white statesman, and the world has talked about it, and I warn the world of it, that the day will come when the races of the world will marshal themselves in great conflict for the survival of the fittest. Men of the Universal Negro Improvement Association, I am asking you to prepare yourselves, and prepare your race the world over, because the conflict is coming, not because you will it, not because you desire it, because you will be forced into it. The conflict between the races is drawing nearer and nearer. You see it; I see it; I see it in the handwriting on the wall, as expressed in the uprising in India. You see the handwriting on the wall of Africa; you see it, the handwriting on the wall of Europe. It is coming; it is drawing nearer and nearer. Four hundred million Negroes of the world, I am asking you to prepare yourselves, so that you will not be found wanting when that day comes. Ah! what a sorry day it will be. I hope it will never come. But my hope, my wish, will not prevent its coming. All that I can do is to warn humanity everywhere, so that humanity may change its tactics, and warn them of the danger. I repeat: I warn the white world against the prejudice they are practicing against Negroes; I warn them against the segregation and injustice they mete out to us, for the perpetuation of these things will mean the ultimate destruction of the present civilization, and the building up of a new civilization founded upon mercy, justice and equality.

I know that we have good men in all races living at the present time. We have good men of the black race, we have good men of the white race, good men of the yellow race, who are endeavoring to do the best they can to ward off this coming conflict. White men who have the vision, go ye back and warn your people of this coming conflict! Black men of vision, go ye to the four corners of the earth, and warn your people of this coming conflict. Yellow men, go ye out and warn your people of this coming conflict, because it is drawing nearer and nearer; nearer and nearer. Oh! if the world will only listen to the heart-throbs, to the soul-beats of those who have the vision, those who have God's love in their hearts.

I see before me white men, black men and yellow men working assiduously for the peace of the world; for the bringing together of this thing called human brotherhood; I see them working through their organizations. They have been working during the last fifty years. Some worked to bring about the emancipation, because they saw the danger of perpetual slavery. They brought about the liberation of 4,000,000 black people. They passed away, and others started to work, but the opposition against them is too strong; the opposition against them is weighing them down. The world has gone mad; the world has become too material; the world has lost its spirit of kinship with God, and man can see nothing else but prejudice, avarice and greed. Avarice and greed will destroy the world, and I am appealing to white, black and yellow whose hearts, whose souls are touched with the true spirit of humanity, with the true feeling of human brotherhood, to preach the doctrine of human love, more, to preach it louder, to preach it longer, because there is great need for it in the world at this time. Ah! if they could but see the danger—the conflict between the races—races fighting against each other. What a destruction, what a holocaust it will be! Can you imagine it?

Just take your idea from the last bloody war, wherein a race was pitted against itself (for the whole white races united as one from a common origin), the members of which, on both sides, fought so tenaciously that they killed off each other in frightful, staggering numbers. If a race pitted against itself could fight so tenaciously to kill itself without mercy, can you imagine the fury, can you imagine the mercilessness, the terribleness of the war that will come when all the races of the world will be on the battlefield, engaged in deadly combat for the destruction or overthrow of the one or the other, when beneath it and as a cause of it lies prejudice and hatred? Truly, it will be an ocean of blood; that is all it will be. So that if I can sound a note of warning now that will echo and reverberate around the world and thus prevent such a conflict, God help me to do it; for Africa, like Europe, like Asia, is preparing for that day. {*Great applause.*}

You may ask yourselves if you believe Africa is still asleep. Africa has been slumbering; but she was slumbering for a purpose. Africa still possesses her hidden mysteries; Africa has unused talents, and we are unearthing them now for the coming conflict. {*Applause.*} Oh, I hope it will never come; therefore, I hope the white world will change its attitude towards the weaker races of the world, for we shall not be weak everlastingly. Ah, history teaches us of the rise and fall of nations, races and empires. Rome fell in her majesty; Greece fell in her triumph; Babylon, Assyria, Carthage, Prussia, the German Empire—all fell in their pomp and power; the French Empire fell from the sway of the great Napoleon, from the dominion of the indomitable Corsican soldier. As they fell in the past, so will nations fall in the present age, and so will they fall in the future ages to come, the result of their unrighteousness.

I repeat, I warn the world, and I trust you will receive this warning as you go into the four corners of the earth. The white race should teach humanity. Out there is selfishness in the world. Let the white race teach humanity first, because we have been following the cause of humanity for three hundred years, and we have suffered much. If a change must come, it must not come from Negroes; it must come from the white race, for they are the ones who have brought about this estrangement between the races. The Negro never hated; at no time within the last five hundred years can they point to one single instance of Negro hatred. The Negro has loved even under the severest punishment. In slavery the Negro loved his master; he protected his master; he safeguarded his master's home. "Greater love hath no man than that he should lay down his life for another." We gave not only our services, our unrequited labor; we gave also our souls, we gave our hearts, we gave our all, to our oppressors.

But, after all, we are living in a material world, even though it is partly spiritual, and since we have been very spiritual in the past, we are going to take a part of the material now, and will give others the opportunity to practice the spiritual side of life. Therefore, I am not telling you to lead in humanity; I am not telling you to lead in the bringing about of the turning of humanity, because you have been doing that for three hundred years, and you have lost. But the compromise must come from the dominant races. We are warning them. We are not preaching a doctrine of hatred, and I trust you will not go back to your respective homes and preach such a doctrine. We are preaching, rather, a doctrine of humanity, a doctrine of human love. But we say love begins at home; "charity begins at home."

We are aggrieved because of this partitioning of Africa, because it seeks to deprive Negroes of the chance of higher national development; no chance, no opportunity, is given us to prove our fitness to govern, to dominate in our own behalf. They impute so many bad things against Haiti and against Liberia, that they themselves circumvented Liberia so as to make it impossible for us to demonstrate our ability for self-government. Why not be honest? Why not be straightforward? Having desired the highest development, as they avowed and professed, of the Negro, why not give him a fair chance, an opportunity to prove his capacity for governing? What better opportunity ever presented itself than the present, when the territories of Germany in Africa were wrested from her control by the Allies in the last war—what better chance ever offered itself for trying out the higher ability of Negroes to govern themselves than to have given those territories to the civilized Negroes, and thus give them a trial to exercise themselves in a proper system of government? Because of their desire to keep us down, because of their desire to keep us apart, they refuse us a chance. The chance that they did give us is the chance that we are going to take. {*Great applause.*} Hence tonight, before I take my seat, I will move a resolution, and I think it is befitting at this time to pass such a resolution as I will move, so that the League of Nations and the Supreme Council of the Nations will understand that Negroes are not asleep; that Negroes are not false to themselves; that Negroes are wide awake, and that Negroes intend to take a serious part in the future government of this world; that God Almighty created him and placed him in it. This world owes us a place, and we are going to occupy that place.

We have a right to a large part in the political horizon, and I say to you that we are preparing to occupy that part.

Go back to your respective corners of the earth and preach the real doctrine of the Universal Negro Improvement Association—the doctrine of universal emancipation for Negroes, the doctrine of a free and a redeemed Africa!★

Emancipation Day

". . . knowing the sufferings of my forefathers I shall give back
to Africa that liberty that she once enjoyed hundreds of years ago,
before her own sons and daughters were taken from her shores
and brought in chains to this Western World."

Liberty Hall, New York City,
January 1, 1922

The Philosophy and Opinions of Marcus Garvey, or Africa for the Africans,
Volume 1

FIFTY-NINE years ago Abraham Lincoln signed the Emancipation Proclamation declaring four million Negroes in this country free. Several

---

★The resolution protesting "against the distribution of the land of Africa by the Supreme Council and the League of Nations among the white nations of the world" followed and was carried "unanimously."

years prior to that Queen Victoria of England signed the Emancipation Proclamation that set at liberty hundreds of thousands of West Indian Negro slaves.

West Indian Negroes celebrate their emancipation on the first day of August of every year. The American Negroes celebrate their emancipation on the first of January of every year. Tonight we are here to celebrate the emancipation of the slaves in this country.

We are the descendants of the men and women who suffered in this country for two hundred and fifty years under that barbarous, that brutal institution known as slavery. You who have not lost trace of your history will recall the fact that over three hundred years ago your forebears were taken from the great continent of Africa and brought here for the purpose of using them as slaves. Without mercy, without any sympathy they worked our forebears. They suffered, they bled, they died. But with their sufferings, with their blood, which they shed in their death, they had a hope that one day their posterity would be free, and we are assembled here tonight as the children of their hope.

I trust each and every one of you therefore will realize that you have a duty which is incumbent upon you; a duty that you must perform, because our forebears who suffered, who bled, who died had hopes that are not yet completely realized. They hoped that we as their children would be free, but they also hoped that their country from whence they came would also be free to their children, their grand-children and great grand-children at some future time. It is for the freedom of that country—that Motherland of ours—that four and a half million Negroes, as members of the Universal Negro Improvement Association, are laboring today.

This race of ours gave civilization, gave art, gave science; gave literature to the world. But it has been the way with races and nations. The one race stands out prominently in the one century or in the one age; and in another century or age it passes off the stage of action, and another race takes its place. The Negro once occupied a high position in the world, scientifically, artistically and commercially, but in the balancing of the great scale of evolution, we lost our place and someone, other than ourselves, occupies the stand we once held.

God never intended that man should enslave his fellow, and the price of such a sin or such a violation of Heaven's law must be paid by everyone. As for me, because of the blessed past, because of the history that I know, so long as there is within me the breath of life and the spirit of God, I shall struggle on and urge others of our race to struggle on to see that justice is done to the black peoples of the world. Yes, we appreciate the sorrows of the past, and we are going to work in the present that the sorrows of our generation shall not be perpetuated in the future. On the contrary, we shall strive that by our labors, succeeding generations of our own shall call us blessed, even as we call the generation of the past blessed today. And they indeed were blest. They were blest with a patience not yet known to man. A patience that enabled them to endure the tortures and the sufferings of slavery for two hundred and fifty years. Why? Was it because they loved slavery so? No. It was because they loved this generation more. Isn't it wonderful? Transcendent? What then are you going to do to show your appreciation of this love, what gratitude are you going to manifest in return for what they have done for you? As for me, knowing the sufferings of my forefathers I shall give back to Africa that liberty that she once enjoyed hundreds of years ago, before her own sons and daughters were taken from her shores and brought in chains to this Western world.

No better gift can I give in honor of the memory of the love of my foreparents for me, and in gratitude of the sufferings they endured that I might be free; no grander gift can I bear to the sacred memory of the generation past than a free and a redeemed Africa—a monument for all eternity—for all times.

As by the action of the world, as by the conduct of all the races and nations it is apparent that not one of them has the sense of justice, the sense of love, the sense of equity, the sense of charity, that would make men happy, and make God satisfied. It is apparent that it is left to the Negro to play such a part in human affairs, for when we look to the Anglo-Saxon we see him full of greed, avarice, no mercy, no love, no charity. We go from the white man to the yellow man, and we see the same unenviable characteristics in the Japanese. Therefore we must believe that the Psalmist had great hopes of this race of ours when he prophesied, "Princes shall come out of Egypt and Ethiopia shall stretch forth her hands unto God."

If humanity is regarded as made up of the children of God and God loves all humanity (we all know that), then God will be more pleased with that race that protects all humanity than with the race that outrages the children of God.

And so tonight we celebrate this anniversary of our emancipation, we do it not with regret, on the contrary we do it with an abiding confidence, a hope and faith in ourselves and in our God. And the faith that we have is a faith that will ultimately take us back to that ancient place, that ancient position that we once occupied, when Ethiopia was in her glory.

Statement on Arrest*

"Jews, Irish and reformers of all races have had their troubles
and trials with their own people, so I am satisfied to bear
the persecution of my own that they might be free."

New York City, January 13, 1922

The Philosophy and Opinions of Marcus Garvey, or Africa for the Africans,
Volume 1

I BELIEVE that true justice is to be found in the conscience of the people,
and when one is deprived of it by the machinations and designs of the
corrupt, there can be no better tribunal of appeal than that of public
opinion, which gives voice to conscience and that is why I now appeal
to the conscience of the American people for justice.

I believe that all races have their peculiar characteristics; the Jew
fights the Jew, the Irish fights the Irish, the Italian fights the Italian, and
so we have the Negro fighting the Negro. As a Negro schooled in the
academy of adversity, with the majority of my race, I have ever had a
whole-souled desire to work for the race's uplift. Recently out of slavery, we have had but a meager chance to rise to the higher heights of
human development as a people. At Emancipation we were flung upon
the civilized world without a program. Unlike the Irish and the Jew we
had no national aspiration of our own. We were left to the tender mercies of philanthropists and humanitarians who helped us to the best of
their ability.

In the Negro's struggle to get somewhere every member of the race
took a selfish course all his own. There was no group program or group
interest. The only cause that held us together as a people was Religion.
During the days of slavery Religion was the only consolation of the
Negro, and then it was given to him by his masters. Immediately after
the Emancipation, when the Negro was thrown back upon his own
resources, the illiterate race preacher took charge of us, and with the eye
of selfishness he exploited the zeal of the religious. Our emotions were
worked upon by our illiterate preacher-leaders of the early days.

The masses of us having found new employment for which we
received pay, were able to contribute to the partial upkeep of our own

---

*See the introductory note for background on Garvey's arrest and subsequent conviction
for mail fraud.

church life, thus making it profitable for the preachers of our race to exploit us in the name of God, without giving us a program by which we could redeem ourselves.

After the illiterate preacher-leader, came the illiterate race-politician who also had no program for the higher temporal development of the race. He, like the preacher, had his selfish plans of using and feeding upon the emotions of the people. These two illiterate parasites, who extracted all that was worth while from the people, travelled hand in hand until we reached the first mile stone of higher intelligence; then the illiterate preacher and politician had to give way to a more intelligent class, who, unfortunately, with only a few exceptions, scattered here and there, followed and are still following in the footsteps of the old preachers and politicians to plunder and exploit the masses, because they had no vision.

And now I come to the source of my troubles, in fighting the battles of the masses. I come to the people in the role of the reformer and say to them, "Awake! the day is upon you, go forth in the name of the race and build yourselves a nation, redeem your country Africa, the land from whence you came and prove yourselves men worthy of the recognition of others."

This is the offence I have committed against the selfish Negro preachers and politicians who have for more than half a century waxed fat at the expense of the people. The shout goes up, "We cannot allow Garvey to preach his reformation and expose us to the people. The people will become too wise. We will lose our standing among them and they will not support us. We must 'get' Garvey. We must discredit him before the people. We cannot do it ourselves, because we have no power. We will frame him up; we will lay traps for him; we will state all manner of charges against him to the various departments of government so that the government will prosecute him for us."

Such have been the ravings, machinations and designs of a certain class of Negro politicians and preachers against me because of my reform work of three and a half years among my people that has over 4,000,000 followers.

Jews, Irish and reformers of all races have had their troubles and trials with their own people, so I am satisfied to bear the persecution of my own that they might be free.

I trust no one from the people would believe that I could be so mean as to defraud a fellow Negro, either directly or indirectly. I have an ideal that is far above money, and that is to see my people really free.

Others of my race oppose me because they fear my influence among the people, and they judge me from their own corrupt, selfish consciences. There is an old adage that says, "A thief does not like to see another man carrying a long bag," and thus the dishonest ones of our preachers and politicians believing that I am of their stamp, try to embarrass me by framing me up with the law.

I have had to dismiss from the employ of the Association, and caused the arrest of many dishonest preachers and politicians, and now their fraternities are out for revenge.

Poor misguided mortals! How can they, when the conscience and soul of a man cannot be incriminated from without?

The Negro ministry needs purging and with the help of God and the people, we shall in a short while show to the world a new race by the purification of those who lead.

I desire to say that I have a great amount of confidence in several of the preachers and politicians of my race today, but the great majority need purging, because among them we have gamblers, thieves, rogues, vagabonds, and these are the ones who are fighting me at this time.

The Hidden Spirit of America

"... history recalls where a race of slaves, through evolution,
through progress has risen to the heights where they ruled
and dominated those who once enslaved them."

Liberty Hall, New York City
February 13, 1922

The Negro World,
February 18, 1922

MY subject for tonight is "The Hidden Spirit of America." Before I speak on the subject I will read to you a bit of news. It is important because it strikes at the vitals of the great matter of the Negro problem— the solution of it. Those of you who are readers of *The Negro World* will remember seeing in the paper this week that bit of news that comes from Mississippi which reads as follows:

"JACKSON, Miss., Jan. 31—Senator McCallum today introduced in the State Senate in session here a concurrent resolution providing for the Legislature of Mississippi to memorialize the President of the United States and the national Congress to secure by treaty, by purchase or other negotiation sufficient territory in Africa to make a suitable and final home for the American Negro, where, under the tutelage of the American Government, he can develop for himself a great republic, to become in time a free and sovereign State and take its place at the council board of the nations of the world.

"Senator McCallum proposes to use such part of the allied war debt as may be necessary to acquire such territorial possessions to the end that America shall become a nation of one blood, as it is in spirit, and, as he says, 'To give the American Negro opportunity for the development of racial rights under the most advantageous circumstances.'"

The subject, "The Hidden Spirit of America," is brought out forcibly in this bit of news that recounts Senator McCallum's intention for proposing that this nation seek in some way or other to establish for the American Negro a sovereign state of his own—a nation of his own in Africa—because he desires that America shall become "a nation of one blood as it is in spirit." I trust you will readily grasp the meaning of that sentence of Senator McCallum's intended resolution.

It brings out without any camouflage the very thing that the Universal Negro Improvement Association has been preaching for four and a half years—that America in spirit at the present time is a white man's country, and it is going to be so in fact; and as far as it will be in fact that is why Senator McCallum is trying in his way to solve the great problem by having the President and Congress decide that America shall establish for the Negroes of America a sovereign State somewhere in Africa. After all, the Universal Negro Improvement Association is not so crazy in thinking about the possibility of an African nation of Negroes. We find that we have a crazy senator who is trying to get the President and Congress and the whole nation crazy also. So that it would appear that the whole country is going crazy with this idea of an African nation for the Negroes of the world.

The same reason why Senator McCallum desires a nation in Africa for the American Negroes is the same reason why other Negroes in other parts of the world who are outside of Africa desire a nation also in Africa; so that we are not only going to have a nation for the American Negroes or a nation for the West Indian Negroes, but we are going to have a nation for all Negroes, and the Universal Negro Improvement Association, I say now without any reserve, is very much in sympathy with Senator McCallum's resolution, because that has been our program for the last four and a half years. We of the Universal Negro Improvement Association realize that for the Negro to encourage himself in the belief that the future will mean peace and happiness for him in these parts of the world where he is hopelessly outnumbered by another race that is prejudiced towards him, is for him to encourage a vain hope. As we can see it, as the two races continue to live side by side in this Western world, and as competition becomes keener between the two races, industrially and politically, that prejudice that is being demonstrated and acted against us now will increase to such an extent that we will suffer the more and we will die the quicker from the results of the prejudice that I have outlined to you.

The thoughtful Negro leader of today will naturally look down the future not only of a day, a week, a month, or a year, but the future of many decades of centuries—as touching our condition. The thoughtful leader can come to no other conclusion than that in another 100 years America will be a changed country, quite different to what it is; that America's attitude towards a weaker race, if that race happens to be here, if that race works in competition with the stronger one that will always be here, that it will mean death for the weaker race.

The thoughtful leader realizes well that industrial, economic and political competition among peoples of different races breeds prejudice, hatred and ends generally in massacres, in civil wars, to the detriment of the weaker group. It has been so in all history; it is so now and it will be so in the future. The stronger group of any race living in any country, let it be America, Europe or anywhere, will not tolerate the keenness of competition industrially or politically with a weaker race within the same bounds. As that stronger race multiplies in numbers, that stronger race will perforce adopt an attitude of hostility toward that weaker race that seeks to compete industrially and politically.

America, as I have said, will be a different country as far as the number of inhabitants is concerned in another 100 years. You are going to have probably three times as many white people in this country in another hundred years as you have now. It will mean that industrial rivalry and competition among them as a people will be keener then and that they will perforce have to protect their own interests as against the interests of any other competitive group, and whether that group happens to be Negroes, Chinese or Japanese, they are going to fare very badly in that day when competition will force the other people to protect their interests industrially, economically and politically.

As we grow more numerous and more determined in demanding our rights in these times when the nation is not fully developed, we will politically arouse the ire and indignation of our fellow citizens of the other race because of our determination to hold political offices that render us politically competitive with the other people who believe that America is theirs if not now in fact, in spirit.

Some of us as leaders flatter ourselves into believing that the problem of black and white will work itself out in America in another few years and that all the Negro has to do is to be humble and submissive and do what he is told to do, and everything will work out well in "the sweet by-and-by." But the keen student will observe this: that a terrible mistake was made then as far as other people were concerned. There was a state of disorganization, and in that state of disorganization certain things happened just by mere chance, and in the chance dozens of black men became Senators, State Senators and Congressmen, and opened up to the eyes of the nation the possibility of the black man governing the white man in these United States of America—the possibility of the black man making laws to govern the white man in these United States of America. The possibility drove them to madness—almost madness—in suddenly rejecting the spirit of the Constitution and the declaration of Lincoln that "all men are created equal," and a determination was arrived at that never again would it be possible for a race of slaves to govern a race of masters within these bounds.

Some of us right now flatter ourselves to believe that this slave race of ours will live right in the United States of America and in the future be lawmakers for the race of our slave masters of sixty years ago. Now let me tell you that nothing of the kind has ever happened in all human history. You students go back in history as far as you possibly can and you cannot show me one instance where a slave race living in the same country— within the same bounds as the race of masters that enslaved them—that slave race being in numbers less than the race of masters and that race has ever yet ruled and governed within the same territory the race of slave masters. It has never yet been in history and it will never be, and the hidden spirit of America is determined that that shall never be; caring not what hopes or promises we get, it will never be. But history recalls where a race of slaves, through evolution, through progress has risen to the heights where they ruled and dominated those who once enslaved them. But that race of slaves has always had to betake themselves to other habitats (probably their own native habitats), and there apart from those who once enslaved them, developed a power of their own, a strength of their own, and in the higher development of that strength and of that power they, like others, have made conquests, and the conquests sometimes have enabled them to enslave those who once enslaved them. In all history you can show me no one instance where a race of slaves ever rose within that nation to govern their masters when their masters outnumbered them as hopelessly as they do now in the United States of America.

So that for us to encourage the idea that one of these days some Negro will be the Attorney General of the United States—for us to encourage the idea that one of these days a Negro will be Postmaster General of these United States or that a Negro will be Vice-President of the United States of America or that a Negro will be Secretary of State of the United States of America, is only to encourage a vain hope that will take you from here into eternity without being realized. If you have any ambition—and all of us (the 15,000,000 who make up the nation at this time) should have some ambition and that ambition should not be less than that of any other men in the nation—if we have ambition, the best thing for us to do is to accept the principles of the Universal Negro Improvement Association—the ideals of the Universal Negro Improvement Association—and that is: All Negroes the world over get together and build up for the race a nation of our own on the continent of Africa. {*Great applause.*} And this race of slaves that cannot get recognition and respect in the country where they were slaves, by using their own ability, by using their power, their genius, would develop for themselves in another country—in their own habitat— a nation of their own and be able to send back from that country—from that native habitat—to that country where they were once enslaved, representatives of their own race that will get as much respect in that country where they were enslaved as any other ambassadors that ever entered that country from any other nation or from any other race. {*Applause.*} What a Southern Senator would not concede to the Negro in the United States he is willing to give to Negroes in Africa. That same Southern Senator who moved this resolution that the President of the United States and the National Congress secure by treaty or purchase, a home in Africa for the American Negro where he can develop a free and sovereign state—a nation that will take its place at the council board of the nations of the world—that Southern Senator who moved that resolution in the Senate of Mississippi is the same Southern Senator who would object and stand behind the objection with his whole life and with the last drop of his blood, for a Negro in the United States of America to dine with the President of the United States at the White House. He would die first than see a Negro in the United States under present conditions be an Attorney General of the United States of America; he would die first than stand and see without protesting that a Negro was Vice-President of the United States of America; yet he says that he wants to see the American Negro develop a nation of his own in Africa that would cause him to take his place at the council board of the nations of the world.

The prejudice of the white folks of the United States of America is not so much because they hate your color; it is because they hate your condition; and it is because they are human beings why they hate. Should you reverse the positions you would do the same thing as they did to us. Why do I say that? There is no man in this hall tonight—no Negro man or woman in this hall tonight—because all of us are human—who would for a whole life time labor and work himself industrially and thriftily to save everything that you possibly can to build up a home of your own and save a little fortune of your own to make yourself happy, and that after you did all that—you have your children; you have your own family to take care of and to look after with that which you individually worked for—there is no one of you who would go out into the street and see a tramp and take that tramp and bring him into your house and let him sleep in the same bed with you; let him occupy your drawing-room, let him enjoy all the comforts of it, and later on have him say to you, "Let me tell you how to run your house." There is no one human being in this building who would do that. Yet that is what we expect the white man to do—we expect that white man to discover his America, to lay the foundation of his nation, to give for his nation, to die for his nation, to build up his nation, and then to say to you who were his slaves, "Come and govern me, go and sit in the Capitol and tell me what I should do."

Although they have not said as much to you, that is how they feel over the question. That is the bone of contention—not because you are black, but because they believe that they are entitled to all the benefits that America can give because they built up America to suit themselves and whatsoever we have done to build up America we did it as slaves and they having used us as slaves they are not responsible for our condition.

I want you to consider that deeply. We have been talking a lot of things about our slave masters and so forth. The slave masters are not so much to be blamed as those who sold us to the slave masters; therefore the obligation of the slave masters is not so much to you; your trouble—my trouble is with the fellow who sold me; that is to say if I buy a dog from someone, I do not know where that dog comes from; he may have picked the dog up somewhere in South America or Central America, but the man brought the dog to me in New York, and being in need of a dog I pay him $5.00 for it. Now, the dog's trouble is with the fellow who caught him down in South America, not with me. {*Laughter.*}

When we get down to a close study of the question of race relationship those are the arguments that the other fellow puts up and we cannot very well defeat him, and those are the arguments that actuate him in acting towards us as he has been doing. As I have said it is a human question, and if the situation was reversed you would do just what he is doing. When we go to Africa, as we will, and build up our civilization, build up our superior government and everything, do you mean to tell me you will allow another class of people to tell you how to run your own government? It is not human, therefore those who tell us a better time is coming and Negroes are going to have big opportunities are endeavoring to deceive us, according to the spirit of the country and the spirit of the nation.

I agree with Senator McCallum and I am going to give every support possible to his resolution and to his program. The quicker we can get this national idea into the minds of white folks and black folks in America, the better it will be for us as a people. It is bound to come if we are to be saved; it must come, and if it does not come and we do not get away from here we are doomed—not as of today, but as for the time that is to confront us.

I feel that the Universal Negro Improvement Association has scored a great victory in having a senator, not even in the North, but in the heart of the South, to move such a resolution, because the problem is in the

South more than anywhere else; and when the Southern white man reaches the point when he or himself will say, let the Negro laborer go from the South; let the peon leave the farm—it means that our case has gone forward. I am not prophesying—because I am not a prophet—but I am going to make this statement, and whether I am alive or not you will remember it: that if things remain as they are—normal—in another 25 years this government will perforce adopt a program of the Universal Negro Improvement Association, whether they give the credit to the organization or not: because it will be the only solution of the great problem. The solution must either come that way, or some of us must make up our minds to die—to die of economic pressure.

Some of us boast that we are 15,000,000 and we are going to be more than 15,000,000 in the future, and therefore the white man cannot get rid of us. The white man can get rid of every Negro in the United States of America in three months. It took McSwiney 75 days to die by starvation, but I don't know the Negro that could last that long. We are so unprepared, we are so unprotected, that when the other race will have become independent of us, that is, economically independent—independent of Negro help in every way—when he arrives at that point, when he has a man for every job and is independent of Negro help, when he gets there—and he is getting there more and more every day—it is only a question of 60 days when the Negro problem is solved. Instead of 15,000,000 Negroes you will have 15,000,000 coffins, and the epitaph will be: "Died from starvation."

I am telling you that is the situation as it is. It is no use any leader coming around telling us the proper time is coming without preparing for that proper time. What we have to do if we desire to ward off economic disaster is to prepare economically for our future, and that is the program of the Universal Negro Improvement Association—the higher industrialization of the Negro as he marches on to his higher political status. Politics without industry means insecurity. A man who is going to talk politics without working is going to be a charge on the state. You cannot live on politics alone; you have to live on industry; industry must be the foundation of your politics, and I am saying to the Negroes of the world that the thing for us to do now is to prepare ourselves industrially, so that if an industrial pressure is brought to bear upon us in the future we will be in a position through independence to protect our own interests.

Some people do not understand the program of the Universal Negro Improvement Association—why we have so many different branches and why we want to start steamships and factories, etc. Those are essentials to the existence of the Negro. Industry is necessary and therefore we have to lay out a program by which we can insure protection to all the people of our race. I am saying to you now that while we are here let us follow this

Universal Negro Improvement Association program, caring not what others say to you about the promise of the future, because you have absolutely no intention and attitude of the future towards you. You cannot expect the other fellow to work for you, to labor for you, to build up a civilization and then hand it over to you. He is not going to do it, because it is not human. The time has come now when we as free men can do for ourselves, and when we start out to do for ourselves this prejudice against us will cease.

Again I repeat, the prejudice against us is not so much because we are black; it is because we have accomplished nothing, and when you, by the encouragement of those who wish to work, go out and do for yourselves, build up a nation, build up a government, you will be as much respected in the country where you were once slaves because then you will be in your own homes.

Many nations of today represented a race of slaves. The great British nation was once a race of slaves; in their own country they were not respected because the Romans went there, brutalized and captured them and took them over to Rome and kept them in slavery. They were not respected in Rome because they were brought as slaves to Rome. What happened? Throughout the world the Britisher is respected today because he went back to his dear Britain and built up a civilization of his own and by his self-reliance and his initiative he forced the respect of the world and he maintains it today; yet he was once a slave, and the position which the Britisher has attained, coming up through slavery, you can attain if you will go out and assiduously work for the development of your race and nation as the Briton has done.

That is my message tonight, and I am saying to you, "Be not weary in well doing." In carrying out and spreading the propaganda of the Universal Negro Improvement Association we have waited for four and one-half years to have a Southern Senator to take this step. We will wait another four years, when the Congress of the United States of America will give its support; and I believe that the time will come, probably within another decade—another 25 years—when this very country—when the white people of this country will help Negroes to found and establish a government of their own in Africa. I believe that because there are many within the nation who wish us well; but they are not going to wish us well if we remain here and compete with them. I am not going to encourage another man to come into my house and boss me, my wife and my children and everybody in there, but I wish him well from a distance. The fellow is my friend if he has his home, but when he comes to my home and wants to meddle into my domestic affairs, we are going to fight it out. That is the position: The other fellow wishes you well away from him; if you are going to go into his house and rule him you are going to be at loggerheads; he is going to hate you; and that is the situation.

The Resurrection of the Negro

"The God you worship is a God that expects
you to be the equal of other men."

Liberty Hall, New York City,
Easter Sunday, April 16, 1922

The Philosophy and Opinions of Marcus Garvey, or Africa for the Africans,
Volume 1

THE Lord is risen! A little over nineteen hundred years ago a man came to this world called JESUS. He was sent here for the propagation of a cause—that of saving fallen humanity. When He came the world refused to hear Him; the world rejected Him; the world persecuted Him; men crucified Him. A couple days ago He was nailed to the cross of Calvary; He died; He was buried. Today He is risen: risen the spiritual leader of creation; risen as the first fruit of them that slept. Today that crucified Lord, that crucified Christ sees the affairs of man from His own spiritual throne on high.

After hundreds of years have rolled by, the doctrine He taught has become the accepted religion of hundreds of millions of human beings. He in His resurrection triumphed over death and the grave; He by His resurrection convinced humanity that His cause was spiritual. The world felt the truth about Jesus too late to have accepted His doctrine in His lifetime. But what was done to Jesus in His lifetime is just what is done to all reformers and reform movements. He came to change the spiritual attitude of man toward his brother. That was regarded in His day as an irregularity, even as it is regarded today. The one who attempts to bring about changes in the order of human society becomes a dangerous imposter upon society, and to those who control the systems of the day.

It has been an historic attitude of man to keep his brother in slavery—in subjection for the purpose of exploitation. When Jesus came the privileged few were taking advantage of the unfortunate masses. Because the teaching of Jesus sought to equalize the spiritual and even the temporal rights of man, those who held authority, sway and dominion sought His liberty by prosecution, sought His life by death. He was called to yield up that life for the cause He loved—because He was indeed a true reformer.

The example set by our Lord and Master nineteen hundred years ago is but the example that every reformer must make up his mind to follow if we are indeed to serve those to whom we minister. Service to humanity means sacrifice. That has been demonstrated by our blessed Lord and Redeemer whose resurrection we commemorate this day. As Christ triumphed nearly two thousand years ago over death and the grave, as He was risen from the dead, so do I hope that 400,000,000 Negroes of today will triumph over the slavishness of the past, intellectually, physically, morally and even religiously; that on this anniversary of our risen Lord, we ourselves will be risen from the slumber of the ages; risen in thought to higher ideals, to a loftier purpose, to a truer conception of life.

It is the hope of the Universal Negro Improvement Association that 400,000,000 Negroes of the world will get to realize that we are about to live a new life—a risen life—a life of knowing ourselves.

How many of us know ourselves? How many of us understand ourselves? The major number of us for ages have failed to recognize in ourselves the absolute masters of our own destiny—the absolute directors and creators of our own fate.

Today as we think of our risen Lord may we not also think of the life He gave to us—the life that made us His instruments, His children—the life that He gave to us to make us possessors of the land that He himself created through His Father? How many of us can reach out to that higher life; that higher purpose; that creative world that says to you you are a man, a sovereign, a lord—lord of the creation? On this beautiful spring day, may we not realize that God made Nature for us; God has given it to us as our province, our dominion? May we not realize that God has created no superior being to us in this world, but Himself? May we not know that we are the true lords and creators of our own fate and of our own physical destiny?

The work of the Universal Negro Improvement Association for the past four and a half years has been that of guiding us to realize that there should be a resurrection in us, and if at no other time I trust that at this Easter-tide we will realize that there is a great need for a resurrection—a resurrection from the lethargy of the past—the sleep of the past—from that feeling that made us accept the idea and opinion that God intended that we should occupy an inferior place in the world.

Men and women of Liberty Hall, men and women of my race, do you know that the God we love, the God we adore, the God who sent His Son to this world nearly two thousand years ago never created an inferior man? That God we love, that God we worship and adore has created man in His own image, equal in every respect, wheresoever he may be; let him be white; let him be yellow; let him be red; let him be black; God has created him the equal of his brother. He is such a loving God. He is such a merciful God. He is such a God that He is no respecter of persons, that He would not in His great love create a superior race and an inferior one. The God that you worship is a God that expects you to be the equal of other men. The God that I adore is such a God and He could be no other.

Some of us seem to accept the fatalist position, the fatalist attitude, that God accorded to us a certain position and condition, and therefore there is no need trying to be otherwise. The moment you accept such an attitude, the moment you accept such an opinion, the moment you harbor such an idea, you hurl an insult at the great God who created you, because you question Him for His love, you question Him for His mercy. God has created man, and has placed him in this world as the lord of the creation, as the sovereign of everything that you see, let it be land, let it be sea, let it be the lakes, rivers and everything therein. All that you see in creation, all that you see in the world, was created by God for the use of man, and you four hundred million black souls have as much right to your possession in this world as any other race.

Created in the image of the same God we have the same common rights, and today I trust that there will be a spiritual and material resurrection among Negroes everywhere; that you will lift yourselves from the doubts of the past; that you will lift yourselves from the slumbers of the past, that you will lift yourselves from the lethargy of the past, and strike out in this new life—in this resurrected life—to see things as they are.

The Universal Negro Improvement Association desires that the four hundred million members of our race see life as the other races see it. The great white race sees life in an attitude of sovereignty; the great yellow race sees life in a similar way, that is to say that man, let him be white or yellow, sees that he is master and owner and possessor of everything that God has created in this world, and given to us in Nature; and that is why by knowing himself, by understanding himself, and by understanding his God, man has gone, throughout the length and breadth of this world, conquering the very elements, harnessing Nature and making a servant of everything that God placed within his reach.

As he has done that for thousands of years pleasing God and justifying his existence, so we are appealing to the members of our race to do that now in this risen life, and if you have never made up your minds before I trust on this Easter Sunday you will do so.

I repeat that God created you masters of your own destiny, masters of your own fate, and you can pay no higher tribute to your Divine Master than function as man, as He created you.

The highest compliment we can pay to our Creator; the highest respect we can pay to our risen Lord and Savior, is that of feeling that He has created us as His masterpiece; His perfect instruments of His own existence, because in us is reflected the very being of God. When it is said that we are created in His own image, we ourselves reflect His greatness, we ourselves reflect the part of God the Father, God the Son, and God the Holy Ghost, and when we allow ourselves to be subjected and create others as our superior, we hurl an insult at our Creator who made us in the fullness of ourselves.

I trust that you will so live today as to realize that you are masters of your own destiny, masters of your fate; if there is anything you want in this world it is for you to strike out with confidence and faith in self and reach for it, because God has created it for your happiness wheresoever you may find it in nature. Nature is bountiful; nature is resourceful, and nature is willing to obey the command of man—Man the sovereign lord; man who is supposed to hold dominion and take possession of this great world of ours.

The difference between the strong and weak races is that the strong races seem to know themselves; seem to discover themselves; seem to realize and know fully that there is but a link between them and the Creator; that above them there is no other but God and anything that bears human form is but their equal in standing and to that form there should be no obeisance; there should be no regard for superiority. Because of that feeling they have been able to hold their own in this world; they have been able to take care of the situation as it confronts them in nature; but because of our lack of faith and confidence in ourselves we have caused others created in a like image to ourselves to take advantage of us for hundreds of years.

For hundreds of years we have been the footstool of other races and nations of the earth simply because we have failed to realize to recognize and know ourselves as other men have known themselves and felt that there is nothing in the world that is above them except the influence of God.

The understanding that others have gotten out of life is the same understanding that 400,000,000 Negroes must get out of this existence of ours. I pray that a new inspiration will come to us as a race; that we will think of nature as our servant; that we will think of man as our partner through life, and go through the length and breadth of this world achieving and doing as other men, as other nations and other races.

Africa for the Africans

"It is hoped when the time comes for American and West Indian Negroes to settle in Africa, they will realize their responsibility and their duty."

New York City
April 18, 1922

The Negro World, April 22, 1922

FELLOW MEN OF THE NEGRO RACE, *Greeting:*

FOR four and a half years the Universal Negro Improvement Association has been advocating the cause of Africa for the Africans—that is, that the Negro peoples of the world should concentrate upon the object of building up for themselves a great nation in Africa.

When we started our propaganda toward this end several of the so-called intellectual Negroes who have been bamboozling the race for over half a century said that we were crazy, that the Negro peoples of the Western world were not interested in Africa and could not live in Africa. One editor and leader* went so far as to say at his Pan-African Congress that American Negroes could not live in Africa, because the climate was too hot. All kinds of arguments have been adduced by these Negro intellectuals against the colonization of Africa by the black race. Some said that the black man would ultimately work out his existence alongside of the white man in countries founded and established by the latter. Therefore, it was not necessary for Negroes to seek an independent nationality of their own. The old-time stories of "African fever," "African bad climate," "African mosquitoes," "African savages," have been repeated by these "brainless intellectuals" of ours as a scare against our people in America and the West Indies taking a kindly interest in the new program of building a racial empire of our own in our Motherland. Now that years have rolled by and the Universal Negro Improvement Association has made the circuit of the world with its propaganda, we find eminent statesmen and leaders of the white race coming out boldly advocating the cause of colonizing Africa with the Negroes of the western world. Not more than two months ago Senator McCullum of the Mississippi Legislature introduced a resolution in the House for the purpose of petitioning the Congress of the United States of America and the President to use their good influence in securing from the Allies sufficient territory in Africa in liquidation of the war debt, which territory should be used for the establishing of an independent nation for American Negroes. Just a few weeks ago Senator France of Maryland gave expression to a similar desire in the Senate of the United States during a speech on the "Soldiers' Bonus and the Allied Duty." He said: "We owe a big duty to Africa and one which we have too long ignored. I need not enlarge upon our peculiar interest in the obligation to the people of Africa. Thousands of Americans have for years been contributing to the missionary work which has been carried out by the noble men and women who have been sent out in that field by the churches of America."

This reveals the real change on the part of prominent statesmen in their attitude on the African question. Now comes another suggestion from Germany, for which Dr. Heinrich Schnee, a former Governor of German East Africa, is author. This German statesman suggests in an

---

*Garvey is referring to W. E. B. DuBois.

interview given out in Berlin and published in New York on the 16th inst., that America take over the mandatories of Great Britain and France in Africa for the colonization of American Negroes. Speaking on the matter, he says, "As regards the attempt to colonize Africa with the surplus American colored population, this would in a long way settle the vexed problem, and under the plan such as Senator France has outlined, might enable France and Great Britain to discharge their duties to the United States, and simultaneously ease the burden of German reparations which is paralyzing economic life."

With expressions as above quoted from prominent world statesmen, and from the demands made by such men as Senators France and McCullum, it is clear that the question of African nationality is not a far-fetched one, but is as reasonable and feasible as was the idea of an American nationality.

I trust that the Negro peoples of the world are now convinced that the work of the Universal Negro Improvement Association is not a visionary one, but very practical and that it is not so far-fetched, but can be realized in a short while if the entire race will only cooperate and work toward the desired end. Now that the work of our organization has started to bear fruit, we find that some of these "doubting Thomases" of three and four years ago are endeavoring to mix themselves up with the popular idea of rehabilitating Africa in the interest of the Negro. They are now advancing spurious "programs" and in a short while will endeavor to force themselves upon the public as advocates and leaders of the African idea.

It is felt that those who have followed the career of the Universal Negro Improvement Association will not allow themselves to be deceived by these Negro opportunists who have always sought to live off the ideas of other people.

It is only a question of a few more years when Africa will be completely colonized by Negroes, as Europe is by the white race. It is for us to welcome the proffered help of such men as Senators McCullum and France. Though their methods are a little different to that of the Universal Negro Improvement Association, yet it is felt that the same object will be achieved. What we want is an independent African nationality, and if America is to help the Negro peoples of the world establish such a nationality, then we welcome the assistance.

It is hoped when the time comes for American and West Indian Negroes to settle in Africa, they will realize their responsibility and their duty. It will not be to go to Africa for the purpose of exercising an over-lordship over the natives, but it shall be the purpose of the Universal Negro Improvement Association to have established in Africa that brotherly cooperation which will make the interest of the African native and the American and West Indian Negro one and the same, that is to say, we shall enter into a common partnership to build up America in the interest of our race.

Everybody knows that there is absolutely no difference between the native African and the American and West Indian Negroes, in that we are descendants from one common family stock. It is only a matter of accident that we have been divided and kept apart for over three hundred years, but it is felt that when the time has come for us to get back together, we shall do so in the spirit of brotherly love, and any Negro who expects that he will be assisted here, there or anywhere by the Universal Negro Improvement Association to exercise a haughty superiority over the fellows of his own race, makes a tremendous mistake. Such men had better remain where they are and not attempt to become in any way interested in the higher development of Africa.

The Negro has had enough of the vaunted practice of race superiority as inflicted upon him by others, therefore he is not prepared to tolerate a similar assumption on the part of his own people. In America and the West Indies, we have Negroes who believe themselves so much above their fellows as to cause them to think that any readjustment in the affairs of the race should be placed in their hands for them to exercise a kind of an autocratic and despotic control as others have done to us for centuries. Again, I say, it would be advisable for such Negroes to take their hands and minds off the now popular idea of colonizing Africa in the interest of the Negro race, because their being identified with this new program will not in any way help us because of the existing feeling among Negroes everywhere not to tolerate the infliction of race or class superiority upon them, as is the desire of the self-appointed and self-created race leadership that we have been having for the last fifty years.

The masses of Negroes in America, the West Indies, South and Central America are in sympathetic accord with the aspirations of the native Africans. We desire to help them to build up Africa as a Negro Empire, where every black man, whether he was born in Africa or in the Western world, will have the opportunity to develop on his own lines under the protection of the most favorable democratic institutions.

It will be useless, as above stated, for bombastic Negroes to leave America and the West Indies to go to Africa, thinking that they will have privileged position to inflict upon the race that bastard aristocracy that they have tried to maintain in this Western world at the expense of the masses. Africa shall develop an aristocracy of its own, but it shall be based upon service and loyalty to race.

Let all Negroes work toward that end. I feel that it is only a question of a few more years before our program will be accepted not only by the few statesmen of America who are now interested in it, but by the strong statesmen of the world, as the only solution to the great race problem. There is no other way to avoid the threatening war of the races that is bound to engulf all mankind, which has been prophesied by the world's greatest thinkers; there is no better method than by apportioning every race to its own habitat.

The time has really come for the Asiatics to govern themselves in Asia, as the Europeans are in Europe and the Western world, so also it is wise for the Africans to govern themselves at home, and thereby bring peace and satisfaction to the entire human family.

I am calling upon Negroes everywhere to lend the support necessary to the Universal Negro Improvement Association for putting over its great Convention program of August of the present year.

As has been outlined in another part of this paper, it is planned to make the immediate establishment of an African nation one of the features of our legislative demands. The best thing that the race can do is to create just at this time a universal sentiment in support of the work of the forthcoming international Convention, so that when our demands are presented to the various Governments that have possessions in Africa, there will be no doubt as to the potency and force of the demands. We have decided to ring the changes in 1922 as never was done before. This year is regarded as a year of racial and national changes. Egypt and Ireland have already secured their freedom for 1922, and it is most likely that before the close of the year India will have gained a larger modicum of self-government. We cannot, therefore, allow the cause of Africa to lag behind. It is for us to force it. Thus the Universal Negro Improvement Association shall leave no stone unturned to win for Africa and the four hundred million Negroes of the world a new position in the racial, national and political affairs of the world. All that is necessary is the moral and financial support of the race everywhere for this great organization. You can contribute your mite now to help this great cause. If you have not done so before, and even if you have, it is your duty to send in a donation to the Universal Negro Improvement Association, 56 West 135th Street, New York City, N.Y., U.S.A., to help this great work for the redemption of Africa and the emancipation of the race.

With very best wishes for your success, I have the honor to be

> Your obedient servant,
> MARCUS GARVEY, President-General
> Universal Negro Improvement Association

Hon. Marcus Garvey Tells of Interview
with the Ku Klux Klan

"The Ku Klux Klan is the invisible government
of the United States of America."

Liberty Hall, New York City
July 9, 1922

The Negro World, July 15, 1922

IN keeping with my duties as leader of a large movement, as one of the
advocates of Negro rights and Negro liberty, as an officer of the largest
Negro organization in the world, I became interested in the activities of
an organization known as the Ku Klux Klan, not because I wanted to be
a member of the Klan, but because I wanted to know the truth about the
Klan's attitude toward the race I represent.

For that reason a conference was arranged between the Acting
Imperial Wizard of the Ku Klux Klan and myself, which took place in
Atlanta, Ga., on the 25th of June. The interview or the report of the conference is to be published in *The Negro World,* the official organ of the
Universal Negro Improvement Association, and I believe it will also be
published in the *Searchlight,* the official organ of the Ku Klux Klan.*
Unfortunately, because of the pressure of business, I have been unable to
read the interview as held to send a copy back to the Imperial Wizard
for his correction as well as for my own, in that it was arranged that the
interview would be handed to each party concerned for his approval or
correction before it was made public. Up to now the corrections have
not been made, and I am to speak tonight not so much from the reported
matter of the interview as from my impression of the Ku Klux Klan as
gained through contact with the leaders of the Klan.

You will understand what it means when two parties enter into an
agreement that no public announcements should be made of certain
things until the two parties had the opportunity of looking over the
copies concerned referring to the matter or the thing; and that has not
been done yet; but since my return to New York I discovered that a large
number of the colored people here are very curious as to the nature of
the visit and what happened, and since I returned to New York I have
received copies of Negro newspapers that have published me as joining
hands with the Ku Klux Klan. I know and you know the attitude of the
Negro press in America—a senseless, ignorant attitude—an attitude that

---

*It was not, however, published in either periodical.

does not tend to help educationally in the development of this race of ours in America, especially to a young, growing race as ours.

From my impressions, from my observations, from my understanding, the Ku Klux Klan is a mighty white organization in the United States of America, organized for the purpose of upholding white supremacy in this country; organized for the purpose of making America a white man's country, pure and simple. The organization has absolutely no apology to make as far as its program is concerned—a program of making America a white man's country. In America we have twelve or fifteen million in a population of 105,000,000 people. The Ku Klux Klan to a large extent represents every white man in the United States of America. I want you to realize that. The Ku Klux Klan represents the spirit, the feeling, the attitude of every white man in the United States of America. Now, what should be the Negro's attitude toward such an organization?

The Negro's attitude toward such an organization should not be to stand off, not knowing its program, not understanding it and saying and writing all kinds of things against it with the intention of aggravating its program and its attitude toward the race, but the duty of the leadership of the Negro race, finding itself in such an unenviable position, is to study the thing, to understand the thing and get as much information as possible about the thing in your own interests. Aggravating the Ku Klux Klan or aggravating any organization in the world organized for the specific purpose of white supremacy is not going to help the race in America, placed at a disadvantage as it is. There is much more beneath the surface of the Ku Klux Klan than you can see on the surface. Some of us Negro leaders and some of us Negro newspapermen get crazy because the *New York World* and *New York American* about two months ago tried to expose the activities of the Ku Klux Klan. Now, let me tell you that the *World* nor the *American* has absolutely no intention to put down the Ku Klux Klan to please Negroes. The *World* and the *American* exposed the activities of the Ku Klux Klan for their own set reason, for their own set purpose, without having in mind the good that would accrue to Negroes by the putting down of the Ku Klux Klan; and let me tell you this, that it was not so much the real intention of their exposé to put down the Ku Klux Klan. Negro editors and Negro leaders got wild and started to lambaste the Ku Klux Klan and write all kinds of things against them. Let me tell you this: that the Ku Klux Klan is really the invisible government of the United States of America, and that there are more people identified with the Klan than you think; that there are more people in sympathy with the activities of the Ku Klux Klan than you think, and that there is more sympathy in this country for the Ku Klux Klan than the ordinary literate Negro newspaperman thinks and sees on the surface.

As proof that the Ku Klux Klan is a worthy organization in the opinion of the white leaders of this country, the exposé of *The New York World* led to what? Led to an investigation of the activities of the Klan by the Congress of the United States; and what has happened up to now? The Ku Klux Klan is still at large, the Ku Klux Klan has grown twice as strong since the exposé as before. The exposé of the Ku Klux Klan was solely a skillful method of advertising the activities of the Klan at very little cost to the Klan.

After the activities of the Ku Klux Klan were exposed, California was besieged with the Ku Klux Klan and New York itself became a stronghold of the Klan, and if I am to take the words of the acting Imperial Wizard, the Ku Klux Klan is stronger in the Northern states than it is in the Southern states of the United States of America.

Now what are you going to do about it? Stand off and refuse to investigate and refuse to understand the attitude of the Klan toward you and in that way expect to solve the problem? Our belief is that the leadership of a large group of people must be intelligent enough to be on guard in protecting the interests or the rights of the people. Because of that intention, because of that feeling, because of that attitude, I interviewed the Imperial Wizard of the Ku Klux Klan to find out the Klan's attitude toward the race. You may believe it or not—I made several statements to him, in which he said this: that the Klan is not organized for the absolute purpose of interfering with Negroes—for the purpose of suppressing Negroes, but the Klan is organized for the purpose of protecting the interests of the white race in America. Now anything that does not spell the interests of the white race in America does not come within the scope of the Ku Klux Klan.

I found out, therefore, that the Ku Klux Klan was purely a racial organization standing up in the interests of white folks exclusive of the interests of others. You cannot blame any group of men, whether they are Chinese, Japanese, Anglo-Saxons or Frenchmen, for standing up for their interests or for organizing in their interest. I am not apologizing for the Klan or endeavoring to excuse the existence of the Klan, but I want a proper understanding about the Ku Klux Klan so that there can be no friction between the Negroes in America and the Ku Klux Klan, because it is not going to help.

The Ku Klux Klan is not an ordinary social club organized around the corner. The Ku Klux Klan is the invisible government of the United States of America. The Ku Klux Klan expresses to a great extent the feeling of every real white American. The attitude of the Ku Klux Klan is that America shall be a white man's country at all hazards, at all costs. The attitude of the Universal Negro Improvement Association is in a way similar to the Ku Klux Klan. Whilst the Ku Klux Klan desires to make America absolutely a white man's country, the Universal Negro Improvement Association wants to make Africa absolutely a black man's country. {*Great applause.*} Whether you wish it or not, that is not the point, because your wish does not amount to anything. The wish of fifteen million Negroes in America does not amount to anything when 95,000,000 other folks wish the thing that you want. That is the disadvantage. We wish liberty; we wish to be good American citizens; we want to be President of the United States; we wish to be Congressmen; we wish to be Senators; we wish to be governors of states; we wish to be mayors of cities; we wish to be police commissioners. It is a wish, all right, but the other fellow wishes the same thing. Now, is he going to allow you to have your wish? That is the attitude. The white people of this country are not going to allow Negroes—ambitious and educated Negroes—to have their wish, and the wish of the educated, ambitious Negro of America is that the Negro has as much right to be President of the United States as President Harding has. The ambition and wish of the Negro in America today is that the Negro has as much right to be a member of the Cabinet as any white man. Now that is your wish. Will the other fellow accede to your wish?

The Ku Klux Klan interprets the spirit of every white man in this country and says, "You shall not pass." What are you going to do? You have the wish, but the odds are against you.

Some of us Negro leaders, some of us newspapermen, before we get down to a serious study of the question and adopt the best possible means of solving the problem, we are working on the surface. My suit is mine, but if a bully comes along and tears it off me it is mine, but it is his now. All of us know that America is as much the Negro's as the white man's, but the white man says, "I am going to make this a white man's country." The only thing for you to do is to get hold of him, beat him and take it away. But can you do that? You cannot do that. Therefore the best thing you can do is to get down to a sober understanding of the Klan and try to the best of your ability to solve the question that concerns you. And the Universal Negro Improvement Association says the only way the problem can be solved is for the Negro to create a government of his own strong enough on the continent of Africa that can compel the respect of all men in all parts of the world.

We are not going to have any fight as an organization with the Ku Klux Klan because it is not going to help. The Ku Klux Klan, as I said a while ago, is the invisible government of the United States of America. What do I mean by that? The Klan represents the spiritual feeling and even the physical attitude of every white man in this country. There are hundreds of other organizations that feel as the Ku Klux Klan feels. There are millions of individuals in America who feel as the Ku Klux

Klan feels, but those individuals, those organizations are not honest enough to make the confession that the Ku Klux Klan makes. I prefer and have a higher regard for the man who intends to take my life who will warn me and say, "Garvey, I am going to take your life," so as to give me time to prepare my soul for my God, rather than the man who will pretend to be my friend, and as I turn my back he ushers me into eternity without even giving me a chance to say my Lord's Prayer.

The Ku Klux Klan comes out openly and says this: "Negroes, we are going to make this country a white man's country; so long as there is a white man in America a Negro shall not be President of the United States; so long as there is a white man in America a Negro shall never be a member of the cabinet; so long as there is a white man in America a Negro shall never again be a Congressman or Senator; so long as there is a white man in America a Negro shall never again be a governor or a lieutenant-governor of a state." Now the man that says that gives you enough information about yourself and about him as to enable you to make some plans to help yourself one way or the other; but the other fellow who comes and says nothing to you, but, on the other hand, flatters you and says, "I am your friend and have the same feeling or attitude toward you as the other fellow who told you"—which is the better friend, the one who tells you or the one who keeps the information from you but means the same thing?

I asked the acting Imperial Wizard of the Ku Klux Klan whether he was interpreting the spirit of just a few people who make up his organization or not, and he said, "No, we are interpreting the spirit of every true white American; but we are honest enough to say certain things that others do not care to say." Now in a nutshell you have the situation. What is the use of staying outside, not understanding the attitude and lambasting those people who are in power? Sentiment cannot put down the Ku Klux Klan; newspaper writings cannot put down the Ku Klux Klan. The Ku Klux Klan is expressing the feeling of over 95,000,000 people. No law can put down the prejudice of a race. You may legislate between now and eternity. If I hate you, no law in the world can make me love you. If I am prejudiced against you for reasons, no law, no constitution in the world can make me change my attitude toward you.

The Ku Klux Klan is therefore expressing the feeling and the sentiment of a large number of people in this country towards us as a race—the attitude of refusing to allow the Negro to enjoy political, economic and social equality. The Ku Klux Klan made me to understand that their attitude is based on the assumption that this country was discovered by white men; this country was first peopled and colonized by white men; that this country's existence was brought about by white men fighting, suffering and dying to create a government of their own and because of the suffering of white men in the past to bequeath to their children of today a country of their own, the children of today are not disposed to give up their rights racially to any other race whether it be Negro, Japanese or any other race on the face of the globe.

Now what are you going to do? This is their attitude. Our lambasting them and publishing all kinds of things without studying them will not help the situation. A lot of Negro leaders are to be found up North who write a lot of stuff, but have not the nerve to go South to give expression to the same sentiments. {*Applause.*} The largest number of Negroes in the United States of America live below the Mason and Dixon line where the Ku Klux Klan rules. It is all right for the fellow up North who does not live under the influence of the Klan to say things about the Klan, but who is going to pay the price of it? The poor unfortunate fellow who lives next door to the Klan and comes in contact with him every day.

The Universal Negro Improvement Association realizes that therefore, and while some of us stand up and say all kinds of things criticizing the Klan, millions of our brothers are suffering because of this criticism up North. We desire to prevent that suffering, and it is for that reason we went down to the South to have a proper understanding to see if we could diplomatically at least help the Negro to throw off the suffering, to throw off this yoke without causing anyone to suffer. That is really the attitude of the organization; that is the reason I interviewed the Imperial Wizard of the Ku Klux Klan. He told me this when I put these pointed questions to him. I asked him: "Mr. Clarke, you will understand that the Negro of today is quite different to the Negro of sixty years ago. Sixty years ago the Negro was a slave, untutored, unintelligent, uncivilized, so to speak; knew nothing about civilized culture or about civilization, and he was satisfied to be a farmer's help—to be a laborer; even to be a slave. Today we have a cultured, civilized Negro, an educated man, a graduate of the best universities in the country and the world. The Negro of sixty years ago had no ambition because he had no civilization, no culture and could not appreciate the benefits and advantages of civilization. Now that he is civilized and cultured he is ambitious and desires the things that every man desires. Now, Mr. Clarke, what is the Klan's attitude toward the Negro who desires to be President of the United States of America?" And he said this: "He shall never be so long as there is one white man living in the United States of America." I said: "Mr. Clarke, what is the attitude of the Klan towards the Negro who wants to be governor of a state?" And he gave the same answer, "Not so long as there is one white man in the United States of America." Again I asked him: "Mr. Clarke, does your organization represent only the group of men in it or the sentiment of your race?" The answer was this: "This organization represents the sentiments of the entire white race." Mr. Clarke did not tell me anything new; he told me what I discovered seven years ago. He told me the thing that caused me to have organized the Universal Negro Improvement Association four and a half years ago. So I was not disturbed, I was not nervous at all. I was speaking to a man who was brutally a white man, and I was speaking to him as a man who was brutally a Negro. He had his interests to protect and I had mine to protect. His one idea, his one greatest hope is to see the great white race the masters of civilization. My one dream, my one hope is to see the great black race the masters of civilization. {*Applause.*} Now I am not going to waste time fighting with the Ku Klux Klan; I am going to use my time fighting for the ideals that we have. And then I asked him: "Mr. Clarke, if your organization is organized for the purpose of offending—or killing—Negroes, or suppressing Negroes, what do you think the end will be?" He said: "We are not organized for that purpose." I then said to him: "I want you to understand that the Negro question is no longer a Southern question or a national question."

It is as President Harding said in his Birmingham speech—that the Negro question is no longer a Southern or a national question in America; it has become an international question. I said to him: "If you are organized for the sole purpose of suppressing Negro ambition and advancement, do you know that Negroes are getting together all over the world and may return the compliment to you?" He said: "I realized that, and it is because of that we have organized. We are not organized to be unfair to the Negro; we want to see the Negro develop as the white man has developed. To be fair, I advise every Negro and those who aspire to leadership to form an organization similar to that of the Ku Klux Klan so that the Negroes may be able to look out for their own interests and not continue to be begging white people to do for them what they ought to do for themselves."

He spoke to me in that frank and open way. I made him to understand that the Universal Negro Improvement Association adopted this attitude—that if the Ku Klux Klan in America was going to outrage Negroes simply because they are black, we may return the compliment somewhere because some other folks do not look like us. He realized that and said: "We are willing to see a great Negro organization with which we can enter into negotiations and understanding to solve this great question of race, and especially the social question of race."

And then we discussed the social side. I said: "Mr. Clarke, what is your attitude on white men raping black women?" And he said: "We are as much against that as any self-respecting Negro can be, and we are organized to see that the purity of the race, and especially the purity of the white race, is upheld, and because of that we would not desire to impose upon you that which we do not intend to accept from you."

I asked him: "What would be your attitude if a white man was to go into a colored neighborhood and endeavor to take advantage of the womanhood of our race?" And he said that his attitude would be against that white man. "Let me tell you this," he said further, "that I would be in sympathy with any Negro organization that would uphold the integrity of the Negro race even as the white organizations are endeavoring to uphold the integrity of the white race."

The Universal Negro Improvement Association is carrying out that doctrine splendidly. When I arrived at Baton Rouge, in Louisiana, I was visited by the president and some officers of the nearby division. They brought to me this report: Three nights ago seven white men came into a colored neighborhood. We found them at midnight sleeping in homes where they had no business, and they flogged them and drove them out of the neighborhood, and the next day they brought them before the judge, and the judge, who was a Ku Kluxer, let go all the colored men and said, "Do some more of that."

So you realize that the Universal Negro Improvement Association is carrying out just what the Ku Klux Klan is carrying out—the purity of the white race down South—and we are going to carry out the purity of the black race not only down South, but all through the world.

I intend in another week or so to publish the nature of the interview and you will have an opportunity of reading word for word what was said and what was done. But before you pass judgment on the Klan, before you go out of your way to criticize any white organization, just find out first how much you will be benefited by the criticism you make. If the criticism is not going to help you I advise you to leave it alone. Just at this time it does not help certain Negroes to go on criticizing everybody and everything. You must realize your position in this country. It is hopeless. You cannot, therefore, adopt an attitude of offense and aggression, because in the retaliation a large number of us are going to suffer.

Let us take the Dyer Anti-Lynching Bill. I believe that bill would have been very much more successful and would have had the support of more of the leading statesmen of this country if a certain organization had not gone forth and made so many claims to the originality of the bill and to the fatherhood of the bill. You cannot successfully put over anything in this country that seeks to change the white man's attitude toward you by taking up an offensive attitude toward the white man if you are dependent upon him to pass the measure for your satisfaction. As proof of what I mean: Since the agitation of the National Association for the Advancement of Colored People about the anti-lynching bill more lynchings have occurred in the Southern states than prior to the agitation of the bill. If more diplomatic steps had been taken we would have had the passage of the bill without anybody knowing who was responsible for it. That we could have achieved by diplomacy without creating any offense. It brings me to this: that our leadership is either ignorant or bankrupt; our leadership has no diplomacy. What is the use of going out of your way to offend somebody whom you cannot discipline or correct? It is like going before a lion and saying, "I am going to hold you." You know the result—you would be destroyed by the lion. It is for you to study the strategy that will enable you to get around the lion and take away its life. That is my subject to you tonight on the Ku Klux Klan. Do not take it as final, because the interview will be published, as I said in the earlier part of my address.

Whether We Will Accept Civilization as It Is or Put It Under a Rigid Examination to Make It What It Ought to Be as Far as Our Race Is Concerned

"To free Africa, we must first free ourselves
mentally, spiritually, and politically."

Third Annual International Convention of the Negro Peoples of the
World
71st Regiment Armory, New York City
August 1, 1922

The Negro World,
August 5, 1922

DEPUTIES, Delegates, Ladies and Gentlemen:

We are assembled here tonight celebrating the opening of the Third Annual International Convention of the Negro Peoples of the World. We have come from the four corners of the world to meet in conference over the great problems that confront our race. It is pleasing to learn that we have representatives from Africa, Australia, Europe, Asia, South and Central America, the West Indies and Canada, and from the forty-eight states of the American Union. Such a representation as you present tonight will give to this convention the aspect of world importance.

We are here as citizens and subjects of the different white governments of the world, but within us is that new spirit that makes each and every one of us an African citizen. We are proud of our racial lineage because out of Africa has come the civilization of the 20th century. It is true that 20th century civilization is corrupt and about to destroy itself, nevertheless the good that is to be found in it can be traced back to the time when our ancestors held up the torch of science, of art, and of literature—when the outer world was groping in darkness and the rest of the human race within the grip of barbarism.

Yet, when the great white race of today had no civilization of its own, when white men lived in caves and were counted as savages, this race of ours boasted of a wonderful civilization on the banks of the Nile; but evolution brings us changes that sometimes make us fail to recognize ourselves even after a lapse of centuries. Today the average Negro fails to understand his own possibilities and potentialities. He lacks confidence and courage, believing that Nature never intended him to do for himself. But the Universal Negro Improvement Association that has brought us together in this third annual international convention is determined to bring to the race a new hope. {*Applause.*} We are determined to point the race to a brighter future, a future that may yet restore to us the ancient glory of our fathers. Africa is looking up, and you, her sons and daughters, are assembled here to give to the race a program and a policy. {*Great applause.*}

The program, to be explained in a few words, is that of universal industrial, educational, religious, social, and political freedom. The stranger will ask, "Why should you want political freedom when Victoria of England gave it to you eighty-four years ago, and Lincoln of America, fifty-seven years ago?" I am tempted to answer for you, and to say that the present-day Negro does not believe in hypocrisy and camouflage. He believes in truth, in honesty, in justice.

The freedom that Lincoln gave us means that half of the population of our race in America is still voteless and voiceless; all of the population of the race in America is deprived of that higher right of citizenship that makes each and everyone an equal under the constitution.

Religiously, we are still slaves to the doctrine of an alien race. It is true that a large number of us here tonight from America, the West Indies, Canada, South and Central America are Christians, whilst others of us are Mohammedans, but for us Christians, have we ever stopped to question the source of our religion; that whilst there is nothing wrong with the teachings of our Blessed Lord and Savior, the lowly Nazarene who suffered and died on the Mount of Calvary to set humanity free, yet that in the practice of His doctrine today is instilled the propaganda that seeks to make the race that you and I represent an inferior unit of the great human family?

Have you ever stopped to think that in the Christian doctrine of today is injected a propaganda that seems to humiliate you and me?

These are things that the Universal Negro Improvement Association questions; these are the things that we are to discuss at our present convention, whether we will accept civilization as it is or put it under a rigid examination to make it what it ought to be as far as our race is concerned.

Not only are we not politically and religiously free as I have aforesaid, but socially we are not free, economically we are not free, and we of the Universal Negro Improvement Association who have called you together in this mighty convention believe that if you must be free, you yourselves must strike the blow. Lincoln cannot free you, Victoria of England cannot free you; if Negroes must be free then four hundred millions of us must organize the world over and strike the blow for our freedom, the freedom we desire. {*Applause.*}

And what do we desire? We desire the emancipation of the entire race, we desire the freedom of our country Africa; free from the domination of an alien race, free from exploitation, free from the pernicious influence of an alien civilization, and an alien creed. {*Applause.*}

This is the time when all peoples are looking forward, yes, on every hand you hear the cry for liberty, and what is liberty? It is that sacred principle for which millions have died in the past, for which millions will die today, and for which millions more will die in the future. Yes, on this principle stood Patrick Henry in the Virginia Legislature one hundred and forty-odd years ago; there he defied the organized power of a mighty empire; I think I can hear the words of that noble patriot ringing through this hall tonight: "I care not what others may say, but as for me, give me liberty or give me death." Such were the words that inspired the early colonists to fight the battle of independence to make America the greatest republic in the world; such are the words that will inspire the four hundred million Negroes throughout the world to fight for the freedom of our Motherland Africa.

To free Africa, we must first free ourselves mentally, spiritually, and politically. So long as we remain the religious slaves of another race, so long as we remain educationally the slaves of another race, so long as we remain politically the slaves of another race, so long shall other men trample upon us and call us an inferior people. But when we lift ourselves from this racial mire to the heights of religious freedom, of political freedom, of social freedom, of educational freedom, then and then only will we start out to become a great race and ultimately make of ourselves a mighty nation.

The new Negro desires Nationhood. We believe if nationhood is good for the Anglo-Saxon race, if nationhood is good for the Anglo-American race, if nationhood is good for the Japanese race, for the Chinese race, or any other race in the world, then it is also good for this great black race of ours. {*Applause.*}

We shall have in this 20th century nothing less than freedom. If it must be won by sacrifice then we are prepared for sacrifice of any kind; if we must give our money we shall give it; if we must give of our intelligence we will give it; if we must give of our physical power, we will give it; if we must give of our blood we shall give it, for by the blood of the fathers, the children are freed. {*Applause.*}

As we assemble ourselves for the thirty-one days and nights of this month, we shall apply ourselves seriously to the solving of the great problems that are upon us. In America we have the problem of lynching, of peonage, and disfranchisement. In the West Indies, South and Central America, we have the problem of peonage, serfdom, and industrial and political governmental inequality; in Africa we have not only peonage, and serfdom, but we have outright slavery, racial exploitation and alien political monopoly. We cannot afford to allow a continuation of these crimes against our race. If we are four hundred million men, women and children worthy of the existence given us by the Divine Creator, then we must either live as free men, or die as men fighting for the great and noble principle of human liberty. We shall take a leaf out of the book of George Washington, yes, we shall be encouraged by the noble exploits of Lafayette, yes, of Garibaldi, and all of those who have stood for the freedom of their countries, for the freedom of humanity, for the establishment of the sacred principle—Liberty. {*Applause.*}

We hear a great deal of talk about Peace. Wilson of America, Lloyd George of England, Clemenceau of France a few years ago prophesied at Versailles a reign of peace. Up to the present many of the leading statesmen of the world have pledged themselves to a program of world peace. Many conferences have been held, political as well as industrial, for the purpose of settling the question of peace; but up to now none of them has laid the foundation for a real peace, for a lasting peace. The peace of the world cannot be settled by political conferences, or by industrial conferences alone. If we are to have a world peace it will only come when a great inter-racial conference is called, when Jew will meet Gentile, when Anglo-Saxon will meet Teuton, when the great Caucasian family will meet the Mongolian, and when all will meet the Negro, and then and there straighten out the differences that have kept us apart for hundreds of years and will continue to keep us apart until doomsday if something is not done to create better racial understanding.

If white men are going to continue to exploit yellow men, if white men are going to continue to exploit black and brown men, if yellow men are gong to exploit brown men and black men, then all we can look forward to is a reign of wars and rumors of wars. So long as Anglo-Saxons oppress Indians, so long as the French race exploits the black race, so long as the Russian murders the Jew, so long will the cause for war be found, and so long will man continue to fight and kill his brother. If England wants peace, if France wants peace, if Italy wants peace, I suggest to them that they pack their bag and baggage and clear out of Africa, because Africa in the future will be to them what Europe has been for the last three hundred years. Europe has been a hotbed of wars, political intrigues, and upheavals for over three centuries, yes, and Europe has changed many a time politically. Once the great Napoleon ruled, the Czars ruled and but recently the German Eagle was the symbol of fear. Today England stands out as the most brilliant star in the European political constellation. But what of tomorrow? Africa with her threatened upheavals will produce the same condition in another century as Europe has done in the past. Can we not realize that we are provoking the sleeping passion of the races? How long do you believe that four hundred million Negroes will allow themselves to be exploited by alien races, robbed and murdered? Just so long until the truth is brought home to them, and then when the sleeping giant awakens, even like Samson he may bring down the pillars of the temple.

The war of 1914–1918 has created a new sentiment throughout the world. Once upon a time weaker peoples were afraid of expressing themselves, of giving vent to their feelings, but today no oppressed race, no oppressed nation is afraid of speaking out in the cause of liberty. Egypt has spoken, Ireland has spoken, Poland has spoken, and Poland is free, Egypt is free, Ireland is also free. Africa is now speaking, and if for seven hundred and fifty years Irishmen found perseverance enough to have carried the cause of freedom on and on until they won, then four hundred million Negroes are prepared to carry on the fight for African liberty even if it takes us to the seat of the Most High, yes, if it takes us until judgment day, we shall fight the cause on and on without relenting. The world may scoff at us, the world may deride us, but there have been many surprises for the world before, and there will be many more. Englishmen scoffed at the colonists when they agitated for independence in America, but their scoffs and derisions did not prevent George Washington from giving us the glorious Stars and Stripes. Men laughed at the propaganda of Tolstoy, the Czar himself impugned the idea of a more liberal Russia, but today Lenin and Trotsky rule; yes, the Louises laughed at the propaganda of the Liberals of France, but the French Monarchy is no more; today Frenchmen take pride in the new democracy of France; so that others may laugh at us today because we are agitating the question of a free and independent Africa, tomorrow who knows, Africa will loom up as the greatest republic of the world.

Men, there is much to live for, and there is much to die for. The man, the race of nation that is not prepared to risk life itself for the possession of an ideal, shall lose that ideal. If you, I repeat, must be free, you yourselves must strike the blow. {*Applause.*} I am not speaking of any other freedom than African freedom because other men are capable of advocating their own causes.

You must not in any way misinterpret the aims and objects of the Universal Negro Improvement Association and of this Convention. We are met for the sole purpose of regulating our affairs as a race. That does not mean that we are to offend any other race. The Universal Negro Improvement Association believes in the fellowship of races. We have a high regard for the white race; we have a high regard for all the other races of the world; but we believe in the Golden rule and its application to all races: "Do unto others as you would that they to you should do." When the white race, and the yellow race, and all the other races are willing to do to the Negro as the Negro is willing to do unto them, then we shall have the reign of peace, I suppose the peace that Lloyd George, Woodrow Wilson and Georges Clemenceau spoke of at the Versailles Conference; until then it becomes the duty of every race to protect itself. We cannot blame the great white race for protecting itself, we shall not blame the great yellow race for protecting itself. And how are they protecting themselves? We see Great Britain with her standing armies and her mighty navy, with a powerful government organized on the latest principles. So of France, so of America, so of Italy, and Japan is also organized with her mighty navy and army, for what purpose? For the purpose of protecting themselves.

We of the Universal Negro Improvement Association are advocating the right for Africa to develop herself as a mighty nation and give to herself the same kind of a naval and military protecting us as the other races. {*Applause.*} Will you blame us for doing that? Then if you blame us, you must blame England; if you blame us then you must blame France; you must blame Italy, you must blame Japan, you must blame all the other civilized peoples and nations of the world, in that we believe if government is good for one race, government is also good for the other race. If the Negro should have no government, if the Negro should have no army, if the Negro should have no navy of his own, then the white race should have no government, the white race should have no army, the white race should have no navy of its own, but, Ladies and Gentlemen, we are not all angels. From the fall of Adam man became a rebellious, wicked, covetous, murderous creature; yes, man from the time of Cain and Abel coveted the property of his brother man, became envious of his brother's success; yes, it was on the principle of injustice that Cain killed Abel, it is on the same principle of injustice that England exploits Africa, that France exploits Africa, that Italy exploits Africa, that Belgium exploits Africa, that the stronger nations of the world exploit the weak. Jesus the great Redeemer came to save man from his fallen state, but man, because of his wickedness, because of his murderous principles, rejected the teachings of Christ, and man was never satisfied until he nailed even the Christ to the Cross of Calvary. Man is wicked, man is envious, man is rebellious, man is murderous, and you can expect very little of man. The only protection against injustice in man is power, physical power, financial power, educational power, scientific power, power of every kind; it is that power that the Universal Negro Improvement Association is encouraging Negroes to get for themselves.

And may I not encourage you at this opening of our Third Annual International Convention to seek the higher scientific power? The battles of the future, whether they be physical or mental battles, will be fought on scientific principles and the race that is able to produce the highest scientific development is the race that will ultimately rule. Men of the Negro race, I implore you to seek the higher scientific knowledge. You must send out your chemists, your engineers, skilled and proficient enough to cope with the scientific men of the other races of the world. If Africa is to be won, if our Motherland is to be redeemed we have to do so through the higher scientific competition. You cannot depend upon your own physical power to bring about the result that we want, and as we discuss these problems during this month of August, let us do so dispassionately, do so with a faith in our own ability, and I feel sure that in another few years, your race and mine will lift itself from its depressed condition of today to the heights of universal respect. {*Applause.*}

Since the adjournment of our last convention, many things of importance have happened to affect our race for good or ill. In September of last year and thereafter the tribesmen of Morocco, our kinsmen, revolted against Spanish imperialism, and they were able to maintain a successful campaign for several months, during which time over one hundred thousand soldiers were lost to Spain. In one battle alone the Moroccans inflicted a casualty of nearly twenty-five thousand, capturing all the armaments of the enemy including aeroplanes and sixteen thousand square miles of land. This is demonstrative of the new spirit that is now permeating the tribesmen of Morocco. It is true that the Moroccans met with many reverses, but when it is considered that the Spaniards had had the advantage of a higher civilization for hundreds of years, you will readily admit that the Moroccans did splendidly against dreadful odds.

The Associated Press reported in January that Reuters had given out the information that a great Pan-African spirit was sweeping all over Africa, and that the propaganda was travelling so fast as to have reached nearly every nook and corner of the Black Continent. Great stress was laid on the strength of the propaganda in the Union of South Africa, French Equatorial Africa, Uganda, Nyasaland, Belgian Congo, Abyssinia and Kenya, East Africa. Reports during the year informed us of a native uprising in Kenya where the natives by the pressure of injustice imposed upon them by their alien masters, rioted, fighting their enemies with wooden spears and leather shields, whilst the enemies charged them with modern artillery, and bombed them from the air in aeroplanes. The uprising was subsequently quelled, and the natives forced to accept the continuation of the iron rule of their foreign alien overlords.

In December of last year a great surprise was sprung upon the race in the award to Rene Maran of the Edmond de Goncourt Prize for the best literary production of the year in France. The volume that won for Maran the prize was *Batauola,* a book in which the author attacked the colonial system of government in Africa, further proving the universality of the dissatisfaction that now exists among far-seeing, self-respecting Negroes, over the mis-government and exploitation that is carried on in Africa by the so-called colonizing and civilizing governments of the world.

Another matter of great interest during the year was the speech of the Honorable Warren G. Harding, President of the United States of America, delivered at Birmingham, Alabama, on the 26th of October, in which he made a plea for race equality, industrially and politically, but suggested that the black and white races maintain a separate and distinct social life. President Harding impressed upon his hearers the fact that the race problem of the South was not only of the South, or of the nation, but that it had become an international question. In the speech, President Harding avowed himself a true friend of the Negro race, even though he has been most senselessly and brutally criticized by a few self-appointed Negro leaders and sycophants.

It was also reported in October that the Kenya colony of East Africa was raided by Abyssinian troops. This suggests a political move of great significance.

In November and December a Disarmament Conference was held in Washington in which several of the first-rate nations of the world took part. Many questions affecting armaments and war in general were discussed at the conference. The Negro was not represented at this conference, neither was he taken into consideration as one of the great possible forces of the future. The conference terminated in a treaty between the United States and the British Empire and Japan and France. Among the items agreed upon were:

1. The high contracting parties agree as between themselves to respect their rights in relation to their insular possessions and insular dominions in the region of the Pacific Ocean. If there should develop between any of the high contracting parties a controversy arising out of any Pacific question, and involving their said rights, which is not satisfactorily settled by diplomacy and is likely to affect the harmonious accord now happily subsisting between them, they shall invite the other high contracting par-

ties to a joint conference to which the whole subject will be referred for consideration and adjustment.

2. If the said rights are threatened by the aggressive action of any other power the high contracting parties shall communicate with one another fully and frankly in order to arrive at an understanding as to the most efficient measures to be taken, jointly or separately, to meet the exigencies of the particular situation.

3. This agreement shall remain in force for ten years from the time it shall take effect, and after the expiration of said period it shall continue to be in force subject to the right of any of the high contracting parties to terminate it upon twelve months' notice.

This agreement was subsequently ratified.

Several other conferences have been held since the adjournment of the Disarmament Conference in Washington, at which many other vital issues have been discussed to the exclusion of the Negro. We are still waiting to see when the other races will recognize us as an integral part of the human family. During the month of July of the present year, the Council of the League of Nations met in London and decided among themselves the apportionment of the late German African colonies. They distributed among themselves the African spoils of war, without taking into consideration the aspirations and feelings of the native Africans and of the Negro race that rendered such signal service during the conflict of 1914-1918. The Council apportioned parts of the Cameroon to England, and other parts to France. Togoland was also given to France, and East Africa was given to England. The high-handed attitude of the members of the League is demonstrative of the spirit of peace. How these statesmen can expect to have permanent peace after such acts of injustice, you and I are unable to tell. We are hoping, however, that one day they will awake to their true sense and realize that peace can only be maintained when humanity universally is satisfied.

I am pleased to report that during the year, Egypt was given her independence, and Ireland was declared a free state. All of us feel glad that the Irish people after a struggle of over seven hundred years have won at last a large modicum of self-government. We must congratulate the Egyptians for the splendid step forward.

It is unfortunate that I have to report the arrest of our friend and co-worker Mahatma Gandhi. Gandhi was arrested by the British authorities in India in March, and sentenced to imprisonment for six years. The incarceration of Gandhi, however, will not affect the non-cooperationist movement of India. New India is marching forward, and with New Africa we hope in a short while there will be a great union of the darker races of the world in self-protection.

America, the hereditary friend of the Negro, has, during the year, through the kind services of President Harding, and Secretary Hughes, extended a loan of five million dollars to Liberia, which is highly appreciated by the thoughtful members of our race. President Harding's government has also brought to a close the American occupation of Santo Domingo, making that Negro country once more free and independent. During the year we were also surprised with the friendly suggestion and effort of Senator McCallum of Mississippi in introducing into the legislature of his state a bill asking that the government of America take steps to create for the Negro race in Africa a racial national government. The effort of Senator McCallum was supported by the state senate, but was subsequently defeated in the House of Representatives. Senator France of Maryland also advocated a similar act on the part of the national government, thereby proving to us that we have many good friends among the white race in America, confined not only to the North but also to be found in the South.

The past year has been a successful one for the work of the Universal Negro Improvement Association, although the enemies within our race have done so much to retard our progress. Many have been the misrepresentations against the organization for the year, made by jealous and unprincipled Negroes. Those who have indulged in the misrepresentation have been men heretofore regarded as leaders of the race. Despite all that has been said and done, our organization has carried on most successfully since the adjournment of the last convention.

Our work has expanded so in Africa, especially in the French colonies, that the French government has become alarmed, believing that the natives are becoming uncontrollable and undisciplined. Why France should act in this manner I am unable to say, because it has always been the belief of a large number of us that France was friendly disposed toward the higher development of the Negro race, but recent happenings have proved to us that France is no better than the other colonial powers that have ravished and exploited Africa for hundreds of years. France continues to keep her black troops on the Rhine, she continues to exploit their military training for the good of France in Europe, without any consideration for the men themselves. For the purpose of counteracting the usefulness of the work of the Universal Negro Improvement Association in Africa, France invited last month a number of African kings and chiefs for the purpose of convincing them of France's unselfish attitude toward Africa, but unfortunately the reception committee made a muddle of the whole affair. Instead of receiving the African kings and chiefs in the way that men of such rank should be received, they unwittingly herded them together in a camp on the outskirts of Paris, which provoked a great deal of resentment on the part of the chiefs, a resentment that I feel sure they will take back to Africa as one of the convincing proofs of the worthiness of the work of the Universal Negro Improvement Association in calling all Negroes to realize that they are all one and have a common cause in the work of racial progress.

I feel sure that you will during this convention adopt measures by which we shall be able to bring about a universal adjustment in racial affairs. Let us go forth loving all humanity, but remembering that we owe a supreme obligation to ourselves of this generation, and to posterity. Our work must not be interpreted as being hostile to any other race.

We are willing now to form an alliance with the great white race for the preservation of civilization, and for the good of a lasting peace, but it must be clearly understood that the new Negro is quite a different man to the Negro of seven or eight years ago. Universally we stand on the platform of human justice, human rights and human liberty. We are not going to yield one bit on these great principles. Men have fought for them, they have died for them in the past and we are willing to fight to see Africa restored to us as our own home. We cede to the Asiatics Asia; we cede to the Caucasians Europe; we also demand for ourselves Africa. Our work in America must be understood as being friendly to our great government. We stand by every principle of the American Constitution. We believe that America's friendship for the Negro is unparalleled and that when the time comes America will do more for us as a race than any other government in the world. We feel that the time is not far distant when our brothers of the white race in America will help us to build up a civilization of our own in Africa. We in our time have helped them to build up a great civilization, a great government in these United States of America, and I feel that common gratitude will suggest to them that they should help us to build up a civilization of our own in the United States of Africa.

It is true that there is a great amount of friction between the two races here at the present time, but that we cannot prevent. Two ambitious races cannot live in peace side by side, when they have to compete with each other economically, politically and socially. It has never been so in all human history and it is unreasonable for us to expect it so in America, unless we are going to have a change of the human heart, and that is not likely. Those of us who lead the Universal Negro Improvement Association can interpret the signs of the times. We foresee the time when the great white race in America will have grown numerically to the point of selfish race exclusion, when no common appeal to humanity will save our competitive race from their prejudice and injustice, hence the Universal Negro Improvement Association warns the Negro of America as well as of the Western world of the dangers of the future, and advises that the best effort of today should be that concentrated on the building up of a national home of our own in Africa. {*Loud and prolonged applause.*}

Climbing Upward

". . . how, in the name of God, with history before you, do you expect to redeem Africa without preparing yourselves, some of us, to die?"

Third Annual International Convention of the Negro Peoples of the World
Liberty Hall, New York City
August 13, 1922

The Negro World,
August 19, 1922

THERE is a great deal of commotion at this time over the activities of the U.N.I.A. We have been hearing a great deal said against the U.N.I.A. and against me personally. Some members are disposed to take the talkers seriously. We who lead the U.N.I.A. in all seriousness have laid down a policy long ago and that policy we have maintained. It is to pay no attention to the man who criticizes unless he is doing something better than what he criticizes. {*Applause.*}

We hear a lot of criticism and most of it from irresponsible individuals about the U.N.I.A. Criticism is very cheap. It does not take an exceptional man; it does not take an abnormal mind; it does not take an intelligent mind to criticize. Even the fool can criticize, and generally it is the fool who criticizes. And at this time we have a large number of fools around New York criticizing the U.N.I.A.

Some of them state that they are solidly against the "Back to Africa" movement, that they are not concerned with Africa and that they have nothing to do with Africa. And some of them are as BLACK as AFRICA. That is the sad part of it. On some of them, you see Africa written all around them. {*Applause.*} And yet they can tell us they have nothing in common with Africa simply because someone who is disposed to continue his disposition as far as we are concerned, about Africa, leads them into what they are thinking.

It suits certain people in the world today to speak disparagingly of Africa, as they have been doing for many centuries. This propaganda of disassociating western Negroes from Africa is not a new one. It is an old one. For hundreds of years the white propagandists have been printing millions of tons of literature to impress the minds of scattered Ethiopia, especially that part within civilization, the idea that Africa is a despised place where no civilized person should go. That Africa is inhabited by a race of cannibals, a race of savages, and that it would be unsafe for civilized human beings to think about settling in Africa, especially black civilized human beings. This propaganda is not new. It is as old as yourselves. It is as old as the hills. But this propaganda is one that is promulgated for the cause that is being realized today. That cause is colonial expansion for those who have waged the propaganda. The Africa that they have taught us of fifty years ago, of eighty years ago, a hundred years ago, as being a hideous place to live in, a place to be avoided, is the Africa that has been parcelled out from north, south, east and west. It is the Africa that caused the bloody war of 1914, and it is the Africa that is going to cause another bloody war. {*Applause.*}

And they have by this propaganda been able to inoculate some of us with the belief that Africa is really a place to be despised, and we are so inoculated that even the blackest son of Africa is now assisting them in carrying out the propaganda that he has nothing in Africa and that he has lost nothing in Africa. I am speaking of William Pickens. Now, everybody who knows Pickens knows that he is as black as anybody in this house, and when any black man in his sober senses gets up anywhere and talks that he has lost nothing in Africa and that he is not going back to Africa, why, he becomes a huge joke to the world. This fellow they call Dean, I wonder what he really means by speaking and writing so disparagingly about Africa. Is it that he has lost his senses? Is it that he has lost his manhood? Is it that he has lost knowledge of himself? You know some of us lose knowledge of ourselves sometimes. In the tropics, where I come from, you will find every well-to-do Negro losing knowledge of himself.

That is, the moment a white man smiles with him; shakes his hand; pats him on the shoulder and invites him to dinner for once, he loses knowledge of himself, and starts to believe that he is a white man. I wonder if anybody has patted Pickens on the shoulder; I wonder if anybody has taken Pickens by the hand; I wonder if anybody has invited Pickens to dinner, and I would not doubt that he has been invited to dinner, because I have seen him recently very much in the company of white folks, and any time a Negro gets into the company of white folks he becomes a dangerous Negro—yes—because he loses knowledge of himself, and whenever you hear a Negro talking about not going back to Africa because he has lost nothing in Africa, believe me, he has lost all trace of racial consciousness and knowledge of himself, and I would not be surprised that this Dean of ours has lost knowledge of himself.

But let me tell Brother Pickens that he is still as black as I am, and if he has lost knowledge of himself, we have not lost our vision, and we can see him just as he has always been.

Now, if these blacks will take our advice, they will throw down this white man's propaganda. I am surprised that men calling themselves Deans and college graduates still have no better sense and judgment than to be continuing the propaganda of these vicious villains who for ages have prepared this propaganda to deceive us so as to be able to rob from us our own heritage. Everybody knows that there is one part of the world that the Negro lays claim to.

Everybody knows that the Negro has no moral nor legal claim to anywhere else outside of Africa. The question of the age is that of political freedom, political liberty and political emancipation for all people. If we are to accept and believe the Divine injunction we must realize that the time is coming when every man and every race must return to its own vine and fig tree. Where in America will Pickens find his own vine and fig tree when everyone starts to look for his? Later on he will tell us he is an Indian or he has Indian cross-blood. So many of us find so many excuses to get out of the race because we are led to believe that the race is unworthy, that it has not accomplished anything—cowards that we are. Any Negro who deserts his race simply because that race has not made good to take its place alongside of the other races of the world can be dubbed nothing else than a coward. The time when we test men, the time when we test the loyalty of individuals is the time when the race or nation is in trouble. And what do we find? At this time when the Negro is in trouble, is endeavoring to lift itself from this condition in which we find ourselves we find so many desiring to desert the ranks and get out of the race by the statements they have made. By their actions they indicate to us that they are slaves and are not with us in the struggle upwards.

When Pickens deserts Africa at this time, when Pickens deserts the manly efforts of Negroes to reclaim their country, what does he do? What is he doing? He is doing that which amounts to treason, because every soldier knows that his nation expects him, if at no other time, at the time when the command is given to march to be loyal and true to his colors. When the general gives the command to march out if the soldier breaks the line you know what happens. And here it is the command is given, because of our conditions, because of our environments; the command is given to go forward for the reclamation of Africa, and whilst we are on the march here steps out one of the soldiers of the mighty host, telling us that he has lost nothing, that he is not concerned about the objective and is willing to compromise the issue of African redemption by being a traitor to the cause of liberty.

We hear them tell us that we are on a fool's errand, because Africa cannot be redeemed in that England, France and the other great powers control Africa, hence there will be no opportunity for the U.N.I.A. to ultimately reclaim Africa and redeem the continent of our forefathers. If other men of other times had argued in that way how many of us of this great human race would be free today? If the early fathers of American Independence had argued about the strength of England would we today have been under the protecting influence of the Stars and Stripes? If the revolutionists of France had compromised with the power of Louis would we today have had a French republic—a French democracy? If the revolutionists of Russia had compromised over the strength of the Czar would we today have a Socialist democracy in Russia? And after all that history teaches—history that these men are supposed to have read—they come back and tell us that because of the great power of England in Africa we cannot redeem Africa, because of the great power of France we cannot redeem Africa, because of the great power of Italy in Africa we cannot redeem Africa.

The power that holds Africa is not divine. The power that holds Africa is human, and it is recognized that whatsoever man has done man can do. {*Applause.*} Until God takes possession of Africa there is no impossibility in the redemption of Africa by the 400,000,000 Negroes of the world, and God has not yet taken possession of Africa. The Englishman is in possession of Africa, the Frenchman is in possession of Africa and the Italian is in possession of Africa. The English, French and Italian are men. What are you? {*Cries of "Men."*}

If you are men how dare anyone say that Africa cannot be redeemed when we have 400,000,000 men who are determined to fight for the redemption of Africa? The redemption of Africa is going to be a spiritual as well as a physical one.

If your heart is not right you cannot redeem Africa. If your soul pulse does not beat correctly you cannot redeem Africa. If you are as cowardly as those who tell us Africa cannot be redeemed then Africa cannot be redeemed. But all of us are not cowards anyhow. We have buried so many cowards and we have resurrected so many bold men who are determined to do or die in the cause of African freedom, we of the U.N.I.A., that we feel, unlike Pickens and his crowd, that Africa can be redeemed.

We know that Africa cannot be redeemed by mere speeches, by mere editorial articles. We know that Africa can only be redeemed by the sacrifice of human blood, and we are prepared to give even the last drop of blood so that one of these days the Red, the Black and the Green will flutter on the loftiest hilltop of our motherland, Africa.

You know the old-time darkey. He does not think of liberty in the terms of blood, and that is why he has never been free. Any sane man, or race, or nation, that desires freedom must first of all think in the terms of blood. Why, even the Heavenly Father tells us that without the shedding of blood there cannot be any remission of sin. And how, in the name of God, with history before you, do you expect to redeem Africa without preparing yourselves, some of us, to die?

The U.N.I.A. is preparing to go the way of all other peoples who have fought for liberty. We are preparing to go the way of George Washington and the noble patriots of this great country. It is the way of the sword and of blood. And let me tell you that the hour is drawing near—nearer than some of us seem to understand—nearer than some of us seem to anticipate! Do you not know, men and women, that in every ten years the world undergoes a change of some kind through warfare? Even in our own country, America, for the last 100 or 150 years, every ten years this country has been at war?

Take the history of the great European powers. Nearly every ten years everyone has been at war, and let me tell you in another few years we are going to come in contact with the bloodiest war mankind has ever seen. The stage is set for a bloody holocaust. You may expect it tomorrow, you may expect it next week, you may expect it next year, you may expect it five years from now or ten years from now, but let me tell you it is coming, and all students of political economy and of political science hear the rumble and see the signs.

It is coming! It is coming!! It is coming!!! And it will soon be here. The U.N.I.A. will not make the mistake of Frederick Douglass, of Samuel Constantine Burke, of Samuel Lewis, of Conrad Reeves, of Booker Washington, for not preparing the minds of the people for the approaching age. No, we won't make the mistake. We are today preparing the minds and hearts and souls and vision of the 400,000,000 Negroes of the world in readiness for the day. It is coming! I say, it is coming, and I want to say it is traveling fast and in a short while it will be here, and when it comes, with God's help, with God's benediction, 400,000,000 of us shall march not on the battle heights of Cuba in the Spanish-American war, not on the battlefields of France and Flanders in the war between the great European powers, but we shall be found walking out on the battlefields of Africa. {*Applause.*} There, once and for all eternity, to declare for the freedom of 400,000,000 oppressed souls.

Men who lack vision, men who lack knowledge, cannot see what we are talking about, cannot see what we are prophesying. But every sober-minded student of history sees and knows the possibilities that we are attempting as an organization. What has been already done by other great groups of people; by other great races at other times, the world seems to think it unnatural for Negroes to be serious about, and because the world takes that attitude some of us and some of our most profound scholars accept the belief that Negroes should not be serious, should not be ambitious. If any other race was agitating the cause that we agitate, the whole world would pronounce the righteousness of it. If Irishmen were agitating for the cause we are agitating, the whole world would believe it righteous; if the Jews were agitating for the cause we agitate, then the world would believe it righteous. But because we are Negroes the world thinks it a joke.

One of these days the joker is going to surprise the world. The sleeping joker may yet become the most serious man of the age and the U.N.I.A. is preparing the race for such an attitude. So that, I trust, you who make up the membership, that none of you will pay any attention to these irresponsible shallow-brained individuals, who have been trying to criticize the U.N.I.A. I say irresponsible because no one of them can show anything done, anything accomplished.

Let us take them individually. We start with Pickens and we end with Chandler Owens. What has Pickens done for the advancement and elevation of the race industrially, commercially, politically, since he has been here?

All that he has done is talk, and everybody has been talking here. Talk is cheap, brother. Everybody can do that except the man who is born dumb. And the things that Pickens is speaking about for the last forty years that he has been here are the things that even a Negro child today is speaking about. So after all, he is no more use than the smallest child. He is no better use to the community than a child, and you know how much use a child is to the community? Any irresponsible idiot can get up in this hall and say that President Harding is no good; that he is not a statesman; that he does not know how to run the American government. Any idiot can get up here and say that Woodrow Wilson was a fool for declaring war against Germany, but that does not make him so. So that I want you to realize that what Pickens has said and is saying any fool can.

The thing is not what you say, but what you do. {*Applause.*}

Now I am willing to be classified as the greatest fool in the world. I am willing to be classified as the greatest idiot in America. I am willing to be classified as an impossible man if, after we have compared the work of Marcus Garvey with W. E. Du Bois and Weldon Johnson, with Pickens and Chandler Owen, and with Randolph, Garvey cannot show accomplishment for accomplishment on a par with the achievement of the other men.

Let us ask what they have done. We have all lived in New York for the last five years. Du Bois lived at first out in Brooklyn, and now he lives at Edgecombe Avenue. Johnson has been living here for the last five years. Now I am willing to stand comparison in the way of achievement with these gentlemen this minute or tomorrow morning.

Let us ask Du Bois what he has done for the Negro people in his immediate vicinity.

Let us ask Johnson what he has done for the Negro people in his own community. Let us ask Pickens what he has done for the Negro people in his immediate vicinity, and let us ask Owens and Randolph the same question and let them ask me the same question, and I will, tomorrow morning at 9 o'clock, take you to 56 West 135th Street and show you between 70 and 80 Negro men and women employed; then I will take you to the various enterprises in Harlem controlled by the U.N.I.A., and I will there show you hundreds of Negro men and women employed in these enterprises, at grocery stores, laundry, hotel, printing establishments, etc. {*Applause.*} I will also show you property owned by the thousands of dollars, all the result of our work in three years. And if you say we cannot be measured by what has been done in the immediate community, I will take you to other parts of America, and I will show you a duplication of the same thing as in New York. Now, if these men can show me where they employ fifty, they employ a hundred, or a thousand Negro men and women, then I am willing to say that I am a big fool; then I am willing to say that I am an idiot, and hand the palm over to Pickens and company. But, my friends, what have they done? {*Cries from the audience: "Nothing!"*} They have been talking for the last ten years, and you have had to pay for their talk. {*Laughter.*} They have been writing for the last ten years, and you have had to buy their trash for ten and fifteen cents every month. That is all their agitation amounts to. Can any race be saved that way? {*Response from the audience: "No!"*}

Every student of political science, every student of political economy, every student of economics, knows that the race can only be saved through a solid industrial foundation {*applause*}; that the race can only be saved through political independence. Take away industry from a race, take away political freedom from a race, and you have a slave race. Thus you realize the usefulness of the Universal Negro Improvement Association in advocating an industrial program for the race. {*Applause.*} Hence you realize the purpose of the Universal Negro Improvement Association in declaring for an independent nation of our own.

The fools who condemn a movement like this are without sense, are without brains! But, men, let me tell you, they are not such fools after all. They are the paid agents of the ancient enemy, to cut you off from the vision that you have husbanded. They are the paid agents of the ancient enemy to disrupt you in this hour of world readjustment. If these ancient enemies of ours obstruct the vision of 400,000,000 Negroes for a while, they will be able ultimately to completely control Africa, and once and for all seal the doom of this race of ours.

It is a bigger question than you seem to understand. These socialists, time-servers, who have been trying to inoculate us with the doctrine of socialism, know nothing about the thing they advocate. If these men had sense, if they had vision, if they had common honesty as Negroes, they would keep as far from socialism as Michael the Archangel keeps from the Devil {*laughter*}; because socialism is only another form of white control that the white man is going to fasten around the neck of the Negro peoples of the world. They tell us that socialism will cause us to be treated with better consideration than other political "isms" which we have followed during the last fifty years in America and the last eighty years in this Western world. Men, can you imagine a change of attitude, a change of action from the same lion {*a voice: "No!"*} that swallowed your brother two days ago, if you cross him today, if some conversion did not take place? Why, these people are asking us to accept socialism from the very same men who have been devouring us for three hundred years! Before you can accept socialism as a cure, you have to change the white man's soul; and that, the Negro socialists have not done yet.

As proof that the socialist soul has not changed yet, he is the same Republican, the same Democrat as other white men, I will refer you to an incident that occurred not very long ago in one of the New York dance halls, where a misguided Negro by the name of Claude McCabe was urged by a socialist editor to attend a dance, saying that he would be treated by white socialists better than by white Republicans; this was an inducement to him to become a member of the socialist party. He was told that Negroes should be socialists, in that the socialists would be kindly disposed to Negroes, would be more sociable, and so forth. He was invited to a dance given by socialists. About 1,000 of his compatriots of his own organization met, and what did they do? They smashed up the dance hall, they closed down the dance because he attempted to dance with a white socialist woman.

So much for the sincerity of socialism. The same thing that happened to Claude McCabe in that socialist gathering is the same thing that would have happened down in Texas or in Georgia—white men would not put up with or stand for a black man dancing with a white woman, or being in a dance hall with white people even if all in attendance were socialists.

Hence you realize that, whether it is socialism or any other political-ism, there is absolutely no change on the part of the other fellow, and the best thing you can do is to devise, to create a politicalism of your own. That is the work, the propaganda of the Universal Negro Improvement Association, and I again present it to you tonight for your favorable con-sideration. {*Great applause.*}

The 'Colored' or Negro Press

"Nearly all the newspapers of the race had entered into
a conspiracy to taboo the term 'Negro' and popularize
the term 'colored' as the proper race term."

Third Annual International Convention
of the Negro Peoples of the World,
New York City, August 15, 1922

The Philosophy and Opinions of Marcus Garvey, or Africa for the Africans,
Volume 2

THE "Colored" or Negro press is the most venal, ignorant and corrupt of our time. This is a broad statement to make against an entire institution, and one so essential to the educational and corporate life of a people; but to be honest and to undeceive the Negro, whom I love above all God's creatures, the truth must be told. I make and again emphasize the statement without any regard for friendship, and with the full knowledge that the said false, vicious and venal press will unmercifully criticize me for telling the truth to the unfortunate of my race.

Unfortunately, the "Colored" or Negro press of today falls into the hands of unprincipled, unscrupulous and characterless individuals whose highest aims are to enrich themselves and to find political berths for themselves and their friends, or, rather, confederates.

The white press of today has its element of venality and corruption, but the higher ethics of the profession are generally observed and maintained, and at no time will you find the influence of white journalism used to debase or humiliate its race, but always to promote the highest ideals and protect the integrity of the white people everywhere.

The Negro press, to the contrary, has no constructive policy nor ideal. You may purchase its policy and destroy or kill any professed ideal if you would make the offer in cash.

Negro newspapers will publish the gravest falsehoods without making any effort to first find out the authenticity; they publish the worst crimes and libels against the race, if it pays in circulation or advertisements. A fair example of the criminality of the Negro press against the race is reflected through its most widely circulated sensational publications, namely, *The Chicago Defender* of Chicago, and *The Afro-American* of Baltimore. These newspapers lead all others in their feature of crime, false news and libels against the race.

The primary motive of Negro newspaper promoters is to make quick and easy money. Several of such promoters are alleged to have made large fortunes through their publications, especially through corrupt politics and bad advertisements that should have been refused in respect for the race.

It is plain to see, and is well known, that the sole and only purpose of these promoters is to make money—with absolutely no race pride or effort to help the race toward a proper moral, cultural and educational growth, that would place the race in the category so much desired by the masses and those honest leaders and reformers who have been laboring for the higher development of the people.

To attempt reform or the higher leadership that would permanently benefit the race, is to court the most vicious and cowardly attack from the promoters of Negro newspapers. If you are not in a "ring" with them to support their newspapers or "split" with them, what they would term the "spoils" then you become marked for their crucifixion. All the Negro leaders or organizations that escape the merciless criticism and condemnation of the Negro press are those who stoop to "feed" their graft or who as fellows of the same fold, "scratch each other's backs." To be honest and upright is to bring down upon your head the heavy hammer of condemnation, as such an attitude would "spoil" the game of the "gang" to enrich itself off the ignorance of the masses who are generally led by these newspapers, their editors and friends.

When I arrived in this country in 1916, I discovered that the Negro press had no constructive policy. The news published were all of the kind that reflected the worst of the race's character in murder, adultery, robbery, etc. These crimes were announced in the papers on front pages by glaring and catchy headlines; other features played up by the papers were dancing and parlor socials of questionable intent, and long columns of what is generally called "social" or "society" news of "Mrs. Mary Jones entertained at lunch last evening Mr. So and So" and "Mr. and Mrs. John Brown had the pleasure of entertaining last evening at their elaborate apartment Miss Minnie Baker after which she met a party of friends." Miss Minnie Baker probably was some Octoroon of questionable morals, but made a fuss of because of her "color," and thus runs the kind of material that made up the average Negro newspaper until *The Negro World* arrived on the scene.

The Chicago Defender, that has become my arch enemy in the newspaper field, is so, because in 1918–1919 I started the *The Negro World* to preserve the term Negro to the race as against the desperate desire of other newspapermen to substitute the term "colored" for the race. Nearly all the newspapers of the race had entered into a conspiracy to taboo the term "Negro" and popularize the term "colored" as the proper race term. To augment this they also fostered the propaganda of bleaching out black skins to light complexions, and straightening out kinky or curly hair to meet the "standard" of the new "society" that was being promoted. I severely criticized *The Chicago Defender* for publishing humiliating and vicious advertisements against the pride and integrity of the race. At that time the *Defender* was publishing full page advertisements about "bleaching the skin" and "straightening the hair." One of these advertisements was from the Plough Manufacturing Company of Tennessee.

There were many degrading exhortations to the race to change its black complexion as an entrant to society. There were pictures of two women, one black and the other very bright and under the picture of the black woman appeared these words: "Lighten your black skin," indicating perfection to be reached by bleaching white like the light woman. There were other advertisements such as "Bleach your dark skin," "take the black out of your face," "If you want to be in society lighten your black skin," "Have a light complexion and be in society," "Light skin beauty over night," "Amazing bleach works under skin," "The only harmless way to bleach the skin white," "The most wonderful skin whitener," "Straighten your kinky hair," "Take the kink out of your hair and be in society," "Knock the kink out," "Straighten hair in five days," etc. These advertisements could also be found in any of the Negro papers published all over the country influencing the poor, unthinking masses to be dissatisfied with their race and color, and to "aspire" to look white so as to be in society. I attacked this vicious propaganda and brought down upon my head the damnation of the "leaders" who sought to make a new race and a monkey out of the Negro.★

The Negro World has rendered a wonderful service to Negro journalism in the United States. It has gradually changed the tone and make-up of some of the papers, and where in 1914–15–16 there was no tendency to notice matters of great importance, today several of the papers are publishing international news and writing intelligent editorials on pertinent subjects. It has been a long and costly fight to bring this about.

I do hope that the statements of truth I have made will further help to bring about a reorganization of the Negro press. I fully realize that very little can be achieved by way of improvement for the race when its press is controlled by crafty and unscrupulous persons who have no pride or love of race.

We need crusaders in journalism who will not seek to enrich themselves off the crimes and ignorance of our race, but men and women who will risk everything for the promotion of racial pride, self-respect, love and integrity. The mistake the race is making is to accept and believe that our unprincipled newspaper editors and publishers are our leaders; some of them are our biggest crooks and defamers.

Situated as we are, in a civilization of prejudice and contempt, it is not for us to inspire and advertise the vices of our people, but, by proper leadership, to form characters that would reflect the highest credit upon us and win the highest opinion of an observant and critical world.

★The Negro World itself began to accept such advertisements within the next year.

The Principles of the Universal
Negro Improvement Association

"The U.N.I.A. stands for the bigger Brotherhood; the U.N.I.A.
stands for human rights, not only for Negroes, but for all races."

Liberty Hall, New York City,
November 25, 1922

The Philosophy and Opinions of Marcus Garvey, or Africa for the Africans,
Volume 2

OVER five years ago the Universal Negro Improvement Association
placed itself before the world as the movement through which the new
and rising Negro would give expression of his feelings. This Association
adopts an attitude not of hostility to other races and peoples of the world,
but an attitude of self-respect, of manhood rights on behalf of
400,000,000 Negroes of the world.

We represent peace, harmony, love, human sympathy, human rights
and human justice, and that is why we fight so much. Wheresoever
human rights are denied to any group, wheresoever justice is denied to
any group, there the U.N.I.A. finds a cause. And at this time among all
the peoples of the world, the group that suffers most from injustice, the
group that is denied most of those rights that belong to all humanity is
the black group of 400,000,000. Because of that injustice, because of
that denial of our rights, we go forth under the leadership of the One
who is always on the side of right to fight the common cause of
humanity; to fight as we fought in the Revolutionary War, as we fought
in the Civil War, as we fought in the Spanish-American War, and as we
fought in the war between 1914–1918 on the battle plains of France
and Flanders. As we fought up the heights of Mesopotamia; even so
under the leadership of the U.N.I.A., we are marshaling the
400,000,000 Negroes of the world to fight for the emancipation of the
race and of the redemption of the country of our fathers.

We represent a new line of thought among Negroes. Whether you call
it advanced thought or reactionary thought, I do not care. If it is reactionary
for people to seek independence in government, then we are reactionary. If
it is advanced though for people to seek liberty and freedom, then we represent the advanced school of thought among the Negroes of this country.
We of the U.N.I.A. believe that what is good for the other fellow is good
for us. If government is something that is worthwhile; if government is
something that is appreciable and helpful and protective to others, then we
also want to experiment in government. We do not mean a government

that will make us citizens without rights or subjects without considerations. We mean the kind of government that will place our race in control, even as other races are in control of their own governments.

That does not suggest anything that is unreasonable. It was not unreasonable for George Washington, the great hero and father of the country, to have fought for the freedom of America giving to us this great republic and this great democracy; it was not unreasonable for the Liberals of France to have fought against the Monarchy to give to the world French Democracy and French Republicanism; it was no unrighteous cause that led Tolstoy to sound the call of liberty in Russia, which has ended in giving to the world the social democracy of Russia, an experiment that will probably prove to be a boon and a blessing to mankind. If it was not an unrighteous cause that led Washington to fight for the independence of this country, and led the Liberals of France to establish the Republic, it is therefore not an unrighteous cause for the U.N.I.A. to lead 400,000,000 Negroes all over the world to fight for the liberation of our country.

Therefore the U.N.I.A. is not advocating the cause of church building, because we have a sufficiently large number of churches among us to minister to the spiritual needs of the people, and we are not going to compete with those who are engaged in so splendid a work; we are not engaged in building any new social institutions, and Y.M.C.A.'s or Y.W.C.A.'s because there are enough social workers engaged in those praise-worthy efforts. We are not engaged in politics because we have enough local politicians, Democrats, Socialists, Soviets, etc., and the political situation is well taken care of. We are not engaged in domestic politics, in church building or in social uplift work, but we are engaged in nation building.

In advocating the principles of this Association we find we have been very much misunderstood and very much misrepresented by men from within our own race, as well as others from without. Any reform movement that seeks to bring about changes for the benefit of humanity is bound to be misrepresented by those who have always taken it upon themselves to administer to, and lead the unfortunate, and to direct those who may be placed under temporary disadvantages. It has been so in all other movements whether social or political; hence those of us in the Universal Negro Improvement Association who lead do not feel in any way embarrassed about this misrepresentation, about this misunderstanding as far as the Aims and Objects of the Negro Improvement Association go. But those who probably would have taken kindly notice of this great movement, have been led to believe that this movement seeks, not to develop the good within the race, but to give expression to that which is most destructive and most harmful to society and to government.

I desire to remove the misunderstanding that has been created in the minds of millions of peoples throughout the world in their relationship to the organization. The Universal Negro Improvement Association stands for the bigger brotherhood; the Universal Negro Improvement Association stands for human rights, not only for Negroes, but for all races. The Universal Negro Improvement Association believes in the rights of not only the black race, but the white race, the yellow race and the brown race. The Universal Negro Improvement Association believes that the white man has as much right to be considered, the yellow man has as much right to be considered, the brown man has as much right to be considered as well as the black man of Africa. In view of the fact that the black man of Africa has contributed as much to the world as the white man of Europe, and the brown man and yellow man of Asia, we of the Universal Negro Improvement Association demand that the white, yellow and brown races give to the black man his place in the civilization of the world. We ask for nothing more than the rights of 400,000,000 Negroes. We are not seeking, as I said before, to destroy or disrupt the society or the government of other races, but we are determined that 400,000,000 of us shall unite ourselves to free our motherland from the grasp of the invader. We of the Universal Negro Improvement Association are determined to unite 400,000,000 Negroes for their own industrial, political, social and religious emancipation.

We of the Universal Negro Improvement Association are determined to unite the 400,000,000 Negroes of the world to give expression to their own feeling; we are determined to unite the 400,000,000 Negroes of the world for the purpose of building a civilization of their own. And in that effort we desire to bring together the 15,000,000 of the United States, the 180,000,000 in Asia, in the West Indies and Central and South America, and the 200,000,000 in Africa. We are looking toward political freedom on the continent of Africa, the land of our fathers.

The Universal Negro Improvement Association is not seeking to build up another government within the bounds or borders of the United States of America. The Universal Negro Improvement Association is not seeking to disrupt any organized system of government, but the Association is determined to bring Negroes together for the building up of a nation of their own. And why? Because we have been forced to it. We have been forced to it throughout the world; not only in America, not only in Europe, not only in the British Empire, but wheresoever the black man happens to find himself, he has been forced to do for himself.

To talk about government is a little more than some of our people can appreciate just at this time. The average man does not think that way, just because he finds himself a citizen or a subject of some country. He seems to say, "Why should there be need for any other government?" We are French, English or American. But we of the U.N.I.A. have studied seriously this question of nationality among Negroes—this American nationality, this British nationality, this French, Italian or Spanish nationality, and have discovered that it counts for nought when that nationality comes in conflict with the racial idealism of the group that rules. When our interests clash with those of the ruling faction, then we find that we have absolutely no rights. In times of peace, when everything is all right, Negroes have a hard time, wherever we go, wheresoever we find ourselves, getting those rights that belong to us, in common with others whom we claim as fellow citizens; getting that consideration that should be ours by right of the constitution, by right of the law; but in the time of trouble they make us all partners in the cause, as happened in the last war, when we were partners, whether British, French or American Negroes. And we were told that we must forget everything in an effort to save the nation.

We have saved many nations in this manner, and we have lost our lives doing that before. Hundreds of thousands—nay, millions of black men, lie buried under the ground due to that old-time camouflage of saving the nation. We saved the British empire; we saved the French empire; we saved this glorious country more than once; and all that we have received for our sacrifices, all that we have received for what we have done, even in giving up our lives, is just what you are receiving now, just what I am receiving now.

You and I fare no better in America, in the British Empire, or in any other part of the white world; we fare no better than any black man wheresoever he shows his head. And why? Because we have been satisfied to allow ourselves to be led, educated, to be directed by the other fellow, who has always sought to lead in the world in that direction that would satisfy him and strengthen his position. We have allowed ourselves for the last 500 years to be a race of followers, following every race that has led in the direction that would make them more secure.

The U.N.I.A. is reversing the old-time order of things. We refuse to be followers any more. We are leading ourselves. That means, if any saving is to be done, later on, whether it is saving this one nation or that one government, we are going to seek a method of saving Africa first. Why? And why Africa? Because Africa has become the grand prize of the nations.

Africa has become the big game of the nation hunters. Today Africa looms as the greatest commercial, industrial and political prize in the world.

The difference between the Universal Negro Improvement Association and the other movements of this country, and probably the world, is that the Universal Negro Improvement Association seeks independence of government, while the other organizations seek to make the Negro a secondary part of existing governments. We differ from the organizations in America because they seek to subordinate the Negro as a secondary consideration in a great civilization, knowing that in America the Negro will never reach his highest ambition, knowing that the Negro in America will never get his constitutional rights. All those organizations which are fostering the improvement of Negroes in the British Empire know that the Negro in the British Empire will never reach the highest of his constitutional rights. What do I mean by constitutional rights in America? If the black man is to reach the height of his ambition in this country—if the black man is to get all of his constitutional rights in America—then the black man should have the same chance in the nation as any other man to become president of the nation, or a street cleaner in New York. If the black man in the British Empire is to have all his constitutional rights it means that the Negro in the British Empire should have at least the same right to become premier of Great Britain as he has to become a street cleaner in the city of London. Are they prepared to give us such political equality? You and I can live in the United States of America for 100 or more years, and our generations may live for 200 years or for 5000 more years, and so long as there is a black and white population, when the majority is on the side of the white race, you and I will never get political justice or get political equality in this country. Then why should a black man with rising ambition, after preparing himself in every possible way to give expression to that highest ambition, allow himself to be kept down by racial prejudice within a country? If I am as educated as the next man, if I am as prepared as the next man, if I have passed through the best schools and colleges and universities as the other fellow, why should I not have a fair chance to compete with the other fellow for the biggest position in the nation? I have feelings, I have blood, I have senses like the other fellow; I have ambition, I have hope. Why should he, because of some racial prejudice, keep me down and why should I concede to him the right to rise above me, and to establish himself as my permanent master? That is where the U.N.I.A. differs from other organizations. I refuse to stultify my ambition, and every true Negro refuses to stultify his ambition to suit any one, and therefore the U.N.I.A. decides if America is not big enough for two presidents, if England is not big enough for two kings, then we are not going to quarrel over the matter; we will leave one president in America, we will leave one king in England, we will leave one president in France and we will have one president in Africa. Hence, the Universal Negro Improvement Association does not seek to interfere with the social and political systems of France, but by the arrangement of things today the U.N.I.A. refuses to recognize any political or social system in Africa except that which we are about to establish for ourselves.

We are not preaching a propaganda of hate against anybody. We love the white man; we love all humanity, because we feel that we cannot live without the other. The white man is as necessary to the existence of the Negro as the Negro is necessary to his existence. There is a common relationship that we cannot escape. Africa has certain things that Europe wants, and Europe has certain things that Africa wants, and if a fair and square deal must bring white and black with each other, it is impossible for us to escape it. Africa has oil, diamonds, copper, gold and rubber and all the minerals that Europe wants, and there must be some kind of relationship between Africa and Europe for a fair exchange, so we cannot afford to hate anybody.

The question often asked is what does it require to redeem a race and free a country? If it takes manpower, if it takes scientific intelligence, if it takes education of any kind, or if it takes blood, then the 400,000,000 Negroes of the world have it.

It took the combined manpower of the Allies to put down the mad determination of the Kaiser to impose German will upon the world and upon humanity. Among those who suppressed his mad ambition were two million Negroes who have not yet forgotten how to drive men across the firing line. Surely those of us who faced German shot and shell at the Marne, at Verdun, have not forgotten the order of our Commander-in-Chief. The cry that caused us to leave America in such mad haste, when white fellow citizens of America refused to fight and said, "We do not believe in war and therefore, even though we are American citizens, and even though the nation is in danger, we will not go to war." When many of them cried out and said, "We are German-Americans and we cannot fight," when so many white men refused to answer to the call and dodged behind all kinds of excuses, 400,000 black men were ready without a question. It was because we were told it was a war of democracy; it was a war for the liberation of the weaker peoples of the world. We heard the cry of Woodrow Wilson, not because we liked him so, but because the things he said were of such a nature that they appealed to us as men. Wheresoever the cause of humanity stands in need of assistance, there you will find the Negro ever ready to serve.

He has done it from the time of Christ up to now. When the whole world turned its back upon the Christ, the man who was said to be the Son of God; when the world cried out, "Crucify Him," when the world spurned Him and spat upon Him, it was a black man, Simon, the Cyrenian, who took up the cross. Why? Because the cause of humanity appealed to him. When the black man saw the suffering Jew, struggling under the heavy cross, he was willing to go to His assistance, and he bore that cross up to the heights of Calvary. In the spirit of Simon, the Cyrenian, 1900 years ago, we answered the call of Woodrow Wilson, the call of a larger humanity, and it was for that that we willingly rushed into the war from America, from the West Indies, over 100,000; it was for that that we rushed into the war from Africa, 2,000,000 of us. We met in France, Flanders and in Mesopotamia. We fought unfalteringly. When the white men faltered and fell back on their battle lines, at the Marne and at Verdun, when they ran away from the charge of the German hordes, the black hell fighters stood before the cannonade, stood before the charge, and again they shouted, "There will be a hot time in the old town tonight."

We made it so hot a few months after our appearance in France and on the various battle fronts, we succeeded in driving the German hordes across the Rhine, and driving the Kaiser out of Germany, and out of Potsdam into Holland. We have not forgotten the prowess of war. If we have been liberal-minded enough to give our life's blood in France, in Mesopotamia and elsewhere, fighting for the white man, whom we have always assisted, surely we have not forgotten to fight for ourselves, and when the time comes that the world will again give Africa an opportunity for freedom, surely 400,000,000 black men will march out on the battle plains of Africa, under the colors of the red, the black and the green.

We shall march out, yes, as black American citizens, as black British subjects, as black French citizens, as black Italians or as black Spaniards, but we shall march out with a greater loyalty, the loyalty of race. We shall march out in answer to the cry of our fathers, who cry out to us for the redemption of our own country, our motherland, Africa.

We shall march out, not forgetting the blessings of America. We shall march out, not forgetting the blessings of civilization. We shall march out with a history of peace before and behind us, and surely that history shall be our breastplate, for how can man fight better than knowing that the cause for which he fights is righteous? How can man fight more gloriously than by knowing that behind him is a history of slavery, a history of bloody carnage and massacre inflicted upon a race because of its inability to protect itself and fight? Shall we not fight for the glorious opportunity of protecting and forevermore establishing ourselves as a mighty race and nation, nevermore to be disrespected by men. Glorious shall be the battle when the time comes to fight for our people and our race.

We should say to the millions who are in Africa to hold the fort, for we are coming 400,000,000 strong.

W. E. Burghardt Du Bois as
a Hater of Dark People

"Calls Own Race 'Black and Ugly,' Judging from the White Man's
Standard of Beauty: Trick of National Association for the Advancement of
Colored People to Solve Problem by Assimilation and Color Distinction"

New York City, February 13, 1923

The Philosophy and Opinions of Marcus Garvey, or Africa for the Africans,
Volume 2

W. E. BURGHARDT DU BOIS, the Negro "misleader," who is editor of the
Crisis, the official organ of the National Association for the Advancement
of "certain" Colored People, situated at 70 Fifth Avenue, New York City,
has again appeared in print. This time he appears as author of an article in
the February issue of the *Century Magazine* under the caption, "Back to
Africa," in which he makes the effort to criticize Marcus Garvey, the
Universal Negro Improvement Association and the Black Star Line. This
"unfortunate mulatto," who bewails every day the drop of Negro blood in
his veins, being sorry that he is not Dutch or French, has taken upon himself the responsibility of criticizing and condemning other people while
holding himself up as the social "unapproachable" and the great "I AM" of
the Negro race. But we will see who Mr. Du Bois is, in that he invites his
own characterization. So we will, therefore, let him see himself as others
see him.

In describing Marcus Garvey in the article before mentioned, he
referred to him as a "little, fat, black man; ugly, but with intelligent eyes
and a big head." Now, what does Du Bois mean by ugly? This so-called
professor of Harvard and Berlin ought to know by now that the standard
of beauty within a race is not arrived at by comparison with another
race; as, for instance, if we were to desire to find out the standard of
beauty among the Japanese people we would not judge them from the
Anglo-Saxon viewpoint, but from the Japanese. How he arrives at his
conclusion that Marcus Garvey is ugly, being a Negro, is impossible to
determine, in that if there is any ugliness in the Negro race it would be
reflected more through Du Bois than Marcus Garvey, in that he himself
tells us that he is a little Dutch, a little French, and a little Negro. Why,
in fact, the man is a monstrosity. So, if there is any ugliness it is on the
part of Du Bois and not on the part of the "little fat, black man with the
big head," because all this description is typical of the African. But this
only goes to show how much hate Du Bois has for the black blood in
his veins. Anything that is black, to him, is ugly, is hideous, is monstrous,
and this is why in 1917 he had but the lightest of colored people in his

office, when one could hardly tell whether it was a white show or a colored vaudeville he was running at Fifth Avenue. It was only after the Universal Negro Improvement Association started to pounce upon him and his National Association for the Advancement of Colored People that they admitted that colored element into the association that could be distinguished as Negro, and it was during that period of time that Weldon Johnson and Pickens got a look-in. But even Pickens must have been "ugly" for Du Bois, for they made it so warm for him up to a few months ago that he had to go a-hunting for another job, the time when Marcus Garvey was willing to welcome him into the Universal Negro Improvement Association.

It is no wonder that Du Bois seeks the company of white people, because he hates black as being ugly. That is why he likes to dance with white people, and dine with them, and sometimes sleep with them, because from his way of seeing things all that is black is ugly, and all that is white is beautiful. Yet this professor, who sees ugliness in being black, essays to be a leader of the Negro people and has been trying for over fourteen years to deceive them through his connection with the National Association for the Advancement of Colored People. Now what does he mean by advancing colored people if he hates black so much? In what direction must we expect his advancement? We can conclude in no other way than that it is in the direction of losing our black identity and becoming, as nearly as possible, the lowest whites by assimilation and miscegenation.

This probably is accountable for the bleaching processes and the hair straightening escapades of some of the people who are identified with the National Association for the Advancement of Colored People in their mad desire of approach to the white race, in which they see beauty as advocated by the professor from Harvard and Berlin. It is no wonder some of these individuals use the lipstick, and it is no wonder that the erudite Doctor keeps a French beard. Surely that is not typical of Africa, it is typical of that blood which he loves so well and which he bewails in not having more in his veins—French.

In referring to the effort of Marcus Garvey and the Universal Negro Improvement Association to establish a building in Harlem, he says in the article: "There was a long, low, unfinished church basement roofed over. It was designed as the beginning of a church long ago, but abandoned. Marcus Garvey roofed it over, and out of this squat and dirty old Liberty Hall he screams his propaganda. As compared with the homes, the business and church, Garvey's basement represents nothing in accomplishment and only waste in attempt."

Here we have this "lazy dependent mulatto" condemning the honest effort of his race to create out of nothing something which could be attributed to their ownership, in that the "dirty old Liberty Hall" he speaks of is the property of Negroes, while in another section of his article he praises the "beautiful and luxurious buildings" he claims to be occupied by other black folk, making it appear that these buildings were really the property of these people referred to, such as, according to his own description, "a brick block on Seventh Avenue stretching low and beautiful from the Y.W.C.A. with a moving picture house of the better class and a colored 5 and 10 cent store, built and owned by black folks." Du Bois knows he lies when he says that the premises herein referred to were built and are owned by black folks. They are the property of industrious Jews who have sought an outlet for their surplus cash in the colored district. The Y.W.C.A. is a donation from the good white people; but he continues by saying "down beyond on One Hundred and Thirty-Eighth Street the sun burns the rising spire of an Abyssinian church, a fine structure built by Negroes who for one hundred years have supported the organization, and are now moving to their luxurious home of soft carpets, stained windows and swelling organ." He also knows that this building has been subscribed to by the Church Extension Society, which is white, and therefore the building is not entirely owned by the members of the Abyssinian church. Finally, he says, "the dying rays hit a low, rambling basement of brick and rough stone." This in reference to Liberty Hall.

Liberty Hall represents the only independent Negro structure referred to in the classification of Du Bois about buildings up in Harlem, but he calls this independent effort "dirty and old," but that which has been contributed by white people he refers to in the highest terms. This shows the character of the man—he has absolutely no respect and regard for independent Negro effort but that which is supported by white charity and philanthropy, and why so? Because he himself was educated by charity and kept by philanthropy. He got his education by charity, and now he is occupying a position in the National Association for the Advancement of Colored People, and it is felt that his salary is also paid by the funds that are gathered in from the charity and philanthropy of white people. This "soft carpet" idea is going to be the undoing of W. E. B. Du Bois. He likes too much the luxurious home and soft carpets, and that is why he is naturally attracted to white folks, because they have a lot of this; but if he were in Georgia or Alabama he would now be stepping on the carpets of Paradise; but that is not all of the man, as far as this is concerned. He ridicules the idea that the Universal Negro Improvement Association should hold a social function in Liberty Hall on the 10th of August, 1922, at which certain social honors were bestowed upon a number of colored gentlemen, such as Knighthood and the creation of the Peerage.

In referring to the matter, he says in the article: "Many American Negroes and some others were scandalized by something which they could but regard as a simple child's play. It seemed to them sinister. This enthronement of a demagogue, a blatant boaster, who with monkey-shines was deluding the people, and taking their hard-earned dollars; and in high Harlem there arose an insistent cry, 'Garvey must go!'" Indeed Du Bois was scandalized by the creation of a Peerage and Knighthood by Negroes, and in truth the person who is responsible for the creation of such a thing should go, because Du Bois and those who think like him can see and regard honor conferred only by their white masters. If Du Bois was created a Knight Commander of the Bath by the British King, or awarded a similar honor by some white Potentate, he would have advertised it from cover to cover of the *Crisis,* and he would have written a book and told us how he was recognized above his fellows by such a Potentate, but it was not done that way. This was an enthronement of Negroes, in which Du Bois could see nothing worthwhile. He was behind the "Garvey must go!" program started in Harlem immediately after the enthronement, because he realized that Garvey and the Universal Negro Improvement Association were usurping the right he had arrogated to himself as being the highest social dignitary, not only in Harlem but throughout the country.

In the seventh paragraph of his article Du Bois has the following to say: "Let us note the facts. Marcus Garvey was born on the northern coast of Jamaica in 1887. He was a poor black boy, his father dying in the almshouse. He received a little training in the Church of England Grammar School, and then learned the trade of printing, working for years as foreman of a printing plant. Then he went to Europe and wandered about England and France working and observing until he finally returned to Jamaica. He found himself facing a stone wall. He was poor, he was black, he had no chance for a university education, he had no likely chance for preferment in any line, but could work as an artisan at small wage for the rest of his life."

Now let us consider Marcus Garvey in comparison with Du Bois. W. E. B. Du Bois was born in Great Barrington, Mass., in 1868. Some wealthy white people became interested in him and assisted in his education. They sent him to Fisk University, from Fisk to Harvard, where he graduated as a commencement orator. He raised part of the money for his later education by giving recitals in white summer hotels. Where he was born—that is, in Great Barrington, Mass.—he had early association with white surroundings. He was brought up with white boys and girls of the better type and more aristocratic class as found in rural towns. He had no love for the poor, even the poor whites in his neighborhood, although he was but a poor, penniless and humble Negro. As proof of that he wrote the following on the tenth page of his book known as *Dark Water:* "I greatly despised the poor Irish and South Germans who slaved in the mills [that is, the mills of the town in which he was born], and I annexed myself with the rich and well-to-do as my natural companions." Marcus Garvey's father, who was also named Marcus Garvey, was one of the best known men in the parish in which he was born, St. Ann, Jamaica. For a number of years he held prominent positions in the parish and was regarded as one of the most independent black men on the island, owning property that ran into thousands of pounds. Through his own recklessness he lost his property and became poor. His poverty did not in any way affect Marcus Garvey, Jr., in that the mother of the latter assumed the responsibility that the father failed to assume, and he therefore got an early education, not through charity, as did Du Bois, but through the support of a loving mother. Marcus Garvey, Jr., never knew the consideration of a father, because at the time when he was born his father had already lost all he had, and had shifted his obligation to his children onto the shoulders of their mother. With the assistance Marcus Garvey got from his mother he educated himself, not only in Jamaica but traveled throughout South and Central America, the West Indies and Europe, where for several years he studied in completing the education that he had already laid the foundation for in his native home. All that was not done by the charity of anyone, but by Marcus Garvey himself, and the support he got from his mother. While, on the other hand, Du Bois, starting even from the elementary stage of his education up to his graduation from Harvard and his passing through Berlin, got all that through the charity and philanthropy of good white people. Admitting that Marcus Garvey was born poor, he never encouraged a hatred for the people of his kind or class, but to the contrary devoted his life to the improvement and higher development of that class within the race which has been struggling under the disadvantage that Du Bois himself portrays in his article.

Marcus Garvey was born in 1887; Du Bois was born in 1868. That shows that Du Bois is old enough to be Marcus Garvey's father. But what has happened? Within the fifty-five years of Du Bois' life we find him still living on the patronage of good white people, and with the thirty-six years of Marcus Garvey's (who was born poor and whose father, according to Du Bois, died in a poorhouse), he is able to at least pass over the charity of white people and develop an independent program originally financed by himself to the extent of thousands of dollars, now taken up by the Negro peoples themselves. Now which of the two is poorer in character and in manhood? The older man, who had all these opportunities and still elects to be a parasite, living off the good will of another race, or the younger man, who had sufficient self-respect to make an effort to do for himself, even though in his effort he constructs a "dirty brick building" from which he can send out his propaganda on race self-reliance and self-respect.

To go back to the motive of Du Bois in the advocacy of the National Association for the Advancement of Colored People is to expose him for what he is. The National Association for the Advancement of Colored People executives have not been honest enough to explain to the people of the Negro race their real solution for the Negro problem, because they are afraid that they would be turned down in their intention. They would make it appear that they are interested in the advancement of the Negro people of America, when, in truth, they are but interested in the subjugation of certain types of the Negro race and the assimilation of as many of the race as possible into the white race.

As proof of the intention underlying the National Association for the Advancement of Colored People we will quote from Du Bois himself. He states in his article:

"We think of our problem here as THE Negro problem, but we know more or less clearly that the problem of the American Negro is very different from the problem of the South African Negro or the problem of the Nigerian Negro or the problem of the South American Negro. We have not hitherto been so clear as to the way in which the problem of the Negro in the United States differs from the problem of the Negro in the West Indies.

"For a long time we have been told, and we have believed, that the race problem in the West Indies, and particularly in Jamaica, has virtually been settled."

Now Du Bois speaks of this settlement of the problem of the race in the West Indies and Jamaica with a great deal of satisfaction. What kind of a settlement is it? Du Bois knows well, but he is not honest enough to admit it, because he himself visited Jamaica and saw the situation there, wherein an arrangement has been effected whereby the white man is elevated to the highest social and economic heights, and between him is socially and economically elevated the mulatto type of Du Bois, and beneath them both is the black man, who is crushed to the very bottom socially and economically.

Du Bois regards this as a settlement of the problem in the West Indies and Jamaica. Now this is the kind of a settlement that he and the National Association for the Advancement of Colored People want in America, and they have not been honest enough to come out and tell us so, that we might act accordingly. This is why Du Bois bewails the black blood in his veins. This is why he regards Marcus Garvey and the Universal Negro Improvement Association as impossible. This is why he calls Marcus Garvey "black and ugly." But while this settlement in Jamaica and the West Indies satisfies Du Bois, and probably would satisfy him in America, he must realize that the fifteen million Negroes in the United States of America do not desire such a settlement; that outside of himself and a half-dozen men of his school of thought, who make up the Executive of the National Association for the Advancement of Colored People, the majority of Negroes are not studying him and his solution of the problem, but all of us colored people of whatsoever hue, are going to fight together for the general upbuilding of the Negro race, so that in the days to come we may be able to look back upon our effort with great pride, even as others worse positioned than ourselves have struggled upward to their present social, economic and political standing among races and nations.

To show the deception and hypocrisy of Du Bois, he pretends, (in the above-quoted paragraph from his article) as if he were not thoroughly acquainted with the problem in the West Indies, when, in another paragraph, he states the following:

"This is the West Indian solution of the Negro problem:

"The mulattoes are virtually regarded and treated as whites, with the assumption that they will, by continued white intermarriage, bleach out their color as soon as possible. There survive, therefore, few white Colonials save newcomers, who are not of Negro descent in some more or less remote ancestor. Mulattoes intermarry, then, largely with the whites, and the so-called disappearance of the color line is the disappearance of the line between the whites and mulattoes and not between the whites and the blacks or even between the mulattoes and the blacks.

"Thus the privileged and exploiting group in the West Indies is composed of whites and mulattoes, while the poorly paid and ignorant proletariats are the blacks, forming a peasantry vastly in the majority, but socially, politically and economically helpless and nearly voiceless. This peasantry, moreover, has been systematically deprived of its natural leadership, because the black boy who showed initiative or who accidentally gained wealth or education soon gained the recognition of the white-mulatto group and might be incorporated with them, particularly if he married one of them. Thus his interest and efforts were identified with the mulatto-white group."

This is the kind of settlement that Du Bois speaks of; and this is the kind of settlement that he wants in the United States of America. Du Bois, you shall not have it!

Du Bois says that "Garvey had no thorough education and a very hazy idea of the technique of civilization." Du Bois forgets that Garvey has challenged him over a dozen times to intellectual combat, and he has for as many times failed to appear. Garvey will back his education against that of Du Bois at any time in the day from early morning to midnight, and whether it be in the classroom or on the public platform will make him look like a dead duck on a frozen lake.

Du Bois seems to believe that the monopoly of education is acquired by being a graduate of Fisk, Harvard and Berlin. Education is not so much the school that one has passed through, but the use one makes of that which he has learned.

If Du Bois' education fits him for no better service than being a lackey for good white people, then it were better that Negroes were not educated. Du Bois forgets that the reason so much noise was made over him and his education was because he was among the first "experiments" made by white people on colored men along the lines of higher education. No one experimented with Marcus Garvey, so no one has to look upon him with surprise that he was able to master the classics and graduate from a university.

Du Bois is a surprise and wonder to the good white people who experimented with him, but to us moderns he is just an ordinarily intelligent Negro, one of those who does not know what he wants.

Du Bois is such a liar when it comes to anything relating to the Universal Negro Improvement Association, the Black Star Line and Marcus Garvey that he will not consider his attacks on the Black Star Line seriously. He lied before in reference to this corporation and had to swallow his vomit. He has lied again, and we think a statement is quite enough to dispose of him in this matter.

This envious, narrow-minded man has tried in every way to surround the Universal Negro Improvement Association and Marcus Garvey with suspicion. He has been for a long time harping on the membership of the Universal Negro Improvement Association as to whether we have millions of members or thousands. He is interested because he wants to know whether these members are all paying dues or not, in that he will become very interested in the financial end of it, as there would be a lot of money available. Du Bois does not know that whether the Universal Negro Improvement Association had money or not he wouldn't have the chance of laying his hands on it, that there are very few "leaders" that we can trust with a dollar and get the proper change. This is the kind of leadership that the Universal Negro Improvement Association is about to destroy for the building up of that which is self-sacrificing; the kind of leadership that will not hate poor people because they are poor, as Du Bois himself tells us he does, but a kind of leadership that will make itself poor and keep itself poor so as to be better able to interpret the poor in their desire for general uplift. He hates the poor. Now, what kind of a leader is he? Negroes are all poor black folk. They are not rich. They are not white; hence they are despised by the great professor. What do you think about this logic, this reasoning, professor? You have been to Berlin, Harvard and Fisk; you are educated and you have the "technique of civilization."

Du Bois harps upon the failure of other Negroes, but he fails to inform the public of his own failures. In his fifty-five years Du Bois personally has made success of nothing. In all his journalistic, personal and other business efforts he has failed, and were it not for Mary White Ovington, Moorefield Storey, Oswald Garrison Villard and Springharn, Du Bois, no doubt, would be eating his pork chops from the counter of the cheapest restaurant in Harlem like many other Negro graduates of Harvard and Fisk.

When it comes to education and ability, Garvey would like to be fair to Du Bois in every respect.

Suppose for the proof of the better education and ability Garvey and Du Bois were to dismantle and put aside all they possess and were placed in the same environment to start life over afresh for the test of the better man? What would you say about this, doctor? Marcus Garvey is willing now because he is conceited enough to believe that in the space of two years he would make you look like a tramp in the competitive rivalry for a higher place in the social, economic world.

Let not our hearts be further troubled over Du Bois, but let fifteen million Negroes of the United States of America and the millions of the West Indies, South and Central America and Africa work toward the glorious end of an emancipated race and a redeemed motherland.

Du Bois cares not for an Empire for Negroes, but contents himself with being a secondary part of white civilization. We of the Universal Negro Improvement Association feel that the greatest service the Negro can render to the world and himself at this time is to make his independent contribution to civilization. For this the millions of members of the Universal Negro Improvement Association are working, and it is only a question of time when colored men and women everywhere will harken to the voice in the wilderness, even though a Du Bois impugns the idea of Negro liberation.

Who and What Is a Negro?

"Some white men, whether they be professors or what not, certainly have a wide stretch of imagination."

New York City,
April 23, 1923

The Philosophy and Opinions of Marcus Garvey, or Africa for the Africans,
Volume 2

THE *New York World* under date of January 15, 1923, published a statement of Drs. Clark Wissler and Franz Boaz (the latter a professor of anthropology at Columbia University), confirming the statement of the French that Moroccan and Algerian troops used in the invasion of

Germany were not to be classified as Negroes, because they were not of that race. How the French and these gentlemen arrive at such a conclusion is marvelous to understand, but I feel it is the old-time method of depriving the Negro of anything that would tend to make him recognized in any useful occupation or activity.

The custom of these anthropologists is: whenever a black man, whether he be Moroccan, Algerian, Senegalese or what not, accomplishes anything of importance, he is no longer a Negro. The question, therefore, suggests itself, "Who and what is a Negro?" The answer is, "A Negro is a person of dark complexion or race, who has not accomplished anything and to whom others are not obligated for any useful service." If the Moroccans and Algerians were not needed by France at this time to augment their occupation of Germany or to save the French nation from extinction, they would have been called Negroes as usual, but now that they have rendered themselves useful to the higher appreciation of France they are no longer members of the Negro race, but can be classified among a higher type as made out by the two professors above mentioned. Whether these professors or France desire to make the Moroccans other than Negroes we are satisfied that their propaganda before has made these people to understand that their destiny is linked up with all other men of color throughout the world, and now that the hundreds of millions of darker peoples are looking toward one common union and destiny through the effort of universal cooperation, we have no fear that the Moroccans and Algerians will take care of the situation in France and Germany peculiar to the interest of Negroes throughout the world.

Let us not be flattered by white anthropologists and statesmen who, from time to time, because of our success here, there or anywhere try to make out that we are no longer members of the Negro race. If we were Negroes when we were down under the heel of oppression then we will be Negroes when we are up and liberated from such thraldom.

The Moroccans and Algerians have a splendid opportunity of proving the real worth of the Negro in Europe, and who to tell that one day Africa will colonize Europe, even as Europe has been endeavoring to colonize the world for hundreds of years.

The white world has always tried to rob and discredit us of our history. They tell us that Tut-Ankh-Amen, a King of Egypt, who reigned about the year 1350 B.C. (before Christ), was not a Negro, that the ancient civilization of Egypt and the Pharaohs was not of our race, but that does not make the truth unreal. Every student of history, of impartial mind, knows that the Negro once ruled the world, when white men were savages and barbarians living in caves; that thousands of Negro professors at that time taught in the universities in Alexandria, then the seat of learning; that ancient Egypt gave to the world civilization and that Greece and Rome have robbed Egypt of her arts and letters, and taken all the credit to themselves. It is not surprising, however, that white men should resort to every means to keep Negroes in ignorance of their history, it would be a great shock to their pride to admit to the world today that 3,000 years ago black men excelled in government and were the founders and teachers of art, science and literature. The power and sway we once held passed away, but now in the twentieth century we are about to see a return of it in the rebuilding of Africa; yes, a new civilization, a new culture, shall spring up from among our people, and the Nile shall once more flow through the land of science, of art, and of literature, wherein will live black men of the highest learning and the highest accomplishments.

Professor George A. Kersnor, head of the Harvard-Boston expedition to the Egyptian Sudan, returned to America early in 1923, and, after describing the genius of the Ethiopians and their high culture during the period of 750 B.C. to 350 A.D. in middle Africa, he declared the Ethiopians were not African Negroes. He described them as dark colored races . . . showing a mixture of black blood. Imagine a dark colored man in middle Africa being anything else but a Negro. Some white men, whether they be professors or what not, certainly have a wide stretch of imagination. The above statements of the professors support my contention at all times that the prejudice against us as Negroes is not because of color, but because of our condition. If black men throughout the world as a race will render themselves so independent and useful as to be sought out by other race groups it will simply mean that all the problems of race will be smashed to pieces and the Negro would be regarded like anybody else—a man to be respected and admired.

More than a year ago the natives of South Africa started to press the limited white population to the wall in the demand of "Africa for the Africans." The prejudiced Boers and others were willing then to let down the color bar and admit to their ranks, socially and otherwise, the half-breed colored people whom they once classified as impossible hybrids, to be despised by both whites and natives. Now they are endeavoring to make common cause with these so-called half-breeds of South Africa, so as to strengthen their position against the threatening ascendency of the demand for a free and redeemed Africa for the blacks of the world.

In an editorial dated March 29, 1923, the Abantu-Batho of Johannesburg states among other things:

"The Cape colored people have been promised absorption by politicians, particularly those of the Dutch race. . . . Indeed we are suspicious that all this talk about absorption is a political trap which has been set to capture the colored vote in the Cape. It is the business of the politician to strengthen his position by getting as many supporters as possible. To do this, he must, of necessity, be diplomatic. That is to say, he must know how to get around the people, and the only way to get around the people is to put before them a beautiful picture of what one intends to do. There can be no doubt that to the Cape colored people the idea of their absorption by the white race presents a beautiful ideal for the attainment of which they are prepared to sacrifice everything. They cannot be blamed for this. As a distinct community they have no past, no traditions, no laws, and no language, which things constitute the pride of every race of mankind. These sons of Hagar are in an awkward position. They despise the people of Hagar, because Hagar's people are despised by the people of Abraham. They are suffering because of the gulf that exists between their mothers' people and those of their fathers. . . . The difference between the treatment meted out to the colored people and the Africans does not in any way signify that the whites have more consideration for the colored people. It will be remembered that when Lord Selborne left this country in 1909, he warned the white people of South Africa against putting the Cape colored people in the same category as Africans because that would unite the two sections of the African peoples to fight for their common rights. Since then the policy has been to differentiate in the treatment of the two sections so as to make combined action impossible. Thus it is not saying too much to aver that the real object of the white race is to make the Cape colored people a buffer between the Africans and Europeans. As a buffer, the Cape colored people can never have the same rights as whites. Now the question is: What are they to do? Will they be satisfied with a position of this kind? Or will they follow the lead of our cousins in America and classify themselves as Africans? In our opinion this is the only way to the salvation of the Cape colored people. They are Africans and not Europeans. And the sooner they realize it the better."

White people will seek every opportunity to fraternize with any race in the world, even the one despised yesterday, if by so doing they can strengthen their position, whether it be in Europe, Africa or elsewhere, but it is for 400,000,000 people who have been discriminated against throughout the world to take a decided stand and for once we will agree with the American white man, that one drop of Negro blood makes a man a Negro? So that 100 percent Negroes and even 1 percent Negroes will stand together as one mighty whole to strike a universal blow for liberty and recognition in Africa.

The World Gone Mad—Force Only Argument to Correct Human Ills

*"We see a new Ethiopia, a new Africa, stretching her hands
of influence throughout the world, teaching man
the way of life and peace, the way to God."*

New York City
May 16, 1923

The Negro World,
May 19, 1923

FELLOW MEN OF THE NEGRO RACE, *Greeting:*

THE world is on fire. The whole human race is gone mad. Man has lost his reason, and now we are in for an age of ruin and destruction that will upset the efforts of the human race for the last five hundred years. All this has been brought about by the drunken greed for power on the part of certain races and nations. We are in such a terrible mix-up that one would not wonder if man gets his hell right now and not hereafter. Everywhere you look, and on every side you turn, you come in contact with the undermining influence of the one race against the other, the one nation against the other. It is apparent that truth, justice, love, mercy have taken their departure, and all that we have is the reign of selfishness and greed which will ultimately be the wreck and ruin of our civilization. In all this terrible muddle four hundred million Negroes are called upon to play their part. It is natural that we must take on the spirit of the age, harmful though we know it to be, but we are so situated that we can do no better than meet the other fellow on his own grounds.

One part of the world is determined to upset the other part. One race is determined to destroy the other for its own selfish existence, and so in this rigid competition for a place and for life we can do no better than strike out in our own direction to save ourselves from this wreck and ruin that threatens.

The Universal Negro Improvement Association steps out speaking in unmistakable terms on behalf of our own group, and in language forcible and uncompromising we call upon each and every member of our race to gird his armor on and be ready for the fray. It is no use talking about settling this human question with prayers and words. It cannot be done; it can only be settled by force. This is the only argument that the races and nations of the world understand in the twentieth century. England is speaking with force, France is speaking with force, all the other European powers are speaking with force as their only language, and the races or the people who cannot present to the world organized force will be naturally dragged under in the tidal wave of race oppression. England and France are more determined than ever to exploit and subjugate their darker citizens and subjects, their professions notwithstanding. It is no use looking to them in the sense of the larger humanity, because they have lost their Christian souls. Englishmen and Frenchmen no longer think of humanity in the terms of Christian brotherhood, but in the terms of pounds and francs.

England wants money, France wants money, Italy wants money, Belgium wants money, Portugal and Spain want money, and the only place that they can grind it from today is Africa; hence, they are making one mad determination to exploit and ravish that country, the land of our fathers, without any consideration for humanity or Christian fellowship. If they profess other than their lust for gold, then we know it is a lie; it is all a farce, pretense, hypocrisy.

Let Robert Cecil talk, and Bryan, and Mussolini; their voices will be lost in the wilderness of African hope, because surely we will not hear them. We heard Chatham before we heard Gladstone, we heard Chamberlain, and out of their profession of human love and brotherly consideration we find that Africa has paid the price in blood and in wealth for the expansion of the British Empire to the loss of millions of native Africans and Negroes everywhere. We are tired of this kind of political hypocrisy; therefore, we are calling upon the four hundred million Negroes of the world to listen to no other voice than that which beckons us on to action. The voice that commands us to go forward in the name of an emancipated race and African redemption, the voice that says, "March on with the hope of a brighter future, with the throwing off of the influences of the past."

We have come to the turning and parting of the ways. The black race needs look no longer to any other race for succor, for advice or for political help. We must naturally look to ourselves. More and more we become disappointed in all our hopes; disappointed in all our ambitions, depending as we have been upon others. In America we are gradually being thrown off politically and disappointed socially and economically. Within the British Empire we are only the scapegoats of a sober and seasoned diplomacy. In France we are only made the dupes of a crafty statesmanship that hopes to profit by the ignorance of those whom they deceive. How, therefore, can we depend upon others? Doing so will mean nothing else but our present and future ruin, such as has been in the past.

The days of slavery are not gone forever. Slavery is threatened for every race and nation that remains weak and refuses to organize its strength for its own protection. Slavery has no day and no time. It is present when the strong race desires to oppress the weaker race. Negroes, be careful of what you do today! No one can tell what our condition will be tomorrow, whether it be slavery or not, if we do not strive toward the goal of racial strength, of racial power, political and national independence. Let us rally around the banner of the Red, the Black and the Green, the universal emblem of African redemption. Let us stand by the colors as Englishmen stand by the Union Jack, as Frenchmen stand by the Tri-Colors, and as white Americans stand by the Stars and Stripes. For us, let the vision be fair, let the vision be one of hope and encouragement.

We need not look to the darkness. Africa shall be redeemed, Negroes shall be emancipated, but all depends upon our present deeds, our present acts. Shall we go backward? The Universal Negro Improvement Association answers, "No!" We have come upon the stage in time to save the entire race from destruction. All that we want is that each and every one will enter the fold of this great and noble organization and let us unitedly march to our destiny. Turn your attention not away from Africa, because Africa shall be the only salvation and solution of this great problem of race in America and the Western World. Africa, the land of our fathers, beckons us home, if not in person, in sympathy, in sentiment and in moral and financial help, so why shouldn't we help her to throw off the shackles placed upon her by an alien civilization and alien races? Why shouldn't we help her put to flight the enemy within her doors who seeks her very vitals? Oh, Mother Africa! Oh, land of our Fathers! to thee we come; to thee we pledge our lives, our manhood, our strength, our all, because through thee, and thee alone, we see the avenue to happiness, to peace, to everlasting glory.

Ethiopia shall once more arise from the ashes of material ruin to the heights of temporal glory. We see a new Ethiopia, a new Africa, stretching her hands of influence throughout the world, teaching man the way of life and peace, the way to God. He, the great Creator Himself, inspired others to say of us that "Princes shall come out of Egypt; Ethiopia shall soon stretch out her hands." This hour we are stretching forth our hands with the desire to teach the world the true principles of mercy and justice.

The Universal Negro Improvement Association [desires] the ascendancy of the Negro race, not for the purpose of brutalizing and destroying the hopes of the human race, but for the purpose of giving further encouragement to man to live, live in the true sense, in the sense of the Brotherhood, in the sense of the common Fatherhood. That is the life that we want, the life that other races have failed to give, that is why the world is in such chaos, that is why the world faces wreck and ruin, that is why the entire world is upset, that is why it faces Africa to save the day.

Negroes, again we appeal to you to come together. Come together in America, the West Indies, South and Central America and let 400,000,000 of us march forward to the sacred duty that falls upon us, that of saving humanity, that of salvaging a sinful world.

You can help the Universal Negro Improvement Association put over this great program by your moral and financial assistance . . .

Your obedient servant,
MARCUS GARVEY, President-General
Universal Negro Improvement Association

Biggest Case in the History of the Negro Race

"Marcus Garvey is afraid of nobody nor
anything at all in the world except God."

Liberty Hall, New York City
May 20, 1923

The Negro World,
May 26, 1923

MY case started last Friday and will continue from tomorrow. It may last for about five or six weeks. As I said before, it is the biggest case that is to be tried in the United States Court, not only in New York, but all over the country. It is a case that involves not Marcus Garvey but the existence of the Universal Negro Improvement Association. The ideals of the Universal Negro Improvement Association are on trial and those of you who are interested in the Universal Negro Improvement Association will naturally be able to weigh the situation in the next few weeks.

Now understand that Marcus Garvey is not concerned a bit about the trial. As far as I am concerned it does not affect me as far as my work goes; that is cut out; my work cannot be destroyed; my work will live through the ages. *{Applause.}* Those who think that they can destroy Marcus Garvey are making a tremendous mistake if they think that by using all the available human physical forces that they can intimidate and destroy Marcus Garvey. Marcus Garvey, as I have often said, did not organize the Universal Negro Improvement Association without calculating its cost— the cost of ingratitude of those whom we are serving; the cost of uncharitableness on the part of those whom he suffers most for. All that does not concern him; their ingratitude does not concern him one bit; so Garvey will not be disappointed about anything in the trial. Nothing can disappoint me; my work is cut out; I have done it and I am still doing it and it will last forever, and those who think that they are getting even with Garvey are only laying the foundation that will destroy themselves in a short while. Let me say this: that Marcus Garvey is not afraid of hell itself, because Marcus Garvey has one conviction, and that is: until the Negro lays a foundation for his own freedom he will never have it and that there is only one way that it can be laid, and it must be laid through sacrifice, through death, through suffering {*applause*} and Marcus Garvey is prepared to go the whole length, and as far as he personally is concerned, it does not matter. I am saying to those who think they are getting even with Garvey, when Garvey dies a million other Garveys will rise up, not in America or not in the West Indies, for where the Negro has lived under the white man's civilization you can hardly make any use of him in this generation, but Marcus Garvey is satisfied that he has stirred Africa from corner to corner and Africa will take care of herself. {*Applause.*} Garvey goes to court like a man. Garvey had no cause to be in court for Garvey; Garvey could be one of the most successful and prosperous Negroes of the twentieth century. I am not going to court because of Garvey, but because of service to the people. Garvey calculated for that and is not surprised.

So don't be disturbed and don't be afraid about Garvey; Garvey knew the consequences and, like a man, he is going to face it. Marcus Garvey has been the target, believing that if they can destroy Garvey they can subsequently destroy the Universal Negro Improvement Association. They may destroy the Universal Negro Improvement Association in America; they may destroy the Universal Negro Improvement Association in the West Indies. If Garvey should die or if Garvey should be imprisoned, let them know it will be only the beginning of the work in Africa. The Negro is in no mood to be tampered with now. The Negro who died on Flanders field—the Negro who died in Mesopotamia, is the same who is willing to do his part towards his race if it means dying in the attempt to put the program over.

So I want the whole world to understand that, like Robert Emmet, Garvey faces the worst; like Roger Casement, Garvey will face the arrows of "hell" for the principles of the Universal Negro Improvement Association. {*Applause.*} You who skin the teeth of ingratitude do not disappoint me one bit; you cannot harm Marcus Garvey; do your worst and Garvey is not affected, nor is he concerned about you; Garvey is concerned about the principles—the sacred principles for which men have died in the past and for which real men will die in the future and for which 400,000,000 Negroes are prepared to die. {*Applause.*} We do not go pussyfooting about this program; we do not go camouflaging and compromising and apologizing. The Universal Negro Improvement Association has not started its real work yet; we have only touched the surface of the great work of the Universal Negro Improvement

Association, and any few Negroes or white men who think that they can destroy the great principles of a rising race are flattering themselves and making the greatest mistake and blunder of the age. Those who try to endanger and imperil and harass the work of the Universal Negro Improvement Association, they know not what they do, for the simple reason they are but piling up sorrows for themselves and for their children, because long after some of us are passed away the principles of the Universal Negro Improvement Association shall live and live on forever. What are you going to do? Can you kill the souls of men? You can destroy the physical body but you cannot destroy the souls of men; you cannot even destroy the mind of man. Now, how can they destroy Garvey when they cannot close Garvey's mouth? Garvey has already spoken to the world and is still speaking to the world and will speak to the world until he reaches the last moment in life, and even then Garvey will just have started to speak to the world. What Garvey cannot do in prison we are going to do otherwise, and as I said, we are not counting so much on the Western world because the Negro in contact with the white man's civilization is practically useless and helpless; he has imbibed the poison of the white man's civilization and he is practically half-dead. If my work had not gone beyond the borders of the Western world, then I would have been disturbed, but, thank God, all Africa is awake—East Africa, North Africa, South Africa, West Africa—thank God, they have all caught the principles and propaganda of the Universal Negro Improvement Association; therefore our work of five years has not been in vain.

The National Association for the Advancement of Colored People, the cheap Negro politicians in Harlem and the brainy white men who have sense enough to know what they want and how to get it, who have combined to fight the Universal Negro Improvement Association, are going to be disappointed, because they cannot harm Garvey. They may waste all their money trying to put me in jail, and hang me and all of that, but you cannot harm Garvey; what you think will harm Garvey has not hurt him in the least, because Garvey knows what he is doing; Garvey knows that the Negro will have to suffer and fight before he gets what he wants. All we want is for the members of the U.N.I.A. to realize and understand what they are up against.

Marcus Garvey is afraid of nobody nor anything at all in the world except God. My father was fearful; my grandfather was fearful, but I did not inherit their fear, because we are living in a new age and in a new world. So that the case is on, and I am not going to talk about it because it may not be proper to discuss it, because I do not want to be misunderstood. Marcus Garvey calculated for all the consequences in a great movement like this; he calculated for the traitors within and the traitors without, so that when they appear he is not in any way surprised.

Marcus Garvey is prepared for the ingratitude of the people whom he serves. Marcus Garvey is prepared for everything, because Garvey was in his sober senses when he founded and started the Universal Negro Improvement Association. I suppose the Kaiser was in his sober senses when he started the war in 1914; therefore, he was satisfied to take what he got. Garvey started to seek the emancipation of 400,000,000 Negroes and the redemption of their country, and anything he gets in the way he is prepared for it, but it is going to react on somebody someday, if not today, at some other time; but remember this, that the principles of the Universal Negro Improvement Association will live forever.

The history of the movement is now being written. Do you know what history means? History is the guidepost of a race; is the inspiration for succeeding generations either to go forward or to stand still; either to revenge or be revenged. Marcus Garvey, when he dies, will not die alone; when Marcus Garvey dies for the principles of the Universal Negro Improvement Association, mark well. Before Garvey goes, Garvey shall have laid a foundation for other Garveys who will be more deadly in their sting than the one who passes off.

So the enemies and traitors are crazy if they think they can damage the Universal Negro Improvement Association. I am speaking to you as the man who founded and organized the Universal Negro Improvement Association, as the man who sacrificed and suffered to bring into existence the Universal Negro Improvement Association. I had a motive and a purpose; it was not the money, because I could have gotten that for myself and been satisfied; it was not position, because I could have got that for myself. What is it? It was the crying voice from the grave that said, "Garvey, we have suffered for 250 years for your day and for your time; we expect something from you at this hour." Let the world understand that Garvey hears the wail and the cry of millions of our forebears crying from the grave—for what? I will not tell you; probably another Garvey will tell you. So let those who fight the U.N.I.A. beware, for some day they will have to reckon with 400,000,000 Negroes, for Garvey is but laying the cornerstone for the incoming of the New Africa—the new Ethiopia that shall stretch forth her hands unto God; the new day when princes shall come out of Egypt.

So you who understand the work of the Universal Negro Improvement Association be not disturbed; keep your peace; keep your minds in good order, because this is only the starting point of the great battle that is to be waged for African redemption, and understand that it is not Marcus Garvey on trial; it is not a question of money on trial; it is the principles of a race fighting for liberty on trial. When you attack Garvey you do not awaken anything in Garvey, but when you attack the principles of the Universal Negro Improvement Association, Garvey goes

to war and shall remain on the firing line until he passes away or until
victory perches on the banner.

So you will understand that for the first time probably in the history
of the Negro you will see a real Negro fight a real battle for racial liberation. {*Applause.*}

The Fight for Negro Rights and Liberty
Begun in Real Earnest

"If the enemy could only know that Marcus Garvey
is but a John the Baptist in the wilderness . . ."

New York City
May 22, 1923

The Negro World,
May 26, 1923

FELLOW MEN OF THE NEGRO RACE, *Greeting:*

THERE comes a time in the history of every race and nation when the
supreme effort must be made to save that race or nation from its enemies,
those within as well as those without. Such a time has come in the history of the Universal Negro Improvement Association in the fight for
Negro liberty and African redemption.

For over three years the enemies of Negro progress laid their plans by
which they hoped they would ultimately destroy the new effort on the
part of Negroes for the realization of a freer, economic, social, educational, and political life.

When the Universal Negro Improvement Association aggressively
started its program in America five years ago, following up its activities
in the West Indies four years prior, the enemies of Negro freedom within
the race, as well as without the race, started to lay the foundation of an
opposition which they calculated they could have used for successfully
destroying the great program of this organization and dash back forever
the hopes of a rising race. They calculated that out of the activities of this
great organization they would have been able to so undermine our
efforts as to make them appear as failures, and thereby strike back at the
movement with what they would think to be irrefutable arguments of
the organization's unworthiness. They tried many schemes, among them
the laying of plans by which the Black Star Line Steamship Corporation

would fail and other business activities connected with the Universal Negro Improvement Association, so that in their argument to the people who make up the Negro race, they would say: "We told you so; we told you so. It could not be done!" The enemies have counted without their hosts. Now is the time for the 400,000,000 Negroes of the world to stand together firmer than ever before, because, in truth, "The enemies shall not pass."

The so-called business failure of the Black Star Line was but a trap set to destroy the Universal Negro Improvement Association. But how silly and simple these small-minded enemies are. Do they believe that they can destroy a spiritual movement in this kind of way? Can they believe in themselves that the Universal Negro Improvement Association can die because of the failure of any business enterprise? The idea of the Black Star Line has not failed, can never fail, because 400,000,000 Negroes are determined that out of Africa shall spring one of the greatest governments of the world, and with the rise of a mighty nation and a great people will come all that contributes to human effort and human endeavors. There shall be a greater Black Star Line; there shall be a Black Star Line that shall belt the world with the industries of black men. So let us think not of failure in the sense that the enemies have laid the trap for it to be.

Smart, brilliant, great and intellectual though you enemies believe yourselves to be, but, gentlemen, you are yet schoolboys in your conceptions. Real men laugh at opposition; real men smile when enemies appear. If you believe you can intimidate and destroy the courage of a race through the destruction of a business enterprise, or by the persecution of an individual, you are crazy, you are foolish, you are mistaken. It might have been so easy with the old Negro, but not with the new. Behind the Universal Negro Improvement Association stands a spiritual force that can never die; no power in the world can destroy it. It is the spirit of liberty, it is the spirit that faces death and smiles. We welcome the opposition of the world, because we are determined to see the battle through. Africa's battle-cry is not yet heard.

What of the day, gentlemen, when Africa shall indeed unfurl her banner of liberty? The persecutions and the sufferings of the past shall be but our breast plates and shields and armour to fight until victory perches upon the banner of Negro liberty. We who are sober in our minds, and our vision, and our outlook, laugh at these children who believe that they can tear to pieces and destroy the principles underlying the Universal Negro Improvement Association as embodied in a Black Star Line, or any other business operation thereto connected.

We have not yet started the battle for liberty, gentlemen; we have just been talking about it. It is a fight that will continue down the ages; it is a fight that is confined to no one generation, but succeeding generations shall fight, the more especially when we write in the present for them a history of injustice and persecution, a history of sufferings as we now undergo them.

What does Marcus Garvey care about persecution by the enemies? If the enemy could only know that Marcus Garvey is but a John the Baptist in the wilderness, that a greater and more dangerous Marcus Garvey is yet to appear, the Garvey with whom you will have to reckon for the injustice of the present generation.

Gentlemen, you may as well sharpen your swords, because it is going to be a bloody conflict. History has been the inspiration of generations past, and what we record shall be the inspiration of black generations yet unborn. Marcus Garvey of the present shall so write a history that Negroes one hundred, two hundred years from now shall not forget, shall not forget, shall not forget.

Gentlemen, remember you are dealing with a serious man living in a serious time. Marcus Garvey does not give a snap for anything human but justice, and that which is based upon righteousness.

With all your trickery, with all your plots, you are just like "chaff before the wind," which shall in a while be blown to atoms. Previous generations have flirted with and fooled with Negroes' liberty. Today it is going to be a battle to the finish. We have no apologies, we have no compromises, we are not begging the issue; we are just determined we are going to live free men or die free men. So let the whole world of Negroes realize that the hour is approaching when black men shall be called upon to take their stand, to play their part, and play it well.

Let the members of the Universal Negro Improvement Association all over the world realize that now is the hour for the manifestation of loyalty and devotion to the cause that we love so well. The enemies think that they are at our door; some of us feel that they are there; now let us get ready to dislodge them. The enemies are not so much from without as from within the race. In the final reckoning, when Ethiopia shall have written her name on the new scroll of empires, when princes shall come out of Egypt, and Africa takes her stand in a new civilization, we will then reckon with the generations of vipers whose names and their children's shall go down to undying posterity.

Fight on, enemies, fight on; it is a battle of the centuries. It is not of Garvey today; it shall be of all times. How long, how long, how long! Answer that for yourselves.

Some men believe themselves smart, some believe themselves wonderfully keen. But, ah! There is no sage who hath not a master! You who think that your small schemes and your secret propaganda to destroy the Universal Negro Improvement Association through its own members can be accomplished make a big mistake. We see that your ambition is to get Garvey out of the way and everything will follow. You said: "We will get Garvey out of the way if we destroy the Black Star Line." Well, Garvey did not go then. "We will get Garvey another way; we will undermine all his business enterprises, and try to make them failures and then tell the people, 'Oh, you see what has happened,' then Garvey is bound to go after that." Well, Garvey did not go. "Well," they said, "what is the matter? Let us attack him in person, then let our slogan be, 'Garvey must go.'" But Garvey did not go. "Well, we will try to get him otherwise, because this Universal Negro Improvement Association idea must be throttled." Ah, but Garvey is here, and both of them shall go down the ages. If Garvey dies, Garvey lives; if the Universal Negro Improvement Association is embarrassed, a greater Universal Negro Improvement Association arises. Gentlemen, what are you going to do? You must first destroy the souls of black men before you can destroy Garvey, and destroy the Universal Negro Improvement Association, and you will have a h—— of a time doing that. Garvey cannot die, the Universal Negro Improvement Association cannot die, because, gentlemen, the thing is not only physical, the individual is not only physical, but there is a spiritual motive, there is a spiritual force back of it that cannot be destroyed.

Great ideals, great principles, great truths never die. Individuals die, the Christ died. Mohammed died; but you did not destroy Christianity or Mohammedanism. Garvey in the flesh can die, and he is ready to die at any time; but, gentlemen, the greater force will live on; one, I repeat, that will go down the ages to tell the story, tell the story of the traitors, tell the story of those who tried to block the passage of the rising Ethiopia, of the new Africa. What shall be your defense before the bar of African redemption, gentlemen? Will you plead innocence; will you plead not knowing better? Ah, ignorance will be no excuse. Our history of the traitors shall go down the ages and shall be written in the black book of time, and even the Angel of Eternity shall lay it before the judgment seat of God.

The traitors are working hard, the enemies are doing their worst; but we smile in their faces. There are combinations of forces working against the Universal Negro Improvement Association, against which it is written by these enemies, "That association and Garvey must be destroyed." They have been using men once placed in positions of trust in this association to help destroy the movement. These traitors we have had to dismiss. Today they, with the rest of our enemies, are determined to tear down the structure that we have built. They have all entered into a conspiracy to sue and embarrass the Universal Negro Improvement

Association . . . The fools, they know no better. Survive we must, go forward we must, so long as there is a God, so long as there is a world, so long as there is a human race. But, members, I repeat, these traitors are endeavoring to embarrass us before the courts, suing us for salaries, trying to force judgments upon us at a time when we are supposed to be fighting the common enemy, so that they could glory in the downfall of the movement. They also are mistaken.

Members and friends, let us pay these traitors, let us pay them off in their bits of silver. Therefore, I appeal to each and every member of the Universal Negro Improvement Association to do this bit of service now; send to the parent body whatsoever financial support you can give to help us pay off these traitors who are endeavoring to sue us. Let us dispose of them that way, and then let us continue the fight against the common enemy. These "bits of silver" shall bring them tears in the years to come. Let us hand them over now, the thirty pieces of silver. That which Judas received did not help him very long; he was willing to return it, but nobody would receive it. These enemies, these traitors, may yet rue the day when they turned their backs upon the Universal Negro Improvement Association, the organization that made them. Did we not make them?

We picked some of them up from the lowest and poorest of the race and made gentlemen of them, because we believed that by their sufferings they would be able to appreciate the service to which they were called. It takes a slave to appreciate liberty; it takes a man who suffers to understand freedom; and that was why we thought that in taking these men and making them gentlemen that we were rendering a service to the race. We made a terrible mistake. It is true all of us make mistakes. Some of these Negroes who never earned more than $25.00 per week, because of their intelligence we thought we could give them a chance to make good and make something of themselves. We gave them grand and noble positions. We tried to make statesmen of them, but they fell by the wayside. Yes, you know that, and you will see them drift back to the condition they were in before they came into the Universal Negro Improvement Association. Our generation and posterity may yet smile in their faces, but let us pay them. And you can do it now by sending your contributions to the "Bit of Silver Fund" to the Secretary-General, Universal Negro Improvement Association, 56 West 135th Street, New York City, U.S.A.

With very best wishes, I have the honor to be

Your obedient servant,
MARCUS GARVEY, President-General
Universal Negro Improvement Association

Last Speech before Incarceration in the Tombs Prison★

"We are not fighting America; we are fighting hypocrisy and lies,
and that we are going to fight to the bitter end."

Liberty Hall, New York City,
June 17, 1923

The Philosophy and Opinions of Marcus Garvey, or Africa for the Africans,
Volume 2

AMONG the many names by which I have been called, I was dubbed by
another name a couple of days ago. The district attorney, with whom I
have been contesting the case for my liberty and for the existence of the
Universal Negro Improvement Association, in his fervid appeal, in his
passionate appeal, to the gentlemen of the jury last Friday cried out:
"Gentlemen, will you let the tiger loose?"

The tiger is already loose, and he has been at large for so long that it is
no longer one tiger, but there are many tigers. The spirit of the Universal
Negro Improvement Association has, fortunately for us, made a circuit of
the world, to the extent that harm or injury done to any one, will in no
way affect the great membership of this association or retard its great program. The world is ignorant of the purpose of this association. The world
is ignorant of the scope of this great movement, when it thinks that by laying low any one individual it can permanently silence this great spiritual
wave that has taken hold of the souls and the hearts and minds of
400,000,000 Negroes throughout the world. We have only started; we are
just on our way; we have just made the first lap in the great race for existence, and for a place in the political and economic sun of men.

Those of you who have been observing events for the last four or five
weeks with keen eyes and keen perceptions will come to no other conclusion than this—that through the effort to strangle the Universal Negro
Improvement Association—through the effort to silence Marcus Garvey—
there is a mad desire, there is a great plan to permanently lay the Negro low
in this civilization and in future civilizations. But the world is sadly mistaken.
No longer can the Negro be laid low; in laying the Negro low you but bring
down the pillars of creation, because 400,000,000 Negroes are determined
to a man, to take a place in the world and to hold that place. The world is
sadly mistaken and rudely shocked at the same time. They thought that the
new Negro would bend; they thought that the new Negro was only bluff-

★See introductory note for background on Garvey's arrest, trial, and subsequent conviction for mail fraud.

ing and would exhibit the characteristic of the old Negro when pushed to the corner or pushed to the wall. If you want to see the new Negro fight, force him to the wall, and the nearer he approaches the wall the more he fights, and when he gets to the wall he is even more desperate.

What does the world think—that we are going back to sixty years ago in America—going back to eighty-five years ago in the West Indies—going back to 300 years ago in Africa? The world is crazy if they indulge that thought. We are not going back; we are going forward—forward to the emancipation of 400,000,000 oppressed souls; forward to the redemption of a great country and the re-establishment of a greater government.

Garvey has just started to fight; Garvey has not given his first exhibition of his fighting prowess yet. Men, we want you to understand that this is the age of men, not of pigmies, not of serfs and peons and dogs, but men, and we who make up the membership of the Universal Negro Improvement Association reflect the new manhood of the Negro. No fear, no intimidation, nothing can daunt the courage of the Negro who affiliates himself with the Universal Negro Improvement Association. The Universal Negro Improvement Association is light, and we have entered into light and shall not go back into darkness. We have entered into the light of a new day; we have seen the light of a new creation; we have seen the light of a new civilization, and we shall follow where that light leads.

I was amused when my friend, the district attorney, said that he was more interested in Negroes than Marcus Garvey. They are so accustomed to the old camouflage that they believe they can plead it everywhere to the satisfaction of every Negro, and to everyone who comes in contact with them. That is the old camouflage that made them our missionaries sixty years ago; it is the same camouflage that made them our leaders since emancipation; but it is the camouflage that will not stand today. It is impossible for a Negro to be more interested in a Jew than a Jew is interested in himself. It is impossible for an Englishman to be more interested in an Irishman than that Irishman is in himself. It is a lie for any Jew to say he is more interested in Negroes than Negroes are in themselves. It is an unnatural lie to talk about one race being more interested in another race than that race is interested in itself. But that only shows how desperate they are. Sometimes we have to beware of Greeks bearing gifts. Unfortunately, I did not have the last word and therefore I was silenced after I placed my defense in; but, nevertheless, the world will know tomorrow the outcome of this case wherein Marcus Garvey and the Universal Negro Improvement Association is involved. One way or the other, the world will not be disappointed. There is no verdict that would disappoint me. I tell you this, that there is to be no disappointment; if they were to give any other verdict than guilty, Marcus Garvey will be very much disappointed; Marcus Garvey knows them so well that Marcus Garvey will expect anything from them; so, whether they give a verdict of guilty or not guilty, it is immaterial to Marcus Garvey; the fight will just then be starting.

Now, understand this is a fight to the finish. We are not fighting this great government, because all Negroes in America—all Negroes all over the world—know that the greatest democracy in the world is the American democracy, the greatest government in the world is the American republic. We are not fighting America; we are fighting hypocrisy and lies, and that we are going to fight to the bitter end. Now, understand me well, Marcus Garvey has entered the fight for the emancipation of a race; Marcus Garvey has entered the fight for the redemption of a country. From the graves of millions of my forebears at this hour I hear the cry, and I am going to answer it even though hell is cut loose before Marcus Garvey. From the silent graves of millions who went down to make me what I am, I shall make for their memory, this fight that shall leave a glaring page in the history of man.

They do not know what they are doing. They brought millions of black men from Africa who never disturbed the peace of the world, and they shall put up a constitutional fight that shall write a page upon the history of human affairs that shall never be effaced until the day of judgment. I did not bring myself here; they brought me from my silent repose in Africa 300 years ago, and this is only the first Marcus Garvey. They have thought that they could for 300 years brutalize a race. They have thought that they could for 300 years steep the soul of a race in blood and darkness and let it go at that. They make a terrible mistake. Marcus Garvey shall revenge the blood of his sires. So don't be afraid of Marcus Garvey. When Marcus Garvey goes to jail the world of Negroes will know. They have come at the wrong time.

I appreciate the splendid way in which you have behaved and conducted yourselves during the trial. We shall observe to the letter the laws of this great country, but Africa shall tell the tale. Marcus Garvey has no fear about going to jail. Like MacSwiney or like Carson, like Roger Casement, like those who have led the fight for Irish freedom, so Marcus Garvey shall lead the fight for African freedom.

I repeat that if they think they can stamp out the souls of 400,000,000 black men, they make a tremendous and terrible mistake. We are no longer dogs; we are no longer peons; we are no longer serfs—we are men. The spirit that actuated George Washington in founding this great republic—the spirit that actuated 6,000,000 black men who are at the present time members of the Universal Negro Improvement Association; it is the spirit that will actuate 400,000,000 Negroes in the redemption of their motherland, Africa. Tell us about fear; we were not born with fear. Intimidation does not drive fear into the soul of Marcus Garvey. There is no fear, but the fear of God. Man cannot drive fear into the heart of man, because man is but the equal of man. The world is crazy and foolish if they think that they can destroy the principles, the ideals of the Universal Negro Improvement Association.

An Appeal to the Conscience of the Black Race to See Itself

"The Negro will have to build his own government, industry, art, science, literature and culture, before the world will stop to consider him."

The Tombs Prison,
New York City, August 14, 1923

The Philosophy and Opinions of Marcus Garvey, or Africa for the Africans,
Volume 2

IT IS said to be a hard and difficult task to organize and keep together large numbers of the Negro race for the common good. Many have tried to congregate us, but have failed, the reason being that our characteristics are such as to keep us more apart than together.

The evil of internal division is wrecking our existence as a people, and if we do not seriously and quickly move in the direction of a readjustment it simply means that our doom becomes imminently conclusive.

For years the Universal Negro Improvement Association has been working for the unification of our race, not on domestic-national lines only, but universally. The success which we have met in the course of our effort is rather encouraging, considering the time consumed and the environment surrounding the object of our concern.

It seems that the whole world of sentiment is against the Negro, and the difficulty of our generation is to extricate ourselves from the prejudice that hides itself beneath, as well as above, the action of an international environment.

Prejudice is conditional on many reasons, and it is apparent that the Negro supplies, consciously or unconsciously, all the reasons by which the world seems to ignore and avoid him. No one cares for a leper, for lepers are infectious persons, and all are afraid of the disease, so, because the Negro keeps himself poor, helpless and undemonstrative, it is natural also that no one wants to be of him or with him.

Progress is the attraction that moves humanity, and to whatever people or race this "modern virtue" attaches itself, there will you find the splendor of pride and self-esteem that never fail to win the respect and admiration of all.

It is the progress of the Anglo-Saxons that singles them out for the respect of all the world. When their race had no progress or achievement to its credit, then, like all other inferior peoples, they paid the price in slavery, bondage, as well as through prejudice. We cannot forget the time when even the ancient Briton was regarded as being too dull to make a good Roman slave, yet today the influence of that race rules the world.

It is the industrial and commercial progress of America that causes Europe and the rest of the world to think appreciatively of the Anglo-American race. It is not because one hundred and ten million people live in the United States that the world is attracted to the republic with so much reverence and respect—a reverence and respect not shown to India with its three hundred millions, or to China with its four hundred millions. Progress of and among any people will advance them in the respect and appreciation of the rest of their fellows. It is such a progress that the Negro must attach to himself if he is to rise above the prejudice of the world.

The reliance of our race upon the progress and achievements of others for a consideration in sympathy, justice and rights is like a dependence upon a broken stick, resting upon which will eventually consign you to the ground.

The Universal Negro Improvement Association teaches our race self-help and self-reliance, not only in one essential, but in all those things that contribute to human happiness and well-being. The disposition of the many to depend upon the other races for a kindly and sympathetic consideration of their needs, without making the effort to do for themselves, has been the race's standing disgrace by which we have been judged and through which we have created the strongest prejudice against ourselves.

There is no force like success, and that is why the individual makes all efforts to surround himself throughout life with the evidence of it. As of the individual, so should it be of the race and nation. The glittering success of Rockefeller makes him a power in the American nation; the success of Henry Ford suggests him as an object of universal respect, but no one knows and cares about the bum or hobo who is Rockefeller's or Ford's neighbor. So, also, is the world attracted by the glittering success of races and nations, and pays absolutely no attention to the bum or hobo race that lingers by the wayside.

The Negro must be up and doing if he will break down the prejudice of the rest of the world. Prayer alone is not going to improve our condition, nor the policy of watchful waiting. We must strike out for ourselves in the course of material achievement, and by our own effort and energy present to the world those forces by which the progress of man is judged.

The Negro needs a nation and a country of his own, where he can best show evidence of his own ability in the art of human progress. Scattered as an unmixed and unrecognized part of alien nations and civilizations is but to demonstrate his imbecility, and points him out as an unworthy derelict, fit neither for the society of Greek, Jew nor Gentile.

It is unfortunate that we should so drift apart, as a race, as not to see that we are but perpetuating our own sorrow and disgrace in failing to appreciate the first great requisite of all peoples—organization.

Organization is a great power in directing the affairs of a race or nation toward a given goal. To properly develop the desires that are uppermost, we must first concentrate through some system or method, and there is none better than organization. Hence, the Universal Negro Improvement Association appeals to each and every Negro to throw in his lot with those of us who, through organization, are working for the universal emancipation of our race and the redemption of our common country, Africa.

No Negro, let him be American, European, West Indian or African, shall be truly respected until the race as a whole has emancipated itself, through self-achievement and progress, from universal prejudice. The Negro will have to build his own government, industry, art, science, literature and culture, before the world will stop to consider him. Until then, we are but wards of a superior race and civilization, and the outcasts of a standard social system.

The race needs workers at this time, not plagiarists, copyists and mere imitators; but men and women who are able to create, to originate and improve, and thus make an independent racial contribution to the world and civilization.

The unfortunate thing about us is that we take the monkey apings of our "so-called leading men" for progress. There is no progress in Negroes aping white people and telling us that they represent the best in the race, for in that respect any dressed monkey would represent the best of its species, irrespective of the creative matter of the monkey instinct. The best in a race is not reflected through or by the action of its apes, but by its ability to create of and by itself. It is such a creation that the Universal Negro Improvement Association seeks.

Let us not try to be the best or worst of others, but let us make the effort to be the best of ourselves. Our own racial critics criticize us as dreamers and "fanatics," and call us "benighted" and "ignorant," because they lack racial backbone. They are unable to see themselves creators of their own needs. The slave instinct has not yet departed from them. They still believe that they can only live or exist through the good graces of their "masters." The good slaves have not yet thrown off their shackles; thus, to them, the Universal Negro Improvement Association is an "impossibility."

It is the slave spirit of dependence that causes our "so-called leading men" (apes) to seek the shelter, leadership, protection and patronage of the "master" in their organization and so-called advancement work. It is the spirit of feeling secured as good servants of the master, rather than as independents, why our modern Uncle Toms take pride in laboring under alien leadership and becoming surprised at the audacity of the Universal Negro Improvement Association in proclaiming for racial liberty and independence.

But the world of white and other men, deep down in their hearts, have much more respect for those of us who work for our racial salvation under the banner of the Universal Negro Improvement Association, than they could ever have, in all eternity, for a group of helpless apes and beggars who make a monopoly of undermining their own race and belittling themselves in the eyes of self-respecting people, by being "good boys" rather than able men.

Surely there can be no good will between apes, seasoned beggars and independent-minded Negroes who will at least make an effort to do for themselves. Surely, the "dependents" and "wards" (and may I not say racial imbeciles?) will rave against and plan the destruction of movements like the Universal Negro Improvement Association that expose them to the liberal white minds of the world as not being representative of the best in the Negro, but, to the contrary, the worst. The best of a race does not live on the patronage and philanthropy of others, but makes an effort to do for itself. The best of the great white race doesn't fawn before and beg black, brown or yellow men; they go out, create for self and thus demonstrate the fitness of the race to survive; and so the white race of America and the world will be informed that the best in the Negro race is not the class of beggars who send out to other races piteous appeals annually for donations to maintain their coterie, but the groups within us that are honestly striving to do for themselves with the voluntary help and appreciation of that class of other races that is reasonable, just and liberal enough to give to each and every one' a fair chance in the promotion of those ideals that tend to greater human progress and human love.

The work of the Universal Negro Improvement Association is clear and clean-cut. It is that of inspiring an unfortunate race with pride in self and with the determination of going ahead in the creation of those ideals that will lift them to the unprejudiced company of races and nations. There is no desire for hate or malice, but every wish to see all mankind linked into a common fraternity of progress and achievement that will wipe away the odor of prejudice, and elevate the human race to the height of real godly love and satisfaction.

An Exposé of the Caste System among Negroes

"Du Bois represents a group that hates the Negro blood in its veins,
and has been working subtly to build up a caste aristocracy . . ."

The Tombs Prison,
New York City, August 31, 1923

The Philosophy and Opinions of Marcus Garvey, or Africa for the Africans,
Volume 2

THE policy of the Universal Negro Improvement Association is so clean-cut, and my personal views are so well known, that no one, for even one moment, could reasonably accuse us of having any other desire than that of working for a united Negro race.

The program of the Universal Negro Improvement Association is that of drawing together, into one universal whole, all the Negro peoples of the world, with prejudice toward none. We desire to have every shade of color, even those with one drop of African blood, in our fold; because we believe that none of us, as we are, is responsible for our birth; in a word, we have no prejudice against ourselves in race. We believe that every Negro racially is just alike, and, therefore, we have no distinction to make, hence wherever you see the Universal Negro Improvement Association you will find us giving every member of the race an equal chance and opportunity to make good.

Unfortunately, there is a disposition on the part of a certain element of our people in America, the West Indies and Africa, to hold themselves up as the "better class" or "privileged" group on the caste of color.

This subject is such a delicate one that no one is honest enough to broach it, yet the evil of it is working great harm to our racial solidarity, and I personally feel it my duty to right now bring it to the attention of all concerned. The Universal Negro Improvement Association is founded on truth, and, therefore, anything that would menace or retard the race must be gotten out of the way, hence our stand in this direction. During the early days of slavery our people were wrested from the bosom of our native land—Africa—and brought into these climes. For centuries, against their will, our mothers were subjected to the most cruel and unfair treatment, the result of which has created among us a diversity of colors and types, to the end that we have become the most mixed race in the world.

The abuse of our race was, up to eighty-five years ago in the West Indies and fifty-seven years ago in America, beyond our control, because we were then but chattel slaves of our masters; but since emancipation we have had full control of our own moral-social life and cannot, therefore, complain against anyone other than ourselves, for any social or moral wrongs inflicted upon us.

The Universal Negro Improvement Association realizes that it is now our duty to socially and morally steady ourselves, hence our desire to bring about a united race should not be blameable to our generation, but to the abuse and advantage taken of us in the past; but that should not be reason for us to further open ourselves to a continuation of this abuse and thereby wreck our racial pride and self-respect. The Universal Negro Improvement Association believes that the time has come for us to call a halt, and thus steady ourselves on the basis of race and not be allowed to drift along in the world as the outcasts or lepers or society, to be laughed at by every other race beneath their social breath.

Some of us in America, the West Indies and Africa believe that the nearer we approach the white man in color the greater our social standing and privilege and that we should build up an "aristocracy" based upon caste of color and not achievement in race. It is well known, although no one is honest enough to admit it, that we have been, for the past thirty years at least, but more so now than ever, grading ourselves for social honor and distinction on the basis of color. That the average success in the race has been regulated by color and not by ability and merit; that we have been trying to get away from the pride of race into the atmosphere of color worship, to the damaging extent that the whole world has made us its laughing stock.

There is no doubt that a race that doesn't respect itself forfeits the respect of others, and we are in the moral-social position now of losing the respect of the whole world.

There is a subtle and underhand propaganda fostered by a few men of color in America, the West Indies and Africa to destroy the self-respect and pride of the Negro race by building up what is commonly known to us as a "blue vein" aristocracy and to foster same as the social and moral standard of the race. The success of this effort is very much marked in the West Indies, and coming into immediate recognition in South Africa, and is now gaining much headway in America under the skillful leadership of the National Association for the Advancement of "Colored" People and their silent but scattered agents.

The observant members of our race must have noticed within recent years a great hostility between the National Association for the Advancement of "Colored" People and the Universal "Negro" Improvement Association, and must have wondered why Du Bois writes so bitterly against Garvey and vice versa. Well, the reason is plainly to be seen after the following explanation:

Du Bois represents a group that hates the Negro blood in its veins, and has been working subtly to build up a caste aristocracy that would socially divide the race into two groups: One the superior because of color caste, and the other the inferior, hence the pretentious work of the National

Association for the Advancement of "Colored" People. The program of deception was well arranged and under way for success when Marcus Garvey arrived in America, and he, after understudying the artful doctor and the group he represented, fired a "bomb" into the camp by organizing the Universal "Negro" Improvement Association to cut off the wicked attempt of race deception and distinction, and, in truth, to build up a race united in spirit and ideal, with the honest desire of adjusting itself to its own moral-social pride and national self-respect. When Garvey arrived in America and visited the office of the National Association for the Advancement of "Colored" People to interview Du Bois, who was regarded as a leader of the Negro people, and who had recently visited the West Indies, he was dumb-founded on approach to the office to find that but for Mr. Dill, Du Bois, himself and the office boy, he could not tell whether he was in a white office of that of the National Association for the Advancement of "Colored" People. The whole staff was either white or very near white, and thus Garvey got his first shock of the advancement hypocrisy. There was no representation of the race there that anyone could recognize. The advancement meant that you had to be as near white as possible, otherwise there was no place for you as stenographer, clerk or attendant in the office of the National Association for the Advancement of "Colored" People. After a short talk with Du Bois, Garvey became so disgusted with the man and his principles that the thought he never contemplated entered his mind—that of remaining in America to teach Du Bois and his group what real race pride meant.

When Garvey left the office of the National Association for the Advancement of "Colored" People, to travel through and study the social life of Negro America, he found that the policy of the Association was well observed in business and professional life, as well as in the drawing room, etc., all over the country. In restaurants, drug stores and offices all over the nation where our people were engaged in business it was discoverable that those employed were the very "lightest" members of the race—as waitresses, clerks and stenographers. Garvey asked, "What's the matter? Why were not black, brown-skin and mulatto girls employed?" And he was told it was "for the good of the trade." That to have trade it was necessary and incumbent to have "light" faces, as near white as possible. But the shock did not stop there. In New York, Boston, Washington and Detroit, Garvey further discovered the activities of the "Blue Vein Society" and the "Colonial Club." The West Indian "lights" formed the "Colonial Club" and the American "lights" the "Blue Vein" Society. The "Colonial Club" would give annual balls beside regular or monthly *soirees* and no one less than a quadroon would be admitted, and gentlemen below that complexion were only admitted if they were lawyers, doctors or very successful business men with plenty of "cash," who were known to uphold the caste aristocracy. At St. Philip's Church, New York, where the Very Rev. Dr. Daniels held sway and dominion, the "society" had things so arranged that even though this man was a brown-skin clergyman, and his rector a very near white gentleman, he had to draw the line and give the best seats in the church and the places of honor to the "Blue Veins" and the others would have a "look in" when they, by fawning before and "humbling" themselves and by giving lavishly to the church, admitted the superiority of caste. (By the way, Dr. Daniels was also an executive officer or director of the National Association for the Advancement of "Colored" People.) In Washington one or two of the churches did the same thing, but in Detroit the Very Rev. "Bob" Bagnall, now director of branches of the National Association for the Advancement of "Colored" People, held sway. In his church no dark person could have a seat in the front, and, to test the truthfulness of it after being told, Garvey, incognito, one Sunday night attempted to occupy one of the empty seats, not so very near the front, and the effort nearly spoiled the whole service, as Brother Bob, who was then ascending the pulpit, nearly lost his "balance" to see such a face so near the "holy of holies." Brother Bob was also an officer of the National Association for the Advancement of "Colored" People. On Garvey's return to New York he made (incognito) a similar test at St. Philip's Church one Sunday, and the Rev. Daniels was nearly ready to fight.

Now, what does all this mean? It is to relate the hidden program and motive of the National Association for the Advancement of "Colored" People and to warn Negro America of not being deceived by a group of men who have as much love for the Negro blood in their veins as the devil has for holy water.

The National Association for the Advancement of "Colored" People is a scheme to destroy the Negro Race, and the leaders of it hate Marcus Garvey, because he has discovered them at their game and because the Universal Negro Improvement Association, without any prejudice to color or caste, is making headway in bringing all the people together for their common good. They hate Garvey because the Universal Negro Improvement Association and the Black Star Line employed every shade of color in the race, according to ability and merit, and put the N.A.A.C.P. to shame for employing only the "lightest" of the race. They hate Garvey because he forced them to fill Shiladay's place with a Negro. They hate Garvey because they had to employ "black" Pickens to cover up their scheme after Garvey had discovered it; they hate Garvey because they have had to employ brown-skin "Bob" Bagnall to make a showing to the people that they were doing the "right" thing by them; they hate Garvey because he has broken up the "Pink Tea Set"; they hate Garvey because they had been forced to recognize mulatto, brown and black talent in the association equally with the lighter element; they hate Garvey because he is teaching the unity of race, without color superiority or prejudice. The gang thought that they would have been able to build up in America a buffer class between whites and Negroes, and thus in another fifty years join with the powerful race and crush the blood of their mothers, as is being done in South Africa and the West Indies.

The imprisonment of Garvey is more than appears on the surface, and the National Association for the Advancement of "Colored" People knows it. Du Bois and those who lead the Association are skillful enough to be using the old method of getting the "other fellow" to destroy himself, hence the activities of "brown-skin" Bagnall and "black" Pickens. Walter White, whom we can hardly tell from a Southern gentleman who lives with a white family in Brooklyn, is kept in the background, but dark Bagnall, Pickens and Du Bois are pushed to the front to make the attack, so that there would be no suspicion of the motive. They are to drive hard and hot, and then the silent influence would bring up the rear, hence the slogan, "Garvey must go!" and the vicious attacks in the different magazines by Pickens, Du Bois and Bagnall.

Gentlemen, you are very smart, but Garvey has caught your tune. The conspiracy to destroy the Negro race is so well organized that the moment anything interferes with their program there springs up a simultaneous action on the part of the leaders. It will be observed that in the September issue of the *Crisis* is published on the very last page of its news section what purports to be the opinion of a Jamaica paper about Marcus Garvey and his case. The skillful editor of the *Crisis,* Dr. Du Bois, reproduces that part of the article that would tend to show the opinion about Garvey in his own country taken from a paper called the *Gleaner,* (edited by one Herbert George de Lisser) and not the property of Negroes.

The article in the original was clipped from the *Gleaner* when it appeared, and was sent by a friend to Garvey, so that he knew all that appeared in it. In it the editor extolled the leadership and virtues of Dr. Du Bois, and said it was the right kind of leadership for the American Negro people, and bitterly denounced Garvey. Du Bois published that part that denounced Garvey, but suppressed the part that gave him the right of leadership; and he failed to enlighten his readers that the editor of the *Gleaner* is a very light man, who hates the Negro blood of his mother and who is part of the international scheme to foster the Blue Vein Society scheme. Dr. Du Bois failed to further enlighten his readers that he visited Jamaica and was part of the "Colonial Society" scheme; he also failed to state that in the plan De Lisser is to "hold down" the West Indian end of the "caste scheme" and he and others to "hold down" the American end, while their agents "hold down" the South African section.

But now we have reached the point where the entire race must get together and stop these schemers at their game. Whether we are light, yellow, black or what not, there is but one thing for us to do, and that is to get together and build up a race. God made us in His own image and He had some purpose when He thus created us. Then why should we seek to destroy ourselves? If a few Du Boises and De Lissers do not want their progeny to remain of our race, why not be satisfied to bide their time and take their peaceful exit? But why try in this subtle manner to humiliate and destroy our race?

We as a people have a great future before us. Ethiopia shall once more see the day of her glory; then why destroy the chance and opportunity simply to be someone else?

Let us work and wait patiently, for our day of racial triumph will come. Let us not divide ourselves into castes, but let us all work together for the common good. Let us remember the sorrow of our mothers. Let us not forget that it is our duty to remedy any wrong that has already been done, and not ourselves perpetuate the evil of race destruction. To change our race is no credit. The Anglo-Saxon doesn't want to be a Japanese; the Japanese doesn't want to be a Negro. Then, in the name of God and all that is holy, why should we want to be somebody else?

Let the National Association for the Advancement of Colored People stop its hypocrisy and settle down to real race uplift.

If Dr. Du Bois, Johnson, Pickens and Bagnall do not know, let me tell them that they are only being used to weaken the race, so that in another fifty or a hundred years the race can easily be wiped out as a social, economic and political force or "menace."

The people who are directing the affairs of the National Association for the Advancement of "Colored" People are keen observers; it takes more than ordinary intelligence to penetrate their motive, hence you are now warned.

All the "gas" about anti-lynching and "social equality" will not amount to a row of pins, in fact, it is only a ruse to raise money to capitalize the scheme and hide the real motive. Negroes, "watch your step" and save yourselves from deception and subsequent extermination.

Statement to Press on Release on Bail Pending Appeal

"My imprisonment of three months has but steeled me for greater service to the people I love so much and who love me."

New York City,
September 10, 1923

The Philosophy and Opinions of Marcus Garvey, or Africa for the Africans,
Volume 2

My detention in jail pending the appeal of my case has in no way affected my vision of justice. To those who are conscious of themselves there can be no incrimination from without, it must be from within.

When a man's conscience convicts him then there is no appeal: Thank Goodness I am not convicted.

I am not peeved at what has been done to me; it is natural and to be expected, that in an effort like mine to serve humanity—and black humanity at that—that powerful enemies will be encountered. The enemies I have are chiefly of my own race, and they have worked hard to discredit and destroy me.

They have only succeeded however in arousing the fighting spirit of millions of black men all over the world. There is nothing to fire a people to action like injustice, and I feel sure that time will tell the good that has been done to my cause, by the injustice meted out to me within the last three months.

The experience I have had will help me greatly in the determination and conduct of the work that is ahead of me. A large number of people only looked at and enjoyed what to them seemed the humorous side of my program. There is no more humor in it than we find in all the other serious reform movements started for the uplift of humanity. The newspapers will, however, make the people laugh as a recreation, and a break in the monotony of a life of economic drudgery and social discord. If I afforded some amusement, I hope that the public will not blame me for it, for I am the direct opposite of the clown. I am serious, I have but one purpose, and that is the uplift and betterment of my race.

My detention in jail after my application for bail pending appeal, was but a reflex of the state of mind of Mr. Maxwell S. Mattuck, the Assistant District Attorney who tried my case for the government.

I am not blaming the government for my conviction and detention in jail. The government cannot represent itself. If at times we meet disappointments in the representation of government, we must reason that all men do not think and act alike. Some persons are worthy of and dignify any position that they hold, others, on the other hand, at their best are but libels to decency and propriety.

The methods that have been used to prejudice the court and the public against me, are of such as to make me shiver in fear that probably hundreds of thousands of innocent persons have lingered and died in prisons from the practice of such a system by unfair and unworthy representatives of governments.

I shall make a fight to bring to the attention of the people and government of this great country the evil methods used to railroad me to prison, to rob me of my name, to destroy my work for the pleasure of rival organizations, and the attempt to prevent me from speaking to the great American conscience by a suppression of free speech, and a muzzling of the press.

I am glad, and feel proud, we have worthy representatives in government to out-balance any singular attempt at misrepresentation and injustice. Our institutions and country shall live forever, so long as the people have such worthy men as representatives to whom we can always appeal from the doings and machinations of the unjust.

I love America for her laws, constitution and her higher sense of fair play and justice. One can always find justice in America.

I have to thank my white friends and the members of my organization, as also the large number of liberal-minded colored citizens, who raised their voice in protest, and who helped generally in my being admitted to bail. I have to thank the judge and all those who had to do with my being liberated.

The few unfair white persons who have acted against us were misinformed, therefore I have no blame for them. They, like the majority, do not understand the Negro, but I hope they will now make a closer study of the tale-bearers of our race who fabricate against their own for special favors.

My imprisonment of nearly three months has but steeled me for greater service to the people I love so much and who love me. I had no money before I was indicted. I had none when I was tried, and none when I was convicted and sentenced, because I gave all to the movement, but the people whom I served, and who know me, did not desert me. They stuck by me and paid for my defense, and subscribed for my bail. These are the people whom my enemies accuse me of defrauding. [Those who] hounded me haven't lost a penny in the ventures of our organization. They never placed a penny in it, yet they are so aggrieved. I feel sure that white America will, when properly informed, agree with us that the only solution of the Negro problem is to give the Negro a country of his own in Africa and for this I am working without any apologies.

I was kindly treated by the warden and prison officials. I shall ever remember the kindly and sympathetic attitude of those worthy representatives of our government. I am also glad to state that not one of my white fellow prisoners believed me guilty of the crime charged against me. It is amazing, but the prisoners seem to keep a tab on all that is going on in the courts. My case was well known to them, so that when I arrived at the jail, they were all surprised and disgusted at the results. They had a kind word of sympathy for me.

Some of the prisoners I met were honest enough to admit their guilt for whatever crimes they were charged, but I believe that there are others who are also innocent victims of circumstances.

Several liberal-minded white friends visited me in jail, and did their best for me in the cause of justice. I am not asking for mercy or sympathy, I am asking for justice, and I have confidence in our constitution to know that it will not be denied me.

First Speech after Release from The Tombs

"I was convicted, not because anyone was defrauded in the
temporary failure of the Black Star Line brought about
by others, but because I represented, even as I do now,
a movement for the real emancipation of my race."

Liberty Hall,
New York City, September 11, 1923★

The Philosophy and Opinions of Marcus Garvey, or Africa for the Africans,
Volume 2

LADIES AND GENTLEMEN:

IT IS needless for me to say that the pleasure of meeting you in Liberty
Hall, the shrine of Negro inspiration, after an enforced absence of three
months, is beyond my ability to express.

The news of the trial of the celebrated case of fraud and my so-called
conviction have made the circuit of the world, and black humanity
everywhere, even to the remotest parts of our homeland, Africa, have
formed their opinion of Western twentieth century civilization and justice, as controlled and administered by the white man.

My absence from you did not leave me despondent, nor desolate, for
in the daily silence of the passing hours in my cell I thought of you, the
warriors of true liberty, who were working for the consummation of our
ideal—a free and redeemed Africa, and my meditations led me into
greater flights of hope that shall strengthen me for the noble work of self-
sacrifice for the cause that we represent.

The amusing part of my trial is that I was indicted along with others
for conspiracy to use the United States mails to defraud in the promotion of the Black Star Line Steamship Company, yet my conviction was
void of conspiracy, in that I alone was convicted, and, if I understand my
conviction clearly, I was convicted for selling stock in the Black Star Line
after I knew it to be insolvent. The difference between us and the trial
court is that they wanted a conviction, caring not how it came about, and
they had it to suit themselves, to the extent that all the others, who had
more to do with the actual selling of stock than I, went free, because they
were not wanted, while I received the fullest penalty that the law could
impose—five years in the penitentiary, the maximum fine of one thou-

---

★This speech is dated September 13 by Amy Jacques Garvey, but September 11 by *The
Negro World*.

sand dollars as provided by law, and the entire cost of the case, a condition not generally imposed but, maybe, once in twenty-five years.

Our point of view is that we cannot defraud ourselves in the sense of promoting the Black Star Line, for the idea of a line of steamships operated by Negroes for the promotion of their industrial, commercial, fraternal and material well-being can never be insolvent or bankrupt; for, as long as the race lasts, and as long as humanity indulges in the pursuit of progress and achievements, the new Negro will be found doing his part to hold a place in the affairs of the world. It is true that we have been defrauded, but it was done, not by those of us who love our work and our race, but by disloyal and dishonest ones, whom we thought had the same feelings as we do, and by crooked white men, who were not even ashamed of hiding their crookedness. One white man said in court that he sold us a ship when he knew it was not worth the money paid for it. Another took $25,000 and an additional $11,000 to buy the *Phyllis Wheatley* to go to Africa, which never materialized, and which money was never returned, the reason of which supplied the legal cause for my indictment. And yet it is said in the law of those who tried me that there was fraud and I should pay the penalty.

The Black Star Line, as we all know, was but a small attempt, or experiment, of the race to fit and prepare ourselves for the bigger effort in the direction of racial self-reliance and self-determination. To say that we have failed, because a few black and white unscrupulous persons deceived and robbed us, is to admit that the colonization scheme of America failed because a few Pilgrim Fathers died at Plymouth, and that the fight of the allies to save the world for a new civilization failed, because the Crown Prince met with early success at Verdun. The Black Star Line was only part of an honest effort on the part of real Negroes to re-establish themselves as a worthy people among the other races and nations of the earth, and but a small contribution in the plan of a free and redeemed African nation for the Negro peoples of the world. The idea of a Black Steamship Line therefore, can only fail when the Negro race has completely passed away, and that means eternity.

I was convicted, not because anyone was defrauded in the temporary failure of the Black Star Line brought about by others, but because I represented, even as I do now, a movement for the real emancipation of my race. I was convicted because I talked about Africa and about its redemption for Negroes. I was convicted because an atmosphere of hostility was created around me. I was convicted because wicked enemies, malicious and jealous members of my own race, misrepresented me to those in authority for the purpose of discrediting and destroying me.

I would not blame the few white persons who contributed to my conviction, neither would I blame the government and the illiberal of the white race who had prejudices against me. They knew no better than the information they received from treacherous, malicious, and jealous Negroes who, for the sake of position and privilege, will sell their own mothers.

I feel, however, that these white persons and the government have now the opportunity of learning the truth, not only about my case and my conviction, but about the differences in the Negro race, that set one against the other.

I have no fear of the ultimate outcome of my case. I shall take it to the highest courts in the land, and from there to the bar of international public opinion, and even though I go to jail because of prejudice, I will have left behind for our generations a record of injustice that will be our guide in the future rise of Ethiopia's glory. Nevertheless, I believe that the higher courts of this country will not mingle prejudice with justice and condemn a man simply because he is black and attempts to do good for his race and his fellow men.

Whatsoever happens, the world may know that the jail or penitentiary has no terrors for me. Guilty men are afraid of jail, but I am as much at home in jail for the cause of human rights as I am in my drawing room, the only difference being that I have not my good wife's company even as I know how glad she would have been to share my lot, but hers must be a life of sacrifice also, painful though it be. When my life is fully given for the cause, and she is left behind, I trust that you will give her the consideration that is due a faithful and devoted wife, who gave up her husband for the cause of human service. During my trial cowards tried to blemish her character, but it is an accepted truth that character is not blemished from without; it is from within, and the noblest souls that ever peopled this world were those maligned and outraged by the vile and wicked.

Service to my race is an undying passion with me, so the greater the persecution, the greater my determination to serve.

As leader of the Universal Negro Improvement Association, of which the Black Star Line was an auxiliary, I must state that the millions of our members in this country and abroad look to America as a national friend, and, citizens and residents as we are, we are jealous of her fair name among the other nations of the world and zealous in the effort to be to her loyal and true.

The Universal Negro Improvement Association seeks to do for Africa similarly what the Pilgrims and later, George Washington sought to do for America. We Negroes want a government of our own in Africa, so that we can be nationally, if not industrially and commercially, removed from competition in race, a condition that will make both races better friends, with malice toward none, but respect and appreciation for each.

Our greatest trouble, however, is with our own people. There are some in the race who are not in sympathy with an independent Negro nation. To them "they have lost nothing in Africa." They believe in the amalgamation of races for the production of new racial and national types; hence their doctrine of social equality and the creating of a new American race. Feeling as they do, divides us into two separate and distinct schools of thought, and, apparently, we are now at war with each other, and they have gained the first victory in having me (through their misrepresentation) indicted and convicted for the purpose of rendering me *hors de combat*.

We who believe in race purity are going to fight the issue out for the salvation of both races, and this can only be satisfactorily done when we have established for the Negro a nation of his own. We believe that the white race should protect itself against racial contamination, and the Negro should do the same. Nature intended us morally (and may I not say socially?) apart, otherwise there never would have been this difference. Our sins will not make the world better; hence, to us of the Universal Negro Improvement Association the time has come to rebuild our ancient and proud race.

My personal suffering for the program of the Universal Negro Improvement Association is but a drop in the bucket of sacrifice. To correct the evils surrounding our racial existence is to undertake a task as pretentious and difficult as dividing the sea or uprooting the Rock of Gibraltar; but, with the grace of God, all things are possible, for in truth there is prophecy that "Ethiopia shall stretch forth her hand, and Princes shall come out of Egypt."

We are expecting the co-operation and support of liberal White America in the promulgation of the ideal of race purity, and the founding of a nation for Negroes in Africa, so that those who, after proper industrial and other adjustments, desire to return to their original native homeland can do so in peace and security.

Now that the world is readjusting itself and political changes and distributions are being made of the earth's surface, there is absolutely no reason why certain parts of Africa should not be set aside absolutely for the Negro race as our claim and heritage. If this is not done, then we may as well look forward to eternal confusion among the races.

Negro men will never always feel satisfied with being ruled, governed and dictated to by other races. As in my case, I would never feel absolutely satisfied with being tried and judged by a white judge, district attorney and jury, for it is impossible for them to correctly interpret the real feelings of my race and appreciate my effort in their behalf; hence, the prejudice from which I suffer. A white man before a black district attorney, judge and jury would feel the same way, and thus we have the great problem that can only be solved by giving the Negro a government of his own. The Black Star Line was an effort in this direction and bore a relationship to the Universal Negro Improvement Association as the Shipping Board does to the government. My effort was not correctly understood, and that is why some people have become prejudiced toward me. Yet in the final presentation of truth the fair-minded is bound to come to the conclusion that the program of the Universal Negro Improvement Association is reasonable and proper for the solution of the vexed question of races.

The Sign by Which We Conquer

"There is no doubt about it that the man who
is doing right is never fearful of anything."

Liberty Hall, New York City
September 16, 1923

The Negro World,
September 22, 1923

MY subject for tonight is "The Sign by Which We Conquer." Perseverance and determination on the part of any people lead ultimately to the goal which they seek. That you are here this evening and hundreds of thousands and millions probably of Negroes are so assembled in different parts of the world in mass meetings tonight carrying out the exercises of the Universal Negro Improvement Association is proof that perseverance and determination will ultimately bring about success for any people.

When we started our movement a few years ago with just a few, the world of other men spurned us, laughed at us, and said that we were wasting time because we could not impress the world. Today that opinion has changed. It has been changed because of the perseverance of the few and the determination of the few. They persevered long enough until they were able to impress not only their immediate community but attract the entire world. And tonight the organization that a few founded four and a half years or five years ago has become the talk of the world and has made such an impress on the world that statesmen everywhere, not only in America but throughout civilization, are worried as to the outcome. We are conscious ourselves what the outcome will be. The outcome for us will be nothing more and nothing less than an independent government for Negroes. {*Applause.*}

It was that vision that attracted us five years ago when just thirteen or a few more of us founded this organization; it is the same vision that attracts us now that we are six million organized; it is the same vision that will attract us until we have completely brought into the fold—if not in active labor, with sentiment and sympathy—the 400,000,000 Negroes of our race. {*Applause.*}

My imprisonment for three months was one of the avenues through which we would get our program presented to the world; and I was not sorry one bit to contribute in that direction to at least impress the world some more about the seriousness of the Universal Negro Improvement Association. That impression of seriousness—the compliment of it is for you, not for me, in that I was placed in a position that I could not help myself more than to write to the world; but that could not move men. The impress that was made upon the world for the last three months was made by you—by your perseverance and by your determination.

The world knows that human achievements and human movements are carried on not by everybody but by the direction of those who lead, and the strategy of a few people has always sought to remove the leaders of movements and if successfully cornered they calculate they would destroy the movement.

Well, they were experimenting with me. They put me in jail to try out if they could destroy the Universal Negro Improvement Association and then they found a greater Universal Negro Improvement Association. {*Applause.*} Now I suppose they will change their tactics; nevertheless the three months has convinced me everywhere that the new Negro is here. Now, what they did to me for three months with the intention of destroying the movement represented by me would have succeeded in another age, and another time prior to this. Ten years ago—twenty-five years ago, if anyone attempted to start a movement as big probably as the Universal Negro Improvement Association and they did what they did to me, naturally as from the attitude of the Negro himself they would have destroyed the movement; but that was the time of the old Negro. They had the plan all right, but they worked the plan in the wrong time. If they had worked that plan ten years ago or fifteen years ago they would have succeeded, but they cannot crush the rising spirit of the Negro in the twentieth century by sending him to jail. They cannot crush the rising spirit of the Negro of the twentieth century by holding a club over his head; you cannot crush the rising spirit of the twentieth century Negro by drawing his blood. The more you do these things the more he will fight. {*Applause.*}

And the Universal Negro Improvement Association has not started yet. Now I am one of those in the Association that know what we are doing, because I happen to be one of the leaders, and we have not started anything yet; we have not done anything yet. Up to now we are just good Sabbath school children; and if acting like good Sabbath school children we create an unrest among other folks, what will happen when we start to behave like men? {*Laughter and applause.*}

There is no doubt about it that the man who is doing right is never fearful of anything. I do not see why the world should be worried about the Universal Negro Improvement Association and worried about Marcus Garvey. If the world has not done anything to Negroes why should it be worried about the activity of Negroes? The world must know that we as a people are not seeking to create any disturbance—to affect the peace of communities and the harmony of races. We are not disposed that way. We are too appreciative of other people's rights to go out of our way to offend them. We are too considerate of other people's happiness to go out of our way to create disturbance; therefore the world of honest people need not be afraid of us; but if there are any dishonest people in the world who have held or are holding what is belonging to other folks—if they have anything belonging to Negroes naturally they will be disturbed because Negroes are going after those things.

We are living in America, but I am speaking not only to you who live in America. As I speak from Liberty Hall I am speaking to Negroes all over the world. America claims she has nothing for us; and England says she has nothing for us; France says so, and the different European governments say they have nothing for us, and we hear some talk now that they have nothing for us in these parts; but we have decided that we have something for ourselves—that we possess something of ourselves, and we have understood that somebody has been keeping it for us. Now we are just about thanking them for being so good in keeping that which was belonging to us, and we are just asking them to cease their kindness for a while and hand over to us what is belonging to us. If somebody gave you something to keep for me and you are honest, when I approach you, you will give it to me. They said we were heathens; we were pagans; we were savages and did not know how to take care of ourselves; that we did not have any religion; we did not have any culture; we did not have any civilization for all those centuries, and that is why they had to be our guardians. Well, we are satisfied that they were our guardians for all this while, because we did not have the civilization; we did not have the culture; we did not have the Christianity. But thank God we have them all now, as we are asking that you hand back to us our own civilization—hand back to us that which you have robbed and exploited us of in the name of God and Christianity for the last 500 years. We are asking England to hand it back; we are asking France to hand it back; we are asking Italy to hand it back; we are asking Belgium to hand it back; we are asking Portugal to hand it back; we are asking Spain to hand it back, and by God, the Moroccans made them hand it back. {*Great applause.*} And if you will not hear the voice of a friend crying out in the wilderness to hand back those things, then, remember, one day you will find, marching down the avenue of time, 400,000,000 black men and women ready to give up, even the last drop of their blood, for the redemption of their motherland, Africa. {*Great applause.*} If you don't want us in Johnstown, Pa.; if you don't want us in Tulsa; if you don't want us in East St. Louis, we want ourselves where we want to be, and we are not going to remain here and create any trouble longer than is necessary. We are not going to leave now. All of us didn't come at the same time and, therefore, all of us won't leave at the same time. {*Laughter.*} They took time bringing us here; so we will take time going there. Some of us have to take our clothes out of pawn {*laughter*}; some of us have to sell our property before we can go. So naturally, we cannot all go at the same time; and then the Black Star Line has not sufficient ships yet. {*Applause.*}

You know they have a peculiar, a queer notion about the Black Star Line. Some people say the Black Star Line has failed. Now, stars don't fall every day. {*Laughter.*} Like the sun, sometimes they go into eclipse, but they come out again, don't they? And sometimes they shine more brilliantly than at other times. And when the Black Star Line comes back she is going to shine for ever more. {*Deafening applause.*} The Black Star Line is the rising hope of a race. And we have placed that star in the firmament of stars. And the Black Star Line shall only fall when the great firmament of stars has passed away. Don't be discouraged. We have been temporarily embarrassed because we did not know ourselves. Believe me, I did not know the Negro when I started to work with the Negro. I had a mistaken notion of the Negro. I believed all Negroes felt like me. What I suffered from the other fellow, what I went through at the hands of the other fellow I thought every Negro went through the same suffering and hardship and felt like me. But all Negroes did not feel like us. We have to sort ourselves. And the big mistake we made in the Black Star Line was that we believed when we started everybody felt like us. But we now know we have a lot of sorting to do, and once bitten we shall be twice shy. So that those of us who are stockholders in the Black Star Line, you need not lose heart. And I trust none of you will tear up your stock certificates or give them away, because these very stock certificates you think little of now will turn up like the German mark twenty years from now. You cannot keep a good thing down. You cannot destroy a good thought. You cannot destroy great minds, great characters. The whole world laughs at Germany now because the mark is low, but the German mind is not low, but the mind of the black man is still active and idealistic. Before you can successfully destroy the Black Star Line, even as before you can successfully destroy German activities, you must destroy the minds of men. Imprisonment cannot destroy that. You cannot destroy the mind. You can only imprison the body. The mind is ever active.

It is impossible at this time to tell any person in the world to hold the minds of the twentieth century Negro. They may as well keep us out of jail as in jail. The thing has gotten away from them. You know we told them, "The more you look, the less you see"; and they were looking in one direction and not in the other. They thought Garvey was the whole show. {*Laughter.*} But they did not seem to know that we have some Garveys scattered all around, and all of them are not in America either. The most of them are now in Africa and raising hell down there. {*Loud applause.*} The thing has gotten away from them, and even if Garvey wanted to call it back it cannot come back. {*Laughter.*} Can't come back. It has gone too far.

But, men, remember this. You at this time can only be destroyed by yourselves, from within and not from without. You have reached the point where the victory is to be won from within and can only be lost from within. The time has come when we have, as I said a while ago, to sort ourselves. I have been placed recently in a very embarrassing position. I have no secrets to keep from you or anybody. I like frankness, honesty of expression of thought and deed. I calculated when I started this movement that we would have worked together and kept our own counsel as a race of people without mixing much with other folks, without going to other folks, and I was successful in keeping to that policy up to three months ago. I calculated that not until the proper time had we to approach the other fellow and tell him what we wanted. That time naturally would come. We could not do everything on this side of the Atlantic without ultimately telling the white man what we want. But I believed the time had not come yet. I do not believe in doing anything prematurely, and I calculated we would have just worked among ourselves until we were ready and then gone to the other fellow and said, "We are ready, and we are asking you to let us come to terms and get this thing done." But, apparently, some of our folks are forcing us to talk with the other fellow before the time comes.

You know we are in a white man's country, not a black man's country. That is our disadvantage, and you can't very well move around the other fellow's country without telling him what you are doing. He becomes suspicious. And we have been moving around for all these years not even paying the other fellow the compliment of letting him know what we are doing. And, because of that, others went and lied and told what we were not doing and got me into a pickle and you in a bad fix. Every fellow believed he was doing a great deed when he started to talk and tell. Well, there are two sides to a story. They told and they thought by telling they would have done us a great deal of harm. They caused me to be sent to jail for five years and caused you to have to put up $5,000 to get me out. But they alone are not going to do the talking. We are going to do some of the talking, too. It is going to be tell for tell. You understand what I mean. Our people are so wicked to themselves that they are not satisfied until they are telling the enemy something about themselves. And because they have resorted—the N.A.A.C.P., the African Blood Brotherhood, the Friends of Negro Freedom—because they have resorted to telling the white man what they do not know about the Universal Negro Improvement Association for the purpose of destroying us, we are not fools to keep our mouths closed, but we are not going to tell about them as they told about us. We are only forced to approach the white man quicker than we anticipated. We were only going to approach him when we were fully organized, but we cannot wait until that time, because, if we do, the enemy will destroy us. So if you see me talking to white folks now, you will know what for.

I am not going to let Du Bois, Weldon Johnson, or Pickens, or Randolph or Owen lie the Universal Negro Improvement Association out of its purpose of emancipating a race, redeeming a motherland. That means, we are going to play politics, too. And I am going to ask something of you. I did not intend to ask you so early, because I felt the time had not come yet. I was hoping in two, three, four, five or six years, politically, we would go to the President of the nation and to the different parties, the Republican and the Democratic and say, "Our program is six million of us want to go back to Africa. We want you to make it a plank in your platform." We wanted to do that in six years' time. But they are forcing it on us now. I am saying to you now: "Get registered wherever you are." If you are not citizens, for your own convenience and for the convenience of carrying on the program you must get naturalized. It won't do you any harm. It will do you a great deal of good, because when the final time comes, we are not going to beg this question, we are going to force it. And if the N.A.A.C.P. feels they can play politics with 200,000, we can play politics with 200,000,000. If they can get one man in jail with 200,000, we can get a dozen men in jail with 2,000,000. So now you quite understand if you see us talking to white folks and bringing them here, you know what we are up to. It is because the other fellow is trying to undermine the cause. And, remember, we are in a white man's country. That is why we have to play this game. We are hoping the time will come when we will be able to deal with our folks other than through the white man. I may not be living then, but my son may be a judge. {*Laughter.*} My son may be a warden of the Tombs some day and he may lock the Tombs and throw away the key. {*Laughter.*}

I thank you for this good humor and I have to thank you for your deep and sincere interest in me. I have no doubt about that . . . I was in no way doubtful during the three months I remained in the Tombs, because you expressed that interest in me day by day. I must thank you for the loans you made to raise my bail bond so that I could be with you tonight and will be with you always. We are still in the fight. Be satisfied, however, that if one general goes down in the fight, other generals will rise. It is a fight that must be carried on, not for a day, not for a limited time, but for all time, and I feel sure that you appreciate the suffering of those who give themselves up for the cause that all of us do love. I thank you all, and I trust we will better understand ourselves and continue the great work for the good of the Universal Negro Improvement Association. {*Loud applause.*}

An Appeal to the Soul of White America

"The Negro must have a country and a nation of his own."

Youngstown, Ohio
October 2, 1923

The Philosophy and Opinions of Marcus Garvey, or Africa for the Africans,
Volume 2

SURELY the soul of liberal, philanthropic, liberty-loving, white America is not dead.

It is true that the glamour of materialism has, to a great degree, destroyed the innocence and purity of the national conscience, but, still, beyond our politics, beyond our soulless industrialism, there is a deep feeling of human sympathy that touches the soul of white America, upon which the unfortunate and sorrowful can always depend for sympathy, help and action.

It is to that feeling that I appeal for four hundred million Negroes of the world, and fifteen millions of America in particular.

There is no real white man in America who does not desire a solution of the Negro problem. Each thoughtful citizen has probably his own idea of how the vexed question of races should be settled. To some the Negro could be gotten rid of by wholesale butchery, by lynching, by economic starvation, by a return to slavery, and legalized oppression, while others would have the problem solved by seeing the race all herded together and kept somewhere among themselves; but a few—those in whom they have an interest—should be allowed to live around as the wards of a mistaken philanthropy; yet, none so generous as to desire to see the Negro elevated to a standard of real progress and prosperity, welded into a homogeneous whole, creating of themselves a mighty nation, with proper systems of government, civilization and culture, to mark them admissible to the fraternities of nations and races without any disadvantage.

I do not desire to offend the finer feelings and sensibilities of those white friends of the race who really believe that they are kind and considerate to us as a people; but I feel it my duty to make a real appeal to conscience and not to belief. Conscience is solid, convicting and permanently demonstrative; belief is only a matter of opinion, changeable by superior reasoning. Once the belief was that it was fit and proper to hold the Negro as a slave, and in this the bishop, priest and layman agreed. Later on, they changed their belief or opinion, but at all times, the conscience of certain people dictated to them that it was wrong and inhuman to hold human beings as slaves. It is to such a conscience in white America that I am addressing myself.

Negroes are human beings—the peculiar and strange opinions of writers, ethnologists, philosophers, scientists and anthropologists notwithstanding. They have feelings, souls, passions, ambitions, desires, just as other men, hence they must be considered.

Has white America really considered the Negro in the light of permanent human progress? The answer is NO.

Men and women of the white race, do you know what is going to happen if you do not think and act now? One of two things. You are either going to deceive and keep the Negro in your midst until you have perfectly completed your wonderful American civilization with its progress of art, science, industry and politics, and then, jealous of your own success and achievements in those directions, and with the greater jealousy of seeing your race pure and unmixed, cast him off to die in the whirlpool of economic starvation, thus getting rid of another race that was not intelligent enough to live, or, you simply mean by the largeness of your hearts to assimilate fifteen million Negroes into the social fraternity of an American race that will neither be white nor black! Don't be alarmed! We must prevent both consequences. No real race-loving white man wants to destroy the purity of his race, and no real Negro conscious of himself wants to die, hence there is room for an understanding, and an adjustment. And that is just what we seek.

Let white and black stop deceiving themselves. Let the white race stop thinking that all black men are dogs and not to be considered as human beings. Let foolish Negro agitators and so-called reformers, encouraged by deceptive or unthinking white associates, stop preaching and advocating the doctrine of "social equality," meaning thereby the social intermingling of both races, intermarriages, and general social co-relationship. The two extremes will get us nowhere, other than breeding hate, and encouraging discord, which will eventually end disastrously to the weaker race.

Some Negroes, in the quest of position and honor, have been admitted to the full enjoyment of their constitutional rights. Thus we have some of our men filling high and responsible government positions, others, on their own account, have established themselves in the professions, commerce and industry. This, the casual onlooker, and even the men themselves, will say carries a guarantee and hope of social equality, and permanent racial progress. But this is the mistake. There is no progress of the Negro in America that is permanent, so long as we have with us the monster evil—prejudice.

Prejudice we shall always have between black and white, so long as the latter believes that the former is intruding upon their rights. So long as white laborers believe that black laborers are taking and holding their jobs, so long as white artisans believe that black artisans are performing the work that they should do; so long as white men and women believe that black men and women are filling the positions that they covet; so long as white political leaders and statesmen believe that black politicians and statesmen are seeking the same positions in the nation's government; so long as white men believe that black men want to associate with and marry white women, then we will ever have prejudice, and not only prejudice, but riots, lynchings, burnings, and God to tell what next will follow!

It is this danger that drives me mad. It must be prevented. We cannot allow white and black to drift along unthinkingly toward this great gulf and danger that is nationally ahead of us. It is because of this that I speak, and now call upon the soul of great white America to help.

It is no use putting off. The work must be done, and it must be started now.

Some people have misunderstood me. Some don't want to understand me. But I must explain myself for the good of the world and humanity.

Those of the Negro race who preach social equality and who are working for an American race that will, in complexion, be neither white nor black, have tried to misinterpret me to the white public, and create prejudice against my work. The white public, not stopping to analyze and question the motive behind criticisms and attacks, aimed against new leaders and their movements, condemn without even giving a chance to the criticized, to be heard. Those of my own race who oppose me because I refuse to endorse their program of social arrogance and social equality, gloat over the fact that by their misrepresentation and under-hand methods, they were able to have me convicted and imprisoned for a crime which they calculate will so discredit me as to destroy the movement that I represent, in opposition to their program of a new American race; but we will not now consider the opposition to a program or a movement, but state the facts as they are, and let deep souled white America pass its own judgment.

In another one hundred years white America will have doubled its population; in another two hundred years it will have trebled itself. The keen student must realize that the centuries ahead will bring us an over-crowded country; opportunities, as the population grows larger, will be fewer; the competition for bread between the people of their own class will become keener, and so much more so will there be no room for two competitive races, the one strong and the other weak. To imagine Negroes as district attorneys, judges, senators, congressmen, assemblymen, aldermen, government clerks and officials, artisans and laborers at work, while millions of white men starve, is to have before you the bloody picture of wholesale mob violence that I fear, and against which I am working.

No preaching, no praying, no presidential edict will control the passion of hungry unreasoning men of prejudice when the hour comes. It will not come, I pray, in our generation, but it is of the future that I think and for which I work.

A generation of ambitious Negro men and women, out from the best colleges, universities and institutions, capable of filling the highest and best positions in the nation, in industry, commerce, society and politics! Can you keep them back? If you do so they will agitate and throw your constitution in your faces. Can you stand before civilization and deny the truth of your constitution? What are you going to do then? You who are just will open the door of opportunity and say to all and sundry, "Enter in." But, ladies and gentlemen, what about the mob, that starving crowd of your own race? Will they stand by, suffer and starve, and allow an opposite, competitive race to prosper in the midst of their distress? If you can conjure these things up in your mind, then you have the vision of the race problem of the future in America.

There is but one solution, and that is to provide an outlet for Negro energy, ambition, and passion, away from the attractions of white opportunity and surround the race with opportunities of its own. If this is not done, and if the foundation for same is not laid now, then the consequence will be sorrowful for the weaker race, and disgraceful to our ideals of justice, and shocking to our civilization.

The Negro must have a country and a nation of his own. If you laugh at the idea, then you are selfish and wicked, for you and your children do not intend that the Negro shall discommode you in yours. If you do not want him to have a country and a nation of his own; if you do not intend to give him equal opportunities in yours, then it is plain to see that you mean that he must die, even as the Indian, to make room for your generations.

Why should the Negro die? Has he not served America and the world? Has he not borne the burden of civilization in this Western world for three hundred years? Has he not contributed of his best to America? Surely all this stands to his credit. But there will not be enough room and the one answer is "find a place." We have found a place; it is Africa, and as black men for three centuries have helped white men build America, surely generous and grateful white men will help black men build Africa.

And why shouldn't Africa and America travel down the ages as protectors of human rights and guardians of democracy? Why shouldn't black men help white men secure and establish universal peace? We can only have peace when we are just to all mankind; and for that peace, and for the reign of universal love, I now appeal to the soul of white America. Let the Negroes have a government of their own. Don't encourage them to believe that they will become social equals and leaders of the whites in America, without first on their own account proving to the world that they are capable of evolving a civilization of their own. The white race can best help the Negro by telling him the truth and not by flattering him into believing that he is as good as any white man without first proving the racial, national, constructive mettle of which he is made.

Stop flattering the Negro about social equality, and tell him to go to work and build for himself. Help him in the direction of doing for himself, and let him know that self-progress brings its own reward.

I appeal to the considerate and thoughtful conscience of white America not to condemn the cry of the Universal Negro Improvement Association for a nation in Africa for Negroes, but to give us a chance to explain ourselves to the world. White America is too big and, when informed and touched, too liberal to turn down the cry of the awakened Negro for "a place in the sun."

What We Believe

"The Universal Negro Improvement Association advocates the uniting and blending of all Negroes into one strong, healthy race."

New York City,
January 1, 1924

The Philosophy and Opinions of Marcus Garvey, or Africa for the Africans,
Volume 2

THE Universal Negro Improvement Association advocates the uniting and blending of all Negroes into one strong, healthy race. It is against miscegenation and race suicide.

It believes that the Negro race is as good as any other, and therefore should be as proud of itself as others are.

It believes in the purity of the Negro race and the purity of the white race.

It is against rich blacks marrying poor whites.

It is against rich or poor whites taking advantage of Negro women.

It believes in the spiritual Fatherhood of God and the Brotherhood of Man.

It believes in the social and political physical separation of all peoples to the extent that they promote their own ideals and civilization, with the privilege of trading and doing business with each other. It believes in the promotion of a strong and powerful Negro nation in Africa.

It believes in the rights of all men.

UNIVERSAL NEGRO IMPROVEMENT ASSOCIATION.
MARCUS GARVEY, President-General.

In Honor of the Return to America of the Delegation Sent to Europe and Africa by the U.N.I.A. to Negotiate for the Repatriation of Negroes to a Homeland of Their Own in Africa

"Africa is the legitimate, moral and righteous home of all Negroes, and . . . the time is coming for all to assemble under their own vine and fig tree . . ."

Madison Square Garden,
New York City, March 16, 1924

The Philosophy and Opinions of Marcus Garvey, or Africa for the Africans,
Volume 2

FELLOW Citizens:

THE coming together, all over this country, of fully six million people of Negro blood, to work for the creation of a nation of their own in their motherland, Africa, is no joke.

There is now a world revival of thought and action, which is causing peoples everywhere to bestir themselves towards their own security, through which we hear the cry of Ireland for the Irish, Palestine for the Jew, Egypt for the Egyptian, Asia for the Asiatic, and thus we Negroes raise the cry of Africa for the Africans, those at home and those abroad.

Some people are not disposed to give us credit for having feelings, passions, ambitions and desires like other races; they are satisfied to relegate us to the back-heap of human aspirations; but this is a mistake. The Almighty Creator made us men, not unlike others, but in His own image; hence, as a race, we feel that we, too, are entitled to the rights that are common to humanity.

The cry and desire for liberty is justifiable, and is made holy everywhere. It is sacred and holy to the Anglo-Saxon, Teuton and Latin; to the Anglo-American it precedes that of all religions, and now come the Irish, the Jew, the Egyptian, the Hindoo, and, last but not least, the Negro, clamoring for their share as well as their right to be free.

All men should be free—free to work out their own salvation. Free to create their own destinies. Free to nationally build up themselves for the upbringing and rearing of a culture and civilization of their own. Jewish culture is different from Irish culture. Anglo-Saxon culture is unlike Teutonic culture. Asiatic culture differs greatly from European culture; and, in the same way, the world should be liberal enough to allow the Negro latitude to develop a culture of his own. Why should the Negro be lost among the other races and nations of the world and to himself? Did nature not make of him a son of the soil? Did the Creator not fashion him out of the dust of the earth?—out of that rich soil to which he bears such a wonderful resemblance?—a resemblance that changes not, even though the ages have flown? No, the Ethiopian cannot change his skin; and so we appeal to the conscience of the white world to yield us a place of national freedom among the creatures of present-day temporal materialism.

We Negroes are not asking the white man to turn Europe and America over to us. We are not asking the Asiatic to turn Asia over for the accommodation of the blacks. But we are asking a just and righteous world to restore Africa to her scattered and abused children.

We believe in justice and human love. If our rights are to be respected, then, we, too, must respect the rights of all mankind; hence, we are ever ready and willing to yield to the white man the things that are his, and we feel that he, too, when his conscience is touched, will yield to us the things that are ours.

We should like to see a peaceful, prosperous and progressive white race in America and Europe; a peaceful, prosperous and progressive yellow race in Asia, and, in like manner, we want, and we demand, a peaceful, prosperous and progressive black race in Africa. Is that asking too much? Surely not. Humanity, without any immediate human hope of racial oneness, has drifted apart, and is now divided into separate and distinct groups, each with its own ideals and aspirations. Thus, we cannot expect any one race to hold a monopoly of creation and be able to keep the rest satisfied.

From our distinct racial group idealism we feel that no black man is good enough to govern the white man, and no white man good enough to rule the black man; and so of all races and peoples. No one feels that the other, alien in race, is good enough to govern or rule to the exclusion of native racial rights. We may as well, therefore, face the question of superior and inferior races. In twentieth-century civilization there are no inferior or superior races. There are backward peoples, but that does not make them inferior. As far as humanity goes, all men are equal, and especially where peoples are intelligent enough to know what they want. At this time all peoples know what they want—it is liberty. When a people have sense enough to know that they ought to be free, then they naturally become the equal of all in the higher calling of man to know and direct himself. It is true that economically and scientifically certain races are more progressive than others; but that does not imply superiority. For the Anglo-Saxon to say that he is superior because he introduced submarines to destroy life, or the Teuton because he compounded liquid gas to outdo in the art of killing, and that the Negro is inferior because he is backward in that direction is to leave one's self open to the retort "Thou shalt not kill," as being the divine law that sets the moral standard of the real man. There is no superiority in the one race economically monopolizing and holding all that would tend to the sustenance of life, and thus cause unhappiness and distress to others; for our highest purpose should be to love and care for each other, and share with each other the things that our Heavenly Father has placed at our common disposal; and even in this, the African is unsurpassed, in that he feeds his brother and shares with him the product of the land. The idea of race superiority is questionable; nevertheless, we must admit that, from the white man's standard, he is far superior to the rest of us, but that kind of superiority is too inhuman and dangerous to be permanently helpful. Such a superiority was shared and indulged in by other races before, and even by our own, when we boasted of a wonderful civilization on the banks of the Nile, when others were still groping in darkness; but because of our unrighteousness it failed, as all such will. Civilization can only last when we have reached the point where we will be our brother's keeper. That is to say, when we feel it righteous to live and let live.

Let no black man feel that he has the exclusive right to the world, and other men none, and let no white man feel that way, either. The world is the property of all mankind, and each and every group is entitled to a portion. The black man now wants his, and in terms uncompromising he is asking for it.

The Universal Negro Improvement Association represents the hopes and aspirations of the awakened Negro. Our desire is for a place in the world; not to disturb the tranquillity of other men, but to lay down our burden and rest our weary backs and feet by the banks of the Niger, and sing our songs and chant our hymns to the God of Ethiopia. Yes, we want rest from the toil of centuries, rest of political freedom, rest of economic and industrial liberty, rest to be socially free and unmolested, rest from lynching and burning, rest from discrimination of all kinds.

Out of slavery we have come with our tears and sorrows, and we now lay them at the feet of American white civilization. We cry to the considerate white people for help, because in their midst we can scarce help ourselves. We are strangers in a strange land. We cannot sing, we cannot play on our harps, for our hearts are sad. We are sad because of the tears of our mothers and the cry of our fathers. Have you not heard the plaintive wail? It is your father and my father burning at stake; but, thank God, there is a larger humanity growing among the good and considerate white people of this country, and they are going to help. They will help us to recover our souls.

As children of captivity we look forward to a new day and a new, yet ever old, land of our fathers, the land of refuge, the land of the Prophets, the land of the Saints, and the land of God's crowning glory. We shall gather together our children, our treasures and our loved ones, and, as the children of Israel, by the command of God, faced the promised land, so in time we shall also stretch forth our hands and bless our country.

Good and dear America that has succored us for three hundred years knows our story. We have watered her vegetation with our tears for two hundred and fifty years. We have built her cities and laid the foundation of her imperialism with the mortar of our blood and bones for three centuries, and now we cry to her for help. Help us, America, as we helped you. We helped you in the Revolutionary War. We helped you in the Civil War, and, although Lincoln helped us, the price is not half paid. We helped you in the Spanish-American War. We died nobly and courageously in Mexico, and did we not leave behind us on the stained battlefields of France and Flanders our rich blood to mark the poppies' bloom, and to bring back to you the glory of the flag that never touched the dust? We have no regrets in service to America for three hundred yers, but we pray that America will help us for another fifty years until we have solved the troublesome problem that now confronts us. We know and realize that two ambitious and competitive races cannot live permanently side by side, without friction and trouble, and that is why the white race wants a white America and the black race wants and demands a black Africa.

Let white America help us for fifty years honestly, as we have helped her for three hundred years, and before the expiration of many decades there shall be no more race problem. Help us to gradually go home, America. Help us as you have helped the Jews. Help us as you have helped the Irish. Help us as you have helped the Poles, Russians, Germans and Armenians.

The Universal Negro Improvement Association proposes a friendly co-operation with all honest movements seeking intelligently to solve the race problem. We are not seeking social equality; we do not seek intermarriage, nor do we hanker after the impossible. We want the right to have a country of our own, and there foster and re-establish a culture and civilization exclusively ours. Don't say it can't be done. The Pilgrims and colonists did it for America, and the new Negro, with sympathetic help, can do it for Africa.

The thoughtful and industrious of our race want to go back to Africa, because we realize it will be our only hope of permanent existence. We cannot all go in a day or year, ten or twenty years. It will take time under the rule of modern economics, to entirely or largely depopulate a country of a people who have been its residents for centuries, but we feel that, with proper help for fifty years, the problem can be solved. We do not want all the Negroes in Africa. Some are no good here, and naturally will be no good there. The no-good Negro will naturally die in fifty years. The Negro who is wrangling about and fighting for social equality will naturally pass away in fifty years, and yield his place to the progressive Negro who wants a society and country of his own.

Negroes are divided into two groups, the industrious and adventurous, and the lazy and dependent. The industrious and adventurous believe that whatsoever others have done it can do. The Universal Negro Improvement Association belongs to this group, and so you find us working, six million strong, to the goal of an independent nationality. Who will not help? Only the mean and despicable "who never to himself hath said, this is my own, my native land." Africa is the legitimate, moral and righteous home of all Negroes, and now that the time is coming for all to assemble under their own vine and fig tree, we feel it our duty to arouse every Negro to a consciousness of himself.

White and black will learn to respect each other when they cease to be active competitors in the same countries for the same things in politics and society. Let them have countries of their own, wherein to aspire and climb without rancor. The races can be friendly and helpful to each other, but the laws of nature separate us to the extent of each and every one developing by itself.

We want an atmosphere all our own. We would like to govern and rule ourselves and not be encumbered and restrained. We feel now just as the white race would feel if they were governed and ruled by the Chinese. If we live in our own districts, let us rule and govern those districts. If we have a majority in our communities, let us run those communities. We form a majority in Africa and we should naturally govern ourselves there. No man can govern another's house as well as himself. Let us have fair play. Let us have justice. This is the appeal we make to white America.

The Work Started

"You are not going to Africa like the Pilgrim Fathers
came to America. Nobody invited them to America."

Liberty Hall, New York City
June 4, 1924

The Negro World,
June 14, 1924

WE ARE making history tonight. It is the brightest chapter in the history
of the Universal Negro Improvement Association. Tonight we finally
send away to Africa a serious and well-prepared group of men. To do
what? To visit Africa? No. This group of men go to the historic country of Liberia, a country founded a little over one hundred years ago by
another serious and responsible group of people, for the purpose of
encouraging a work just like this.

It was in the minds of the people who constituted the American
Colonization Society over one hundred years ago that this hour would
come in the history of the black people, in the development of the black
people in the only independent nation on the West Coast of Africa. The
people who live in Liberia today are blood of our blood and flesh of our
flesh, especially the ruling element, the Americo-West Indian Liberians.
They represent in Liberia today the offspring of an earlier generation of
Negroes who went from this country and from the West Indies one hundred years ago, eighty years ago, fifty years ago, one-quarter of a century
ago to make it possible to find and have freedom, a freedom that would,
indeed, be worthwhile not only for themselves, but for the rest of their
kind. And the hour has come.

Years ago, a small group of Negroes left this country. Some went from
Maryland, some from the Carolinas, to found that new home that they
call Liberia, the Liberia that is now attracting us. They got together there
and they made laws among themselves, imitative of the laws of this great
republic, for the purpose of insuring and perpetuating their society.
Coming down the ages they have developed it to the extent that today
Liberia is one of the recognized nations of the world. Her constitution
is as liberal and as modern as that of any other nation, only that in that
constitution and in the laws they made, because they had an eye to the
future, an eye to this hour, they saw to it that the constitution was
so made and the law was so constructed that that country would be
preserved not only for them, but their children and for succeeding
generations of Negroes exclusively. So much so, that because of these
protecting laws they were able to keep out alien intruders, alien self-

seekers who desired to have robbed them of their country years ago under the guise of friendship and diplomacy. But because of the keenness of our fathers who founded the Liberian Republic, and because of their loyalty to their race and to their native land, Africa, they held that country even against odds, tremendous difficulties, insomuch that the world seems to misunderstand them to the extent of saying that for one hundred years they have done nothing.

But if they have done nothing, they had a method in not doing anything. There was a method in their madness. If they had attempted to do anything, the something that the outer world desired, there would have been no Liberia today, and there would have been no free country on the continent of Africa. But we are satisfied with what our fathers did, what the rulers and directors of Liberia have done for the one hundred years they have occupied the country. They have been able to arouse the sleeping consciousness of the four hundred million Negroes of the world to go to the rescue, to help build Liberia and make her one of the greatest nations of the world.

And we are going to do it. The answer of the six million active members of the Universal Negro Improvement Association in the Western world, the answer of the four hundred million Negroes who have got the vision of the Universal Negro Improvement Association is that, "Yes, we are going to do it." And I feel sure that with the men we are sending out as forerunners in practical work, in practical achievement, give us twenty-five years and we will compel the world to change its opinion about the backwardness of Liberia and the inability of the Negro to demonstrate the ability of government.

We are asking the world for a fair chance. That is all we ask for. We are asking the world for a fair chance to assist the people of Liberia in developing that country, as the world is giving the Jew a fair chance to develop Palestine. And, if they do not give us a fair chance, we are going to raise hell. {*Applause.*} The world will have to make room for us or we will realize the world has no sympathy for us, and if we must die we may as well die fighting with our backs to the wall. But I feel sure a sensible world will not inflict that much upon us because the world ought to know that the Negro, like everybody else, is entitled to just, liberal and fair consideration. That is all we ask. We ask that of liberal America. We ask America to help us in this enterprise. As they have helped different countries of Europe, Russia, France, Belgium, Serbia, so do we ask the liberal white man of America to help the Universal Negro Improvement Association put over this program for the development of a country of our own in Africa. We ask the liberal minds of Europe for the same consideration that they have shown to other people seeking self-development.

We are going there on a peaceful mission, a mission for the industrial, agricultural, commercial and cultural development of that country. We want to prove our worth. And, surely, men, we are going to prove it. We have already demonstrated our worth in helping others to climb the ladder of success. We have splendidly helped America for 300 years to her position in the world today. We have splendidly helped the British Empire for over 300 years to her position. We have for nearly 300-odd years helped France build the French Empire, and we are asking them for nothing more than for their friendly encouragement and consideration in this program of self-help.

We want to help ourselves, and we feel sure that when the appeal is made to the conscience of America, America will respond to us as we responded to the call of America. We have never failed America in any circumstances. From the revolutionary period to this we have been willing and ready to answer the call of America, the adopted home of 15,000,000 of us. We have never failed the British when they called. From the time of the Ashanti war, from the time of the Zulu war, to the war of 1918, British Negroes, millions of them, never failed the British and their call to service and to help. The Negroes have never failed the French. From the first days of French colonizing in Africa to the guard on the Rhine, the French Negro never failed to hearken to the call of France. And, now, we are making a similar appeal, a similar call for help to these great peoples and these great nations. If they hear us not, it is because they have lost the sense of humanity, it is because they have lost the sense of justice and fair play. And if their souls are so dead, surely we will not be responsible for the consequences in dealing with dead souls.

We are a serious group of people just at this time. We want a chance to live because we know that if we do not exert ourselves to live we are bound to die, and we are not going to allow anybody to kill us before our time. We know the consequences if we do not start out on our own initiative and our own account. And that is why we do not understand our critics and those who seem to condemn us. What do they mean? Do they mean we must sit down and prepare ourselves to die as the world intends weak and inactive people to do? They cannot be our friends if they do not want us to be active and up and doing. But we count our friends by the million, outside even this race of ours because the world must be sober enough to understand in an age like this you cannot keep so many people down, four hundred millions of them. Some of us at least are alive to this, and the Universal Negro Improvement Association is thinking for the race, and we are presenting the program for the Negro, the program of self-development and initiative. We are going to try it, at least, if nothing more. I feel sure, men and women, that as these men go away from us in a few days they will take with them our best wishes and our united determination to stand by them to the last. So long as I am President-General, they shall be in want of nothing in their desire to carry out the program of the Universal Negro Improvement Association. {*Applause.*}

They are going, I say, to do serious work. They are going to prepare for the group of those of us who will sail from this country in another few months. As you know, we are preparing that the first group of colonists sail from New York in September. They will arrive in Liberia around the first week in October. By the time these men sail and land and by the time you get there these men are supposed to have ready for you certain accommodations. You are not going to Africa like the Pilgrim Fathers came to America. Nobody invited them to America. They came of their own accord and they did not know where they were going, and the storm drove them around the New England coast, and they got off the boats and made the trees their home, and they lived in and under those trees for a long while. Now, we have been invited home. We have been requested to come home, and then we have been told how to get ready to come home, and the sending of these experts is a part of the arrangements under which we are to go home. We are not going home to live under trees. We are going home, and when we get off the boat these men are going to have ready for us temporary homes in which we will live until we build permanently for ourselves. And please leave your native laziness behind. {*Laughter.*} Don't think these men will furnish you with homes. You will get busy and build permanent homes of your own. Negroes like to pay too much rent anyhow. We will introduce a new system. We are going to pay so much rent. This engineer of ours is going to lay out plans whereby every industrious man and woman can have a home of his own when you get there. As I said before, we do not want any bums to go to Africa now. And if I have any friends who are bums, take my advice and stay where you are, because we will put you in jail. If you look up the engineer's plans you will find one of the first buildings to be erected is a jail. {*Laughter.*} The fellow who has a grudge or a spite against the other fellow's goods, please stay in Harlem, in America, and make the best you can with the Irish cop.

Leave that part of the white man's civilization in New York, in Harlem, in America, because we have a new civilization in Africa.

We have made arrangements whereby every industrious family going to Liberia will have twenty-five acres of land which you can develop agriculturally or industrially, and in addition to that you will get a free house lot in the city to build your home, and after you have built your house on it the government will give you a free title in fee simple for the occupation of the land. If you are single you will get fifteen acres of land. If you are a woman you will get ten acres for industrial or agricultural development and a free house lot. You will get five acres for every child you have. We have a list of thousands of people who want to go this year and next year. We want all to get busy. Work hard so that you can land in Liberia with at least two or three hundred dollars to start with, because a bum in Liberia is just as bad as a bum in Harlem. Society has no use for such a character at this time.* {*Loud applause.*}

The Negro Is Dying Out

"How can any Negro leader flatter us about progress and the rest of it, when the world is preparing more than ever to bury the entire race?"

The Fourth International Convention of the Negro Peoples of the World
Carnegie Hall, New York City,
August 1, 1924.

The Philosophy and Opinions of Marcus Garvey, or Africa for the Africans,
Volume 2

Delegates to the Fourth International Convention of the Negro
Peoples of the World, Ladies and Gentlemen:

THE pleasure of addressing you at this hour is great. You have re-assembled yourselves in New York, coming from all parts of the world to this Annual Convention, because you believe that by unity you can alleviate the unfortunate condition in which racially we find ourselves.

We are glad to meet as Negroes, notwithstanding the stigma that is placed upon us by a soulless and conscienceless world because of our backwardness.

As usual, I am not here to flatter you, I am not here to tell you how happy and prosperous we are as a people, because that is all false. The Negro is not happy, but, to the contrary, is extremely miserable. He is miserable because the world is closing fast around him, and if he does not strike out now for his own preservation, it is only a question of a few more decades when he will be completely out-done in a world of strenuous competition for a place among the fittest of God's creation.

The Negro is dying out, and he is going to die faster and more rapidly in the next fifty years than he has in the past three hundred years. There is only one thing to save the Negro, and that is an immediate realization of his own responsibilities. Unfortunately we are the most careless and indifferent people in the world! We are shiftless and irresponsible, and that is why we find ourselves the wards of an inherited materialism that has lost its soul and its

---

*Garvey misstated or misunderstood the position of Liberia, which did not invite or allow settlement by U.N.I.A. members.

conscience. It is strange to hear a Negro leader speak in this strain, as the usual course is flattery, but I would not flatter you to save my own life and that of my own family. There is no value in flattery. Flattery of the Negro for another quarter of a century will mean hell and damnation to the race. How can any Negro leader flatter us about progress and the rest of it, when the world is preparing more than ever to bury the entire race? Must I flatter you when England, France, Italy, Belgium and Spain are all concentrating on robbing every square inch of African territory—the land of our fathers? Must I flatter you when the cry is being loudly raised for a white America, Canada, Australia and Europe, and a yellow and brown Asia? Must I flatter you when I find all other peoples preparing themselves for the struggle to survive, and you still smiling, eating, dancing, drinking and sleeping away your time, as if yesterday were the beginning of the age of pleasure? I would rather be dead than be a member of your race without thought of the morrow, for it portends evil to him that thinketh not. Because I cannot flatter you I am here to tell, emphatically, that if we do not seriously reorganize ourselves as a people and face the world with a program of African nationalism our days in civilization are numbered, and it will be only a question of time when the Negro will be as completely and complacently dead as the North American Indian, or the Australian Bushman.

You talk about the progress we have made in America and elsewhere, among the people of our acquaintance, but what progress is it? A progress than can be snatched away from you in forty-eight hours, because it has been built upon sand.

You must thank God for the last two generations of whites in our western civilization; thank God that they were not made of sterner stuff, and character and a disposition to see all races their rivals and competitors in the struggle to hold and possess the world, otherwise, like the Indian, we would have been nearly all dead.

The progress of the Negro in our civilization was tolerated because of indifference, but that indifference exists no longer. Our whole civilization is becoming intolerant, and because of that the whole world of races has started to think.

Can you blame the white man for thinking, when red and yellow men are knocking at his door? Can you blame the tiger for being on the defensive when the lion approaches? And thus we find that generations ago, when the Negro was not given a thought as a world competitor he is now regarded as an encumbrance in a civilization to which he has materially contributed little. Men do not build for others, they build for themselves. The age and our religion demand it. What are you going to expect, that white men are going to build up America and elsewhere and hand it over to us? If we are expecting that we are crazy, we have lost our reason.

If you were white, you would see the rest in hell before you would deprive your children of bread and give it to others. You would give that which you did not want, but not that which is to be the sustenance of your family, and so the world thinks; yet a Du Bois and the National Association for the Advancement of Colored People will tell us by flattery that the day is coming when a white President of the United States of America will get out of the White House and give the position to a Negro, that the day is coming when a Mr. Hughes will desert the Secretaryship of State and give it to the Negro, James Weldon Johnson; that the time is just around the corner of constitutional rights when the next Ambassador to the Court of Saint James will be a black man from Mississippi or from North Carolina. Do you think that white men who have suffered, bled and died to make America and the world what it is are going to hand over to a parcel of lazy Negroes the things that they prize most?

Stop flattering yourselves, fellowmen, and let us go to work. Do you hear me? Go to work! Go to work in the morn of a new creation and strike, not because of the noonday sun, but plod on and on, until you have succeeded in climbing the hills of opposition and reached the height of self-progress, and from that pinnacle bestow upon the world a civilization of your own, and hand down to your children and posterity of your own a worthy contribution to the age of human materialism.

We of the Universal Negro Improvement Association are fair and just. We do not expect the white man to rob himself, and to deprive himself, for our racial benefit. How could you reasonably expect that, in an age like this, when men have divided themselves into racial and national groups, when the one group has its own interest to protect as against that of the other?

The laws of self-preservation force every human group to look after itself and protect its own interest; hence so long as the American white man or any other white man, for that matter, realizes his responsibility, he is bound to struggle to protect that which is his and his own, and I feel that the Negro today who has been led by the unscrupulous of our race has been grossly misguided, in the direction of expecting too much from the civilization of others.

Immediately after emancipation, we were improperly led in the South by this same group and ultimately lost our vote and voice. The carpetbagger and the thoughtless, selfish Negro politician and leader sold the race back into slavery. And the same attempt is now being made in the North by that original group, prompted by the dishonest white political boss and the unscrupulous Negro politician. The time has come for both races to seriously adjust their differences and settle the future of our respective peoples. The selfish of both races will not stop to think and act, but the responsibility becomes more so ours, who have the vision of the future.

Because of my attempt to lead my race into the only solution that I see would benefit both groups, I have been maliciously and wickedly maligned, and by members of our own race. I have been plotted against, framed up, indicted and convicted, the story which you so well know. That was responsible for our not having a Convention last year. I thank you, however, for the tribute you paid me during that period in postponing the Convention through respect to my enforced absence. Last August I spent three months in the Tombs in New York, but I was as happy then as I am now. I was sent there by the evil forces that have always fought and opposed reform movements, but I am as ready now to go back to the Tombs or elsewhere as I was when I was forced to leave you. The jail does not make a criminal, the criminal makes himself. There are more criminals out of jail than in jail, the only difference is that the majority of those who are out, are such skillful criminals that they know how to keep themselves out. They have tried to besmirch my name so as to prevent me doing the good that I desire to do in the interest of the race. It amuses me sometimes to hear the biggest crooks in the Negro race referring to me as a criminal. As I have said before, Negro race leaders are the biggest crooks in the world. It is because of their crookedness that we have not made more progress. If you think I am not telling the truth in this direction you may quiz any of the white political bosses, and those who will tell the truth will reveal a tale most shocking as far as our Negro leaders are concerned. This is true of the group of fellows of our race that lead universally as well as nationally. They will sell the souls of their mothers and their country into perdition. That is why the Universal Negro Improvement Association has to make such a fight, and that is why the opposition is as hard and marked. You can pay the Negro leader to hang his race and block every effort of self-help. This is not commonly so among other races. We must give credit to the great white race, to the extent that they will fight among themselves, that they will cheat each other in business, but when it approaches the future and destiny of the race, a halt is immediately called. Not so with the Negro; he does not know when and where to stop in hurting himself.

I repeat that we must reorganize ourselves as a people, if we are to go forward, and I take this opportunity, as you assemble yourselves here from all parts of the world, to sound the warning note.

To review the work of our Association for the past two years is to recount the exploits of a continuous struggle to reach the top. Our organization has been tested during the past two years beyond that of any other period in the history of Negro movements. I am glad to say, however, that we have survived all the intrigues, barriers, and handicaps placed in the way. Some of our enemies thought that they would have been able to crush our movement when I was convicted and sentenced to prison. They had depended upon that, as the trump card in their effort to crush the new spirit of freedom among Negroes, but like all such efforts, it was doomed to failure. I will bring to your recollection a similar effort made a little over nineteen hundred years ago when on Calvary's Mount, the Jews, after inspiring the Romans, attempted to crucify the man, Christ, the leader of the Christian religion. They thought that after the crucifixion, after he was buried, that they would have silenced the principles of Christianity forever, but how successful they were, is made manifest today when we find hundreds of millions of souls the world over professing the principles for which the man died on Calvary's cross. As in the rise of Christianity, so do we have the spiritual rise of the Universal Negro Improvement Association throughout the world. They tried to crucify it in America, and it has arisen in Africa a thousandfold. They tried to crucify it on the American continent, and it is now sweeping the whole world. You cannot crucify a principle; you cannot nail the souls of men to a cross; you cannot imprison it; you cannot bury it. It will rise like the spirit of the Great Redeemer and take its flight down the ages, until men far and near have taken up the cry for which the principle was crucified.

We of the Universal Negro Improvement Association are stronger today than we ever were before. We are strong in spirit, strong in determination; we are unbroken in every direction; we stand firm facing the world, determined to carve out and find a place for the four hundred millions of our suffering people. We call upon humanity everywhere to listen to the cry of the new Negro. We ask the human heart for a response, because Africa's sun cannot be downed. Africa's sun is rising, gradually rising, and soon shall take its place among the brilliant constellations of nations. The Negro wants a nation, nothing less, nothing more; and why shouldn't we be nationally free, nationally independent, nationally unfettered? We want a nationality similar to that of the English, the French, the Italian, the German, to that of the white American, to that of the yellow Japanese; we want nationality and government because we realize that the American nation in a short while will not be large enough to accommodate two competitive rivals, one black and the other white.

There is no doubt about it that the black man of America today aspires to the White House, to the Cabinet, and to the Senate, and the House. He aspires to be head of state and municipal governments. What are you going to do with him? He cannot be satisfied in the midst of a majority group that seeks to protect its interest at all hazards; then the only alternative is to give the Negro a place of his own. That is why we appeal to the sober white minds of America, and not the selfish ones. The selfish ones will see nothing more than the immediate present, but the deeply thinking white man will see the result of another fifty or one hundred years, when these two peoples will be brought together in closer contact of rivalry. As races we practically represent a similar intelligence today. We have graduated from the same schools, colleges and universities. What can you do with men who are equally and competently fitted in mind, but give them an equal chance, and if there is no chance of equality, there must be dissatisfaction on the one hand. That dissatisfaction we have in our midst now. We have it manifested by W. E. B. Du Bois, by James Weldon Johnson; we have it manifested by the organization known as the National Association for the Advancement of Colored People, that seeks to bring about social equality, political equality, and industrial equality, things that are guaranteed us under the Constitution, but which, in the face of a majority race, we cannot demand, because of the terrible odds against us. In the midst of this, then, what can we do but seek an outlet of our own, unless we intend to fight a losing game. Reason will dictate that there is no benefit to be derived from fighting always a losing game. We will lose until we have completely lost our stand in America.

To repeat myself, we talk about progress. What progress have we made when everything we do is done through the good will and grace of the liberal white man of the present day? But can he always afford to be liberal? Do you not realize that in another few decades he will have on his hands a problem of his own—a problem to feed his own children, to take care of his own flesh and blood? In the midst of that crisis, when he finds not even enough to feed himself, what will become of the Negro? The Negro naturally must die to give way, and make room for others who are better prepared to live. That is the danger, men; and that is why we have the Universal Negro Improvement Association. The condition that I have referred to will not only be true of America and of continental Europe; it will be true wherever the great white race lives. There will not be room enough for them, and others who seek to compete with them. That is why we hear the cry of Egypt for the Egyptians, India for the Indians, Asia for the Asiatics, and we raise the cry of Africa for the Africans; those at home and those abroad. That is why we ask England to be fair, to be just and considerate; that is why we ask France, Italy, Spain and Belgium to be fair, just and considerate; that is why we ask them to let the black man restore himself to his own country; and that is why we are determined to see it done. No camouflage, and no promise of good-will, will solve the problem. What guarantee have we, what lease have we on the future that the man who treats us kindly today will perpetuate it through his son or his grandson tomorrow?

Races and peoples are only safeguarded when they are strong enough to protect themselves, and that is why we appeal to the four hundred million Negroes of the world to come together for self-protection and self-preservation. We do not want what belongs to the great white race, or the yellow race. We want only those things that belong to the black race. Africa is ours. To win Africa we will give up America, we will give up our claim in all other parts of the world; but we must have Africa. We will give up the vain desire of having a seat in the White House in America, of having a seat in the House of Lords in England, of being President of France, for the chance and opportunity of filling these positions in a country of our own.

That is how the Universal Negro Improvement Association differs from other organizations. Other organizations, especially in America, are fighting for a political equality which they will never get, and never win, in the face of a majority opposition. We win so much today and lose so much tomorrow. We will lose our political strength in the North in another few years, as we lost it in the South during Reconstruction. We fill one position today, but lose two tomorrow, and so we will drift on and on, until we have been completely obliterated from Western civilization.

You may ask me what good has the Universal Negro Improvement Association done, what has it accomplished within the last six years? We will point out to you the great changes that have taken place in Africa, the West Indies and America. In the West Indies, black men have been elevated to high positions by the British Government, so as to off-set and counteract the sweeping influence of the Universal Negro Improvement Association. Several of the Colonies have been given larger constitutional rights. In Africa, the entire West Coast has been benefited. Self-government has been given to several of the African Colonies, and native Africans have been elevated to higher positions, so as to offset the sweeping spirit of the Universal Negro Improvement Association throughout the Continent of Africa. In America, several of our men have been given prominent positions; Negro commissions have been appointed to attend to affairs of state; Negro Consuls have been appointed. Things that happened in America within the last six years to advance the political status, the social and industrial status of the Negro were never experienced before. All that is traceable to the Universal Negro Improvement Association within the last six years. In the great game of politics you do not see the immediate results at your door, but those who are observant will be able to trace the good that is being done from the many directions whence it comes. If you were to take a survey of the whole world of Negroes you will find that we are more highly thought of in 1922 than we were in 1914. England, France and the European and Colonial powers regard the Universal Negro Improvement Association with a certain amount of suspicion because they believe that we are antagonistic. But we are not. We are not antagonistic to France, to England or Italy, nor any of the white powers in Europe. We are only demanding a square deal for our race. Did we not fight to help them? Did we not sacrifice our blood, give up our all, to save England, to save France, Italy and America during the last war? Then why shouldn't we expect some consideration for the service rendered? That is all we ask; and we are now pressing that claim to the throne of white justice. We are told that God's throne is white, although we believe it to be black. But if it is white, we are placing our plea before that throne of God, asking Him to so touch the hearts of our fellow-men as to let them yield to us the things that are ours, as it was right to yield to Caesar the things that were Caesar's.

As we deliberate on the many problems confronting us during the month of August, let us not lose control of ourselves; let us not forget that we are the guardians of four hundred millions; let us not forget that it is our duty to so act and legislate as to help humanity everywhere, whether it be black or white. We shall be called upon during this month to take up certain matters that are grave, but dispassionately we shall discuss them; and whenever the interest of the different race groups clash, let it be our duty to take the other fellow's feelings into our consideration. If we must be justly treated, then we ourselves must treat all men similarly. So, let no prejudice cause us to say or do anything against the interest of the white man, or the yellow man; let us realize that the white man has the right to live, the yellow man has the right to live, and all that we desire to do is to impress them with the fact that we also have the right to live.

First Message to the Negroes of the World from Atlanta Prison ("The Whirlwind Speech")

"Look for me in the whirlwind or the storm, look for me all around you, for, with God's grace, I shall come and bring with me countless millions of black slaves who have died in America and the West Indies and the millions in Africa to aid you in the fight for Liberty, Freedom and Life."

February 10, 1925

The Philosophy and Opinions of Marcus Garvey, or Africa for the Africans,
Volume 2

FELLOW MEN OF THE NEGRO RACE, *Greeting:*

I am delighted to inform you, that your humble servant is as happy in suffering for you and our cause as is possible under the circumstances of being viciously outraged by a group of plotters who have connived to do their worst to humiliate you through me, in the fight for real emancipation and African Redemption.

I do trust that you have given no credence to the vicious lies of white and enemy newspapers and those who have spoken in reference to my surrender. The liars plotted in every way to make it appear that I was not willing to surrender to the court. My attorney advised me that no mandate would have been handed down for ten or fourteen days, as is the custom of the courts, and that would have given me time to keep speaking engagements I had in Detroit, Cincinnati and Cleveland. I hadn't left the city for ten hours when the liars flashed the news that I was a fugitive. That was good news to circulate all over the world to demoralize the millions of Negroes in America, Africa, Asia, the West Indies and Central America, but the idiots ought to know by now that they can't fool all the Negroes at the same time.

I do not want at this time to write anything that would make it difficult for you to meet the opposition of the enemy without my assistance. Suffice it to say that the history of the outrage shall form a splendid chapter in the history of Africa redeemed, when black men will no longer be under the heels of others, but have a civilization and country of their own.

The whole affair is a disgrace, and the whole black world knows it. We shall not forget. Our day may be fifty, a hundred or two hundred years ahead, but let us watch, work and pray, for the civilization of injustice is bound to crumble and bring destruction down upon the heads of the unjust.

The idiots thought that they could humiliate me personally, but in that they are mistaken. The minutes of suffering are counted, and when God and Africa come back and measure out retribution these minutes may multiply by thousands for the sinners. Our Arab and Riffian friends will be ever vigilant, as the rest of Africa and ourselves shall be. Be assured that I planted well the seed of Negro or black nationalism which cannot be destroyed even by the foul play that has been meted out to me.

Continue to pray for me and I shall ever be true to my trust. I want you, the black peoples of the world, to know that W. E. Du Bois and that vicious Negro-hating organization known as the Association for the Advancement of "Colored" People are the greatest enemies the black people have in the world. I have so much to do in the few minutes at my disposal that I cannot write exhaustively on this or any other matter, but be warned against these two enemies. Don't allow them to fool you with fine sounding press releases, speeches and books; they are the vipers who have planned with others the extinction of the "black" race.

My work is just begun, and when the history of my suffering is complete, then future generations of Negroes will have in their hands the guide by which they shall know the "sins" of the twentieth century. I, and I know you, too, believe in time, and we shall wait patiently for two hundred years, if need be, to face our enemies through our posterity.

You will cheer me much if you will now do even more for the organization than when I was among you. Hold up the hands of those who are carrying on. Help them to make good, so that the work may continue to spread from pole to pole.

I am also making a last minute appeal for support to the Black Cross Navigation and Trading Company. Please send in and make your loans so as to enable the directors to successfully carry on the work.

All I have I have given to you. I have sacrificed my home and my loving wife for you. I entrust her to your charge, to protect and defend her in my absence. She is the bravest little woman I know. She has suffered and sacrificed with me for you; therefore, please do not desert her at this dismal hour, when she stands alone. I have left her penniless and helpless to face the world, because I gave you all, but her courage is great, and I know she will hold up for you and me.

After my enemies are satisfied, in life or death I shall come back to you to serve even as I have served before. In life I shall be the same; in death I shall be a terror to the foes of Negro liberty. If death has power, then count on me in death to be the real Marcus Garvey I would like to be. If I may come in an earthquake, or a cyclone, or plague, or pestilence, or as God would have me, then be assured that I shall never desert you and make your enemies triumph over you. Would I not go to hell a million times for you? Would I not like Macbeth's ghost, walk the earth forever for you? Would I not lose the whole world and eternity for you? Would I not cry forever before the footstool of the Lord Omnipotent for you? Would I not die a million deaths for you? Then, why be sad? Cheer up, and be assured that if it takes a million years the sins of our enemies shall visit the millionth generation of those that hinder and oppress us.

Remember that I have sworn by you and my God to serve to the end of all time, the wreck of matter and the crash of worlds. The enemies think that I am defeated. Did the Germans defeat the French in 1870? Did Napoleon really conquer Europe? If so, then I am defeated, but I tell you the world shall hear from my principles even two thousand years hence. I am willing to wait on time for my satisfaction and the retribution of my enemies. Observe my enemies and their children and posterity, and one day you shall see retribution settling around them.

If I die in Atlanta my work shall then only begin, but I shall live, in the physical or spiritual to see the day of Africa's glory. When I am dead wrap the mantle of the Red, Black and Green around me, for in the new life I shall rise with God's grace and blessing to lead the millions up the heights of triumph with the colors that you well know. Look for me in the whirlwind or the storm, look for me all around you, for, with God's grace, I shall come and bring with me countless millions of black slaves who have died in America and the West Indies and the millions in Africa to aid you in the fight for Liberty, Freedom and Life.

The civilization of today is gone drunk and crazy with its power and by such it seeks through injustice, fraud and lies to crush the unfortunate. But if I am apparently crushed by the system of influence and misdirected power, my cause shall rise again to plague the conscience of the corrupt. For this I am satisfied, and for you, I repeat, I am glad to suffer and even die. Again, I say, cheer up, for better days are ahead. I shall write the history that will inspire the millions that are coming and leave the posterity of our enemies to reckon with the hosts for the deeds of their fathers.

With God's dearest blessings, I leave you for awhile.

African Fundamentalism

*"We must canonize our own saints, create our own martyrs,
and elevate to positions of fame and honor black men and women
who have made their distinct contributions to our racial history."*

Atlanta, Georgia, Federal Penitentiary
June 1925

The Negro World,
June 6, 1925

FELLOWMEN OF THE NEGRO RACE, *Greeting:*

THE time has come for the Negro to forget and cast behind him his hero worship and adoration of other races, and to start out immediately to create and emulate heroes of his own.

We must canonize our own saints, create our own martyrs, and elevate to positions of fame and honor black men and women who have made their distinct contributions to our racial history. Sojourner Truth is worthy of the place of sainthood alongside of Joan of Arc; Crispus Attucks and George William Gordon are entitled to the halo of martyrdom with no less glory than that of the martyrs of any other race. Toussaint L'Overture's brilliancy as a soldier and statesman outshone that of a Cromwell, Napoleon and Washington; hence, he is entitled to the highest place as a hero among men. Africa has produced countless numbers of men and women, in war and in peace, whose lustre and bravery outshine that of any other people. Then why not see good and perfection in ourselves?

We must inspire a literature and promulgate a doctrine of our own without any apologies to the powers that be. The right is ours and God's. Let contrary sentiment and cross opinions go to the winds. Opposition to race and independence is the weapon of the enemy to defeat the hopes of an unfortunate people. We are entitled to our own opinions and not obligated to or bound by the opinions of others.

If others laugh at you, return the laughter to them; if they mimic you, return the compliment with equal force. They have no more right to dishonor, disrespect and disregard your feeling and manhood than you have in dealing with them. Honor them when they honor you; disrespect and disregard them when they vilely treat you. Their arrogance is but skin deep and an assumption that has no foundation in morals or in law. They have sprung from the same family tree of obscurity as we have; their history is as rude in its primitiveness as ours; their ancestors ran wild and naked, lived in caves and in the branches of trees, like monkeys, as ours; they made human sacrifices, ate the flesh of their own dead and the raw meat of the wild beast for centuries even as they accuse us of doing; their cannibalism was more prolonged than ours; when we were embracing the arts and sciences on the banks of the Nile their ancestors were still drinking human blood and eating out of the skulls of their conquered dead; when our civilization had reached the noonday of progress they were still running naked and sleeping in holes and caves with rats, bats and other insects and animals. After we had already unfathomed the mysteries of the stars and reduced the heavenly constellations to minute and regular calculus they were still backwoodsmen, living in ignorance and blatant darkness.

The world today is indebted to us for the benefits of civilization. They stole our arts and sciences from Africa. Then why should we be ashamed of ourselves? Their MODERN IMPROVEMENTS are but DUPLICATES of a grander civilization that we reflected thousands of years ago, without the advantage of what is buried and still hidden, to be resurrected and reintroduced by the intelligence of our generation and our prosperity. Why should we be discouraged because somebody laughs at us today? Who to tell what tomorrow will bring forth? Did they not laugh at Moses, Christ and Mohammed? Was there not a Carthage, Greece and Rome? We see and have changes every day, so pray, work, be steadfast and be not dismayed.

As the Jew is held together by his RELIGION, the white races by the assumption and the unwritten law of SUPERIORITY, and the Mongolian by the precious tie of BLOOD, so likewise the Negro must be united in one GRAND RACIAL HIERARCHY. Our UNION MUST KNOW NO CLIME, BOUNDARY, or NATIONALITY. Like the great Church of Rome, Negroes the world over MUST PRACTICE ONE FAITH, that of Confidence in themselves, with One God! One Aim! One Destiny! Let no religious scruples, no political machination divide us, but let us hold together under all climes and in every country, making among ourselves a Racial Empire upon which "the sun shall never set."

Let no voice but your own speak to you from the depths. Let no influence but your own raise you in time of peace and time of war. Hear all, but attend only that which concerns you.

Your first allegiance shall be to your God, then to your family, race and country. Remember always that the Jew in his political and economic urge is always first a Jew; the white man is first a white man under all circumstances, and you can do no less than being first and always a Negro, and then all else will take care of itself. Let no one inoculate you for their own conveniences. There is no humanity before that which starts with yourself. "Charity begins at home." First to thyself be true, and "thou canst not then be false to any man."

God and Nature first made us what we are, and then out of our own creative genius we make ourselves what we want to be. Follow always that great law.

Let the sky and God be our limit, and Eternity our measurement. There is no height to which we cannot climb by using the active intelligence of our own minds. Mind creates, and as much as we desire in Nature we can have through the creation of our own minds. Being at present the scientifically weaker race, you shall treat others only as they treat you; but in your homes and everywhere possible you must teach the higher development of science to your children; and be sure to develop a race of scientists par excellence, for in science and religion lies our only hope to withstand the evil designs of modern materialism. Never forget your God. Remember, we live, work and pray for the establishing of a great and binding RACIAL HIERARCHY, the rounding of a RACIAL EMPIRE whose only natural, spiritual and political limits shall be God and "Africa, at home and abroad."

Message of Marcus Garvey to Membership of U.N.I.A. from Atlanta Prison

"... ever remember that from nothing I raised up an organization through which you may see the light ..."

Atlanta, Georgia, Federal Penitentiary,
August 1, 1925

The Philosophy and Opinions of Marcus Garvey, or Africa for the Africans,
Volume 2

FELLOW members of the Universal Negro Improvement Association and co-workers in the cause of African Redemption:

It is with feeling of deep love and thoughts of a great future for the Negro race that I address you.

My months of forcible removal from among you, being imprisoned as a punishment for advocating the cause of our real emancipation, have not left me hopeless or despondent; but to the contrary, I see a great ray of light and the bursting of a mighty international political cloud which will bring you complete freedom.

We have gradually won our way back into the confidence of the God of Africa, and He shall speak with the voice of thunder that shall shake the pillars of a corrupt and unjust world, and once more restore Ethiopia to her ancient glory.

Our enemies have seemingly triumphed for a while, but the final battle when staged will bring us complete success and satisfaction.

The wicked and obstructive elements of our own race who have tried to defeat us shall meet their Waterloo, and when they fall we feel sure they shall not rise again. for many years since our general emancipation, certain elements composed chiefly of a few octoroons and quadroons who hate the blood of our race (although part of us) with greater venom, scorn and contempt than the most prejudiced of other races, have tried to undermine and sell us out to the mighty powers of oppression, and within recent years, they have succeeded in getting the ear of the leading statesmen of the world, and have influenced them to treat the bulk of us Negroes as dogs, reserving for themselves, their kind and class, all the privileges and considerations that, as a race, would have been otherwise granted us and merited.

The National Association for the Advancement of Colored People, although pretending to be interested in and working for the race, is really and truly the active representative of this class. I trust you will not believe that my opposition to the National Association for the Advancement of Colored People is based upon any other motive than that of preventing them from destroying the Negro race that they so much despise and hate.

I am always glad and ever willing to cooperate with all Negro organizations that mean good by the race, but I am perfectly convinced and satisfied that the present executive personnel of the National Association for the Advancement of Colored People is not serious nor honest in intent toward the black race.

When they shall have removed their white and colored officers who believe in the racial extermination of the Negro type, and honestly promote a program for race uplift, then we can cooperate with them for the general good, until then we regard them as among the greatest enemies of our race. They teach race amalgamation and inter-marriage as the means of destroying the moral purity of the Negro race and our absorption within the white race which is nothing less than race suicide.

You must not forget that we have enemies also within our own organization—men whose motives are selfish and who are only seeking the "loaves and fishes" and not honest in heart in serving the people. Yet we have to make the "wheat and tare" grow together till the day of harvest. It is impossible to know all our enemies at one and the same time. Some are our enemies because they do not want to see the Negro rise; some because the organization supplies the opportunity for exploitation; others because they are unable to resist the temptation of the evil one who would have them betray us in our most righteous efforts of racial love and freedom.

I feel that my imprisonment has helped to open the eyes of the world to your true position, and has made friends to your cause. Men and women of other races who were misinformed and deceived by our enemies, are now seeing the light. The graves that the enemies of race pride and purity dug for us may yet entomb them.

Hold fast to the ideal of a dignified Negro race. Let us work together as one people, whether we are octoroons, quadroons, mulattoes or blacks for the making of a nation of our own, for in that alone lies our racial salvation.

The few who do not want to be with us will find out their mistake sooner or later, but as for us, let us all unite as one people. It is no fault of ours that we are what we are—if we are black, brown, yellow or near white, the responsibility for the accident is not ours, but the time has now come for us to get together and make of ourselves a strong and healthy race.

The National Association for the Advancement of Colored People wants us all to become white by amalgamation, but they are not honest enough to come out with the truth. To be a Negro is no disgrace, but an honor, and we of the Universal Negro Improvement Association do not want to become white. We do not seek for the white man's company more than he would seek after ours. We are proud and honorable. We love our race and respect and adore our mothers. We are as proud as our fathers were in the days of old, and even though we have passed through slavery in the Western world, we shall not hang down our heads for Ethiopia shall again return to her glory.

The Universal Negro Improvement Association is a union of all groups within the race. We love each other with pride of race and great devotion and nothing in the world shall come between us.

The truth has to be told so that we may know from whence our troubles cometh. Yet we must never, even under the severest pressure, hate or dislike ourselves. Even though we oppose the present leaders of the National Association for the Advancement of Colored People, we must remember that we are all members of one race, rent asunder by circumstances. Let us help them by advice and conversion. Men like Du Bois need our sympathy. We should teach them to love themselves, at least, have respect for the blood of their mothers—our mothers, who have suffered so much to make us what we are. We should take the truth to the innocent members of the National Association and save them from the mis-leadership of the white and colored persons who seek to destroy our race by miscegenation and use them as a pawn towards that end, and to foster their own class interest. Let us reach out and convert these unfortunate people and thus save them from a grave error. They should not be left to the tender mercies of their vile leaders, for they are good people and of our race, they mean good, but are misdirected.

I have to return many thanks to you, the members of the Universal Negro Improvement Association, for the loyal support you have given me during my trials and troubles, suffered for you. I can realize that you have at all times done your best for me, even as I have done the best for you, as God has directed me to see. If it were not for you I would have been left helpless and comfortless. I shall never forget you. If it were not for you, the members and some of the officers of local divisions, I would have been left penniless and helpless to fight my enemies and the great powers against me, and to even in the slightest way give protection to my wife whom I neglected and cheated for the cause that I so much love.

It is surprising how those we serve and help most can be ungrateful and unkind in our absence, and generally seek to take advantage of the one who cannot help himself. My name I leave with you the people. For you I have built up an organization of international standing. Every sacrifice has been made. My youth, money and ability were freely given for the cause. The cause you now see. It was not made in a day, but it took years of steady work and sacrifice. Others will now try to take advantage of my predicament to rob and exploit you in my name and blame the absent and helpless, but ever remember that from nothing I raised up an organization through which you may see the light; let others, if they may, show the ability to carry on that which they have found, and not seek to exploit, to ruin and then blame the absent one as is so easy to do. It was during my absence in the West Indies when I was helpless to act, that the traitors within and enemies without did the deeds of dishonor that placed me for the Black Star Line where I am. Let not the same characters succeed to enrich themselves at the cost of the name of one who cannot protect himself or protect you. You must protect yourselves—the time has come. My full tale of warning is not to be told here, but suffice it to say that on you I rely for the ultimate success of our great effort, and but for you I would have been hopelessly defeated in the great struggle to "keep the fire burning." Probably I should not have expected better for even our Blessed Master feared worse when his chief disciples failed him. I am not complaining, but I warn you against treachery, deceit, self-seeking, dishonesty and racial disloyalty. Personally, as I have so often stated, I counted the cost years ago, but the responsibility is not all mine, but equally that of the one whom I love with great devotion and fondness. You, I feel sure, have done your duty by her and will continue to shield and protect her, while, because of my imprisonment for you, I find it impossible to do my duty.

The God of our Fathers will raise up friends for the cause of Africa, and we who have struggled in the wilderness for all this time shall surely see the promised land.

Hold fast to the Faith. Desert not the ranks, but as brave soldiers march on to victory. I am happy, and shall remain so, as long as you keep the flag flying.

I hope to be with you again with greater energy and force to put the program over. I have yet to let my real voice and soul be heard in Europe, Asia and continental America in plea for the Negro's rights and for a free and redeemed Africa. Yet, I have not spoken. I await the summons of my God for the greater work that must be done. In the meanwhile pray for success and pray for me.

Statement of Conviction

"I am satisfied of having won a glorious
victory over all my enemies . . ."

Atlanta, Georgia, Federal Penitentiary,
circa September 1925

The Philosophy and Opinions of Marcus Garvey, or Africa for the Africans,
Volume 2

"Let Fate do her worst; there are relics of joy
Bright dreams of the past, which she cannot destroy;
Which come in the night—time of sorrow and care,
And bring back the features that joy used to wear.
Long, long be my heart with such memories filled,
Like the vase in which roses have once been distilled—
You may break, you may shatter the vase if you will,
But the scent of the roses will hang round it still."

JUSTICE, in modern jurisprudence, is doubtful, and much more so than that of other ages, with all things considered proportionately.

It is sad to make this confession, after so many improvements have been added to our boasted civilization. Justice, however, is left more to the feeling, like or dislike of the individual or group of individuals charged with the responsibility of administering it, rather than to its ethical interpretation or the corporate demands of the community or society; hence, if the individuals are wrong, we suffer from the result, and not because our civilization, in that respect, is altogether imperfect.

If you have friends and influence; if you are powerfully allied with the party in control of government; if you are potently rich or if you are born to the silver spoon and among the elect of society, you may have "justice" your way, whether you are guilty or not. Sometimes it is invoked by the "call" on the telephone, the chat around the dinner table, over the "glass" at the club or by the "written" letter. If the request is made by the friend of the particular individual in power, then with a "clap" on the shoulder, a "shake" of the hand, or a "kick off" of the feet with the hands in the pockets the promise is made, "well, I will see," I will "fix it all right," and there goes a fair sample of "modern justice." It was so with the Greeks and Romans, it is so now, and may be yet for a long while.

The poor wretch who has no such affiliation or means of approach "gets it in the neck," and for him "justice" is clear and positive without the hope of appeal. For his petty or minor crime, he is made "an example" of, and the able jurist admonishes with high-sounding morals, and by the heaviest of sentences imposed "purges" the atmosphere surrounding a privileged society, by locking away in some prison or penitentiary the unfortunate creature, who is looked upon as a menace to established order, an evil-doer and breaker of the solemn and sacred laws of the land.

In such an atmosphere, being a Negro who sought the higher liberties and rights of his people, was I charged, convicted and sentenced to a long term of imprisonment. The facts surrounding my case constitute a moral public scandal for which any people, and even those of despised Russia or Turkey, ought to hang their heads in shame, judged by the professed standards of civilization.

Like the Jews who "framed" the Man Christ because he sought to do good, other Negroes, jealous of my success and power among the masses as a leader, "framed" me for the convenience and satisfaction of those who sought my elimination and desired to be rid of me because of their fear of my personality in the body politic and international.

During the summation of the prosecutor before the jury at my trial, he was bold enough to acknowledge that the witnesses who testified against me were liars and some of them thieves; but that was immaterial as the desire was to convict me. After such a brazen statement and confession, a jury—not of my race, but of the race from which I desired to free the Negro so as to save him from extermination as threatened through the hidden plans of a superior intelligence that now materially rules the world—convicted me of using the mails in a "scheme" to defraud a person I never met, did not know, had nothing to do nor corresponded with, even though he testified that he could not remember what was sent to him, by some one, surely not me, in an empty envelope bearing the rubber stamp imprint of the Black Star Line. To be convicted for using the mails to defraud on the evidence of a rubber stamped, empty envelope that could have been stamped and posted by any enemy or hired agent with the intent that prompted the prosecution is a departure in our system that may lead to the incrimination and conviction of any man in our civilization who trespasses within the bounds or province where there is such a law. In modern jurisprudence, controlled as it is by politics, wealth and power, the "marked" person falls a prey to the hunter who sets the "legal" trap that never fails to "catch" the individual when badly "wanted." It is only a question of time when every individual "sought" or "wanted" is "caught" by the legal entanglements prepared for the purpose of rendering harmless and permanently silent those not desired or who may constitute themselves a stumbling block in the way of privileged and hereditary power. Somebody says (but if it were not said, then I say it now), that "the laws of our civilization have but one interpretation for the poor and ignorant, and for those of wealth and power, there are many interpretations, hence the poor are generally convicted on the one meaning, while the rich are freed on the many interpretations."

I am satisfied of having won a glorious victory over all my enemies, in that they found it beyond their own power and ability to defeat me, hence the resort to and use of the sovereign power of government to destroy me. It took the power of the Roman State to destroy the physical person and influence of Christ who sought to save the souls of men. His enemies failed of themselves, and because He was Christ, after three days he demonstrated his power over all. In my case, and that of other reformers, blessed with only physical power, we take satisfaction in seeing the thing we suffer for survive and become of benefit to our fellowmen.

I sought to emancipate the millions of Negroes all over the world from political and industrial thraldom, which was too big an effort for rivals within my own race to stand; and those of other races who profit by their exploitation and servitude regarded me as a dangerous menace to be rid of by all means, hence the combined effort to use the greater power of the state to silence and destroy me. How well they have succeeded the future will tell; but I am of the firm belief that "truth one day will get a hearing" and then the shame and disgrace, if any, will be rightly placed.

Ideals of liberty, freedom and righteousness do not prosper in the 20th century except they coincide with oil, rubber, gold, diamond, coal, iron, sugar, coffee and such other minerals and products desired by the privileged, capitalists and leaders who control the systems of government.

Righteousness and justice in the 20th century are interpreted to mean class interest whether it be of the abused "bourgeoisie," "plutocrats" or "communists."

The fiery communists are fighting against one class interest for the enthronement of theirs—a group of lazy men and women who desire to level all initiative and intelligence and set a premium on stagnation—and so our world goes wrong.

I am against the brand of communism that is taught in America, because it is even more vicious than all the other "isms" put together. In America it constitutes a group of liars, plotters and artful deceivers who twist—a one-third truth to a whole big lie, and give it out to the unthinking clientele for consumption. Communism among Negroes in 1920–21 was represented in New York by such Negroes as Cyril Briggs and W. A. Domingo, and my contact with, and experience of them, and their methods are enough to keep me shy of that kind of communism for the balance of my natural life. A group of men of any ism or party who would seek to kill or illegally or improperly dispose of a political adversary because he doesn't agree with their particular brand of politics are no associates for those who seek the perfection of government. Because I sought to build up in Africa a democratic Negro state and not a commune the Negro communists preferred me dead than alive. Such class interest is dangerous, and it is foolish for the masses, as they are now situated, to jump from the frying pan into the fire. The American Negro is warned to keep away from communism, as it is taught in this country; he should work, watch and wait for his own opportunity, which is largely to his own making. Such a doctrine as this makes me unpopular to both extremes, with some of my own race thrown in, hence my predicament.

I pray the day will never come for the Negro and America when the government falls into the hands of such representatives of communism. I would rather be dead than live under government administered by such characters.

To be convicted as I was does not mean anything. Anyone could have been thus incriminated. No one is responsible for the lies of others and for the vengeance of his enemies. To be "framed" up and convicted in an atmosphere over which you have no control, or even a fair chance to make yourself clear by having the truth told, doesn't make one a criminal.

For a man who never plays cards and doesn't know the difference between poker and any other game, to be ruthlessly lied upon by even an assistant district attorney, as being a player of such a game, and to be convicted by a jury on such testimony is to leave the subject of conviction surprised, but amused, at the way things are done, or rather, crimes committed in the name of justice. In addition to being called a poker player, a game I knew nothing about, I was also accused of "playing the races," "a white slaver," "a character before whom Jessie James pales into insignificance," all such lies and nonsense were paraded before the jury to arouse prejudice, and added to all these I was supposed to be a cold-blooded murderer who killed one man, or caused him to be killed and had planned the killing of the judge, district attorney and the entire jury. All these lies were manufactured to ensure the conviction of one man whose only crime is the love of his race. But didn't the prosecutor himself claim in open court in his address to the jury and by statement before the court that he loved Negroes more than Marcus Garvey did, and it was because of his love of them why he wanted him convicted, because he was their greatest enemy? Now don't laugh, it is serious, for when a child I was told the story of the spider and the fly, and it seems so applicable in this case of love, that I would not have you lose the moral for anything in the world. For witnesses to look you in the face and lie to you about things that never happened, and then to be convicted on such testimony and to hear a judge moralize upon your behavior because of that, is to make you frown upon modern justice and regard it as a farce. Imagine that all these things happened to you and then you will become better appreciative of the strain I underwent during the eventful days of my trial and confinement.

My head is as high as Olympus. My character is as firm as Gibraltar's rock, and no judge, jury or prosecutor in the world shall make me a criminal when I am not. In prison I feel happy knowing that I am only occupying a cell intended for others whose morality is below mine, and whose consciences can make them nothing but cowards.

I believe in God. I believe in a final judgment of the soul. I am satisfied to wait until then to face my accusers and condemners and may the Lord have mercy on their souls.

If the white man's God is not a myth, I wonder how some of the race will face Him? Is He a God of moods, prejudices and passions? If He is not, then white man, where do you expect and intend to spend eternity? Probably Mr. Bryan will tell us when he has completely disarmed the evolutionists. But whether this God exists in reality for the white man or not, there is an eternity, and I intend to take no chances with not getting there right. Resting on my conscience I defy a world to make a criminal of me, and I am more satisfied to rest in the honor and cleanliness of my own soul and character than to merit the good will of the agents of injustice and corruption.

A district attorney once had condemned and subsequently electrocuted an innocent man charged with murder. His skillful prosecution and brilliant effort to convict the accused on manufactured and circumstantial evidence were with the eye of creating a reputation for future success in his profession. Subsequently the innocence of the electrocuted man was discovered, but the attorney had already built up a large practice and made his reputation through the case. Oh! for the reputations that have been made and built upon the dead bones and the wrecked lives of innocents. What man can look his fellows in the eye having made his name and reputation by stealing the characters of others? What place can such an individual find in society when at every turn the graves of his victims rise before him and the shadows of the wrecked lives, like Banquo's ghost, haunt him? To take success thus attained is to forfeit every impulse of manhood. I would rather be a hangman!

DOVER·THRIFT·EDITIONS

FICTION

FLATLAND: A ROMANCE OF MANY DIMENSIONS, Edwin A. Abbott. 96pp. 27263-X

SHORT STORIES, Louisa May Alcott. 64pp. 29063-8

WINESBURG, OHIO, Sherwood Anderson. 160pp. 28269-4

PERSUASION, Jane Austen. 224pp. 29555-9

PRIDE AND PREJUDICE, Jane Austen. 272pp. 28473-5

SENSE AND SENSIBILITY, Jane Austen. 272pp. 29049-2

LOOKING BACKWARD, Edward Bellamy. 160pp. 29038-7

BEOWULF, Beowulf (trans. by R. K. Gordon). 64pp. 27264-8

CIVIL WAR STORIES, Ambrose Bierce. 128pp. 28038-1

"THE MOONLIT ROAD" AND OTHER GHOST AND HORROR STORIES, Ambrose Bierce (John Grafton, ed.) 96pp. 40056-5

WUTHERING HEIGHTS, Emily Brontë. 256pp. 29256-8

THE THIRTY-NINE STEPS, John Buchan. 96pp. 28201-5

TARZAN OF THE APES, Edgar Rice Burroughs. 224pp. (Not available in Europe or United Kingdom.) 29570-2

ALICE'S ADVENTURES IN WONDERLAND, Lewis Carroll. 96pp. 27543-4

THROUGH THE LOOKING-GLASS, Lewis Carroll. 128pp. 40878-7

MY ÁNTONIA, Willa Cather. 176pp. 28240-6

O PIONEERS!, Willa Cather. 128pp. 27785-2

PAUL'S CASE AND OTHER STORIES, Willa Cather. 64pp. 29057-3

FIVE GREAT SHORT STORIES, Anton Chekhov. 96pp. 26463-7

TALES OF CONJURE AND THE COLOR LINE, Charles Waddell Chesnutt. 128pp. 40426-9

FAVORITE FATHER BROWN STORIES, G. K. Chesterton. 96pp. 27545-0

THE AWAKENING, Kate Chopin. 128pp. 27786-0

A PAIR OF SILK STOCKINGS AND OTHER STORIES, Kate Chopin. 64pp. 29264-9

HEART OF DARKNESS, Joseph Conrad. 80pp. 26464-5

LORD JIM, Joseph Conrad. 256pp. 40650-4

THE SECRET SHARER AND OTHER STORIES, Joseph Conrad. 128pp. 27546-9

THE "LITTLE REGIMENT" AND OTHER CIVIL WAR STORIES, Stephen Crane. 80pp. 29557-5

THE OPEN BOAT AND OTHER STORIES, Stephen Crane. 128pp. 27547-7

THE RED BADGE OF COURAGE, Stephen Crane. 112pp. 26465-3

MOLL FLANDERS, Daniel Defoe. 256pp. 29093-X

ROBINSON CRUSOE, Daniel Defoe. 288pp. 40427-7

A CHRISTMAS CAROL, Charles Dickens. 80pp. 26865-9

THE CRICKET ON THE HEARTH AND OTHER CHRISTMAS STORIES, Charles Dickens. 128pp. 28039-X

A TALE OF TWO CITIES, Charles Dickens. 304pp. 40651-2

THE DOUBLE, Fyodor Dostoyevsky. 128pp. 29572-9

THE GAMBLER, Fyodor Dostoyevsky. 112pp. 29081-6

NOTES FROM THE UNDERGROUND, Fyodor Dostoyevsky. 96pp. 27053-X

THE ADVENTURE OF THE DANCING MEN AND OTHER STORIES, Sir Arthur Conan Doyle. 80pp. 29558-3

THE HOUND OF THE BASKERVILLES, Arthur Conan Doyle. 128pp. 28214-7

THE LOST WORLD, Arthur Conan Doyle. 176pp. 40060-3

DOVER · THRIFT · EDITIONS

FICTION

A JOURNAL OF THE PLAGUE YEAR, Daniel Defoe. 192pp. 41919-3
SIX GREAT SHERLOCK HOLMES STORIES, Sir Arthur Conan Doyle. 112pp. 27055-6
SHORT STORIES, Theodore Dreiser. 112pp. 28215-5
SILAS MARNER, George Eliot. 160pp. 29246-0
JOSEPH ANDREWS, Henry Fielding. 288pp. 41588-0
THIS SIDE OF PARADISE, F. Scott Fitzgerald. 208pp. 28999-0
"THE DIAMOND AS BIG AS THE RITZ" AND OTHER STORIES, F. Scott Fitzgerald. 29991-0
MADAME BOVARY, Gustave Flaubert. 256pp. 29257-6
THE REVOLT OF "MOTHER" AND OTHER STORIES, Mary E. Wilkins Freeman. 128pp.
  40428-5
A ROOM WITH A VIEW, E. M. Forster. 176pp. (Available in U.S. only.) 28467-0
WHERE ANGELS FEAR TO TREAD, E. M. Forster. 128pp. (Available in U.S. only.) 27791-7
THE IMMORALIST, André Gide. 112pp. (Available in U.S. only.) 29237-1
HERLAND, Charlotte Perkins Gilman. 128pp. 40429-3
"THE YELLOW WALLPAPER" AND OTHER STORIES, Charlotte Perkins Gilman. 80pp. 29857-4
THE OVERCOAT AND OTHER STORIES, Nikolai Gogol. 112pp. 27057-2
CHELKASH AND OTHER STORIES, Maxim Gorky. 64pp. 40652-0
GREAT GHOST STORIES, John Grafton (ed.). 112pp. 27270-2
DETECTION BY GASLIGHT, Douglas G. Greene (ed.). 272pp. 29928-7
THE MABINOGION, Lady Charlotte E. Guest. 192pp. 29541-9
"THE FIDDLER OF THE REELS" AND OTHER SHORT STORIES, Thomas Hardy. 80pp. 29960-0
THE LUCK OF ROARING CAMP AND OTHER STORIES, Bret Harte. 96pp. 27271-0
THE HOUSE OF THE SEVEN GABLES, Nathaniel Hawthorne. 272pp. 40882-5
THE SCARLET LETTER, Nathaniel Hawthorne. 192pp. 28048-9
YOUNG GOODMAN BROWN AND OTHER STORIES, Nathaniel Hawthorne. 128pp. 27060-2
THE GIFT OF THE MAGI AND OTHER SHORT STORIES, O. Henry. 96pp. 27061-0
THE NUTCRACKER AND THE GOLDEN POT, E. T. A. Hoffmann. 128pp. 27806-9
THE ASPERN PAPERS, Henry James. 112pp. 41922-3
THE BEAST IN THE JUNGLE AND OTHER STORIES, Henry James. 128pp. 27552-3
DAISY MILLER, Henry James. 64pp. 28773-4
THE TURN OF THE SCREW, Henry James. 96pp. 26684-2
WASHINGTON SQUARE, Henry James. 176pp. 40431-5
THE COUNTRY OF THE POINTED FIRS, Sarah Orne Jewett. 96pp. 28196-5
THE AUTOBIOGRAPHY OF AN EX-COLORED MAN, James Weldon Johnson. 112pp. 28512-X
DUBLINERS, James Joyce. 160pp. 26870-5
A PORTRAIT OF THE ARTIST AS A YOUNG MAN, James Joyce. 192pp. 28050-0
THE METAMORPHOSIS AND OTHER STORIES, Franz Kafka. 96pp. 29030-1
THE MAN WHO WOULD BE KING AND OTHER STORIES, Rudyard Kipling. 128pp. 28051-9
YOU KNOW ME AL, Ring Lardner. 128pp. 28513-8
SELECTED SHORT STORIES, D. H. Lawrence. 128pp. 27794-1
GREEN TEA AND OTHER GHOST STORIES, J. Sheridan LeFanu. 96pp. 27795-X
THE CALL OF THE WILD, Jack London. 64pp. 26472-6
FIVE GREAT SHORT STORIES, Jack London. 96pp. 27063-7
THE SEA-WOLF, Jack London. 248pp. 41108-7
WHITE FANG, Jack London. 160pp. 26968-X
DEATH IN VENICE, Thomas Mann. 96pp. (Available in U.S. only.) 28714-9
IN A GERMAN PENSION: 13 Stories, Katherine Mansfield. 112pp. 28719-X
THE NECKLACE AND OTHER SHORT STORIES, Guy de Maupassant. 128pp. 27064-5
BARTLEBY AND BENITO CERENO, Herman Melville. 112pp. 26473-4
THE OIL JAR AND OTHER STORIES, Luigi Pirandello. 96pp. 28459-X
THE GOLD-BUG AND OTHER TALES, Edgar Allan Poe. 128pp. 26875-6
TALES OF TERROR AND DETECTION, Edgar Allan Poe. 96pp. 28744-0

DOVER·THRIFT·EDITIONS

FICTION

THE QUEEN OF SPADES AND OTHER STORIES, Alexander Pushkin. 128pp. 28054-3

THE STORY OF AN AFRICAN FARM, Olive Schreiner. 256pp. 40165-0

FRANKENSTEIN, Mary Shelley. 176pp. 28211-2

THE JUNGLE, Upton Sinclair. 320pp. (Available in U.S. only.) 41923-1

THREE LIVES, Gertrude Stein. 176pp. (Available in U.S. only.) 28059-4

THE BODY SNATCHER AND OTHER TALES, Robert Louis Stevenson. 80pp. 41924-X

THE STRANGE CASE OF DR. JEKYLL AND MR. HYDE, Robert Louis Stevenson. 64pp. 26688-5

TREASURE ISLAND, Robert Louis Stevenson. 160pp. 27559-0

GULLIVER'S TRAVELS, Jonathan Swift. 240pp. 29273-8

THE KREUTZER SONATA AND OTHER SHORT STORIES, Leo Tolstoy. 144pp. 27805-0

THE WARDEN, Anthony Trollope. 176pp. 40076-X

FIRST LOVE AND DIARY OF A SUPERFLUOUS MAN, Ivan Turgenev. 96pp. 28775-0

FATHERS AND SONS, Ivan Turgenev. 176pp. 40073-5

ADVENTURES OF HUCKLEBERRY FINN, Mark Twain. 224pp. 28061-6

THE ADVENTURES OF TOM SAWYER, Mark Twain. 192pp. 40077-8

THE MYSTERIOUS STRANGER AND OTHER STORIES, Mark Twain. 128pp. 27069-6

HUMOROUS STORIES AND SKETCHES, Mark Twain. 80pp. 29279-7

AROUND THE WORLD IN EIGHTY DAYS, Jules Verne. 160pp. 41111-7

CANDIDE, Voltaire (François-Marie Arouet). 112pp. 26689-3

GREAT SHORT STORIES BY AMERICAN WOMEN, Candace Ward (ed.). 192pp. 28776-9

"THE COUNTRY OF THE BLIND" AND OTHER SCIENCE-FICTION STORIES, H. G. Wells. 160pp. (Not available in Europe or United Kingdom.) 29569-9

THE ISLAND OF DR. MOREAU, H. G. Wells. 112pp. (Not available in Europe or United Kingdom.) 29027-1

THE INVISIBLE MAN, H. G. Wells. 112pp. (Not available in Europe or United Kingdom.) 27071-8

THE TIME MACHINE, H. G. Wells. 80pp. (Not available in Europe or United Kingdom.) 28472-7

THE WAR OF THE WORLDS, H. G. Wells. 160pp. (Not available in Europe or United Kingdom.) 29506-0

ETHAN FROME, Edith Wharton. 96pp. 26690-7

SHORT STORIES, Edith Wharton. 128pp. 28235-X

THE AGE OF INNOCENCE, Edith Wharton. 288pp. 29803-5

THE PICTURE OF DORIAN GRAY, Oscar Wilde. 192pp. 27807-7

JACOB'S ROOM, Virginia Woolf. 144pp. (Not available in Europe or United Kingdom.) 40109-X

MONDAY OR TUESDAY: Eight Stories, Virginia Woolf. 64pp. (Not available in Europe or United Kingdom.) 29453-6

NONFICTION

POETICS, Aristotle. 64pp. 29577-X

POLITICS, Aristotle. 368pp. 41424-8

NICOMACHEAN ETHICS, Aristotle. 256pp. 40096-4

MEDITATIONS, Marcus Aurelius. 128pp. 29823-X

THE LAND OF LITTLE RAIN, Mary Austin. 96pp. 29037-9

THE DEVIL'S DICTIONARY, Ambrose Bierce. 144pp. 27542-6

THE ANALECTS, Confucius. 128pp. 28484-0

CONFESSIONS OF AN ENGLISH OPIUM EATER, Thomas De Quincey. 80pp. 28742-4

THE SOULS OF BLACK FOLK, W. E. B. Du Bois. 176pp. 28041-1

DOVER · THRIFT · EDITIONS

NONFICTION

NARRATIVE OF THE LIFE OF FREDERICK DOUGLASS, Frederick Douglass. 96pp. 28499-9

SELF-RELIANCE AND OTHER ESSAYS, Ralph Waldo Emerson. 128pp. 27790-9

THE LIFE OF OLAUDAH EQUIANO, OR GUSTAVUS VASSA, THE AFRICAN, Olaudah Equiano. 192pp. 40661-X

THE AUTOBIOGRAPHY OF BENJAMIN FRANKLIN, Benjamin Franklin. 144pp. 29073-5

TOTEM AND TABOO, Sigmund Freud. 176pp. (Not available in Europe or United Kingdom.) 40434-X

LOVE: A Book of Quotations, Herb Galewitz (ed.). 64pp. 40004-2

PRAGMATISM, William James. 128pp. 28270-8

THE STORY OF MY LIFE, Helen Keller. 80pp. 29249-5

TAO TE CHING, Lao Tze. 112pp. 29792-6

GREAT SPEECHES, Abraham Lincoln. 112pp. 26872-1

THE PRINCE, Niccolò Machiavelli. 80pp. 27274-5

THE SUBJECTION OF WOMEN, John Stuart Mill. 112pp. 29601-6

SELECTED ESSAYS, Michel de Montaigne. 96pp. 29109-X

UTOPIA, Sir Thomas More. 96pp. 29583-4

BEYOND GOOD AND EVIL: Prelude to a Philosophy of the Future, Friedrich Nietzsche. 176pp. 29868-X

THE BIRTH OF TRAGEDY, Friedrich Nietzsche. 96pp. 28515-4

COMMON SENSE, Thomas Paine. 64pp. 29602-4

SYMPOSIUM AND PHAEDRUS, Plato. 96pp. 27798-4

THE TRIAL AND DEATH OF SOCRATES: Four Dialogues, Plato. 128pp. 27066-1

A MODEST PROPOSAL AND OTHER SATIRICAL WORKS, Jonathan Swift. 64pp. 28759-9

CIVIL DISOBEDIENCE AND OTHER ESSAYS, Henry David Thoreau. 96pp. 27563-9

SELECTIONS FROM THE JOURNALS (Edited by Walter Harding), Henry David Thoreau. 96pp. 28760-2

WALDEN; OR, LIFE IN THE WOODS, Henry David Thoreau. 224pp. 28495-6

NARRATIVE OF SOJOURNER TRUTH, Sojourner Truth. 80pp. 29899-X

THE THEORY OF THE LEISURE CLASS, Thorstein Veblen. 256pp. 28062-4

DE PROFUNDIS, Oscar Wilde. 64pp. 29308-4

OSCAR WILDE'S WIT AND WISDOM: A Book of Quotations, Oscar Wilde. 64pp. 40146-4

UP FROM SLAVERY, Booker T. Washington. 160pp. 28738-6

A VINDICATION OF THE RIGHTS OF WOMAN, Mary Wollstonecraft. 224pp. 29036-0

All books complete and unabridged. All 5³⁄₁₆" x 8¹⁄₄," paperbound. Available at your book dealer, online at **www.doverpublications.com**, or by writing to Dept. GI, Dover Publications, Inc., 31 East 2nd Street, Mineola, NY 11501. For current price information or for free catalogs (please indicate field of interest), write to Dover Publications or log on to **www.doverpublications.com** and see every Dover book in print. Dover publishes more than 500 books each year on science, elementary and advanced mathematics, biology, music, art, literary history, social sciences, and other areas.